THE BUDDHA SIDE

Topics in Contemporary Buddhism
GEORGE J. TANABE, JR., EDITOR

Establishing a Pure Land on Earth: The Foguang Buddhist Perspective on Modernization and Globalization
STUART CHANDLER

Buddhist Missionaries in the Era of Globalization
LINDA LEARMAN, EDITOR

Being Benevolence: The Social Ethics of Engaged Buddhism
SALLIE B. KING

Japanese Temple Buddhism: Worldliness in a Religion of Renunciation
STEPHEN G. COVELL

Zen in Brazil: Quest for Cosmopolitan Modernity
CRISTINA ROCHA

Land of Beautiful Vision: Making a Buddhist Sacred Place in New Zealand
SALLY MCARA

Attracting the Heart: Social Relations and the Aesthetics of Emotion in Sri Lankan Monastic Culture
JEFFREY SAMUELS

The Buddha Side: Gender, Power, and Buddhist Practice in Vietnam
ALEXANDER SOUCY

TOPICS IN
CONTEMPORARY
BUDDHISM

THE BUDDHA SIDE

Gender, Power, and Buddhist Practice in Vietnam

ALEXANDER SOUCY

University of Hawai'i Press
Honolulu

17 16 15 14 13 12   6 5 4 3 2 1

Library of Congress Cataloging-in-Publication Data

Soucy, Alexander Duncan.
   The Buddha side : gender, power, and Buddhist practice in Vietnam / Alexander Soucy.
     p. cm. — (Topics in contemporary Buddhism)
   Includes bibliographical references and index.
   ISBN 978-0-8248-3598-9 (hardcover : alk. paper)
   1. Buddhism—Vietnam—Hanoi—Customs and practices.   2. Women in Buddhism—Vietnam—Hanoi.   3. Buddhism—Social aspects—Vietnam—Hanoi.   4. Buddhism and state—Vietnam.   I. Title.   II. Series: Topics in contemporary Buddhism.
   BQ4960.V5S68 2012
   294.309597—dc23
                              2012004375

Printed by Sheridan Books, Inc.

Contents

Series Editor's Preface

Often when scholars expand their research beyond Buddhism and include Buddhists, the results challenge the usual definitions of that religion based on its teachings and practices. In this wide-ranging study of Vietnamese Buddhists, Alexander Soucy presents such a challenge by showing the vital connections between religion and superstition, orthodoxy and heterodoxy, temple and community, Buddhist and non-Buddhist beliefs, spirituality and fun. As if this were not comprehensive enough, he takes readers beyond these binary relationships and offers a hard and fascinating look at the added complicities of age, gender, and politics. The result is a landscaped portrait of Buddhists in contemporary Vietnam and how they live their faith.

George J. Tanabe, Jr.
SERIES EDITOR

Acknowledgments

There is a long list of people who deserve my thanks for the part that they played in the creation of this work. My wife's family has supported me and helped me in a myriad of ways since we first met during my fieldwork in Hanoi. Thank you, Bố, Mẹ, Em Hương, Em Hà, Em Hùng, and Em Khánh. Also thanks to Em Hòa and Chú Đại. You made Vietnam a home rather than a field site.

There are many people who helped me extensively in Vietnam, without whom my research would have gone nowhere. Professor Phan Huy Lê and the Center for Vietnamese and Intercultural Studies were very helpful in getting me the necessary papers, orienting me, and providing me with excellent Vietnamese lessons in 1997–1998. My teacher Cô Lan did far more for me than teach Vietnamese language: she offered advice when I ran into sticky situations and gave me useful information. The secretary of the Center, Anh Hùng, was also very helpful. Of course, there were many others who became good friends and helped make Hanoi a home: Em Khánh, Em Mai, Em Thiện, Anh Don, Em Tâm, Em Hà, Em Thủ, Em Tuấn, Hùng, Em Hợp, Em Mỹ, Em Hoa, Hải, Em Phương, Anh Hùng, Chị Thu, Em Ngọc, Em Hồng, Em Lãnh, Em Ánh, Em Lan Hương, Em Ngọc Hương, Em Huyền, Em Tương Anh, Em Ha, Em Trung, Em Vân; Ông Châu, Ông Lâm, Anh Anh, Thầy Trung, Thầy Bình, Thầy Thịnh, Thầy Hùng, Ông Dũng, Cô Định, Bà Thảo, Cô Chính, Chị Hương, Cô Phương, Em Quỳnh, Ông Thang, Chú Ký, Ông Cừ, Cô Đài, Em Nhung, Ông Linh, and Bà Duyên.

My Ph.D. supervisor, Kathryn Robinson, was a patient, supportive, and constructive mentor. David Marr and his family (especially Michael and Huyền) helped me prepare for Vietnam and gave me very useful guidance and friendship after returning. Andrew Kipnis gave me helpful comments, intellectual stimulation, and a great deal of encouragement in my project. Jim Fox offered intellectual and logistical support that made my stay in Canberra a great deal more comfortable than it would have been if he were not around. Thank you for all of your support.

Lisa Law, Peter Raftos, and Andrew Walker all helped by reading drafts at an earlier stage. I would like to thank them all from the bottom of my heart. Tim Curtis, Đỗ Thiện, Kevin Ormes, Phạm Thu Thủy, and Ian Scales helped me with a number of details, for which I express my gratitude. Philip Taylor has always been a strong supporter and his encouragement at a crucial time brought me back to academia when I thought I had no chance to continue. His words and help have played a pivotal role in the trajectory of my life.

My colleagues at Saint Mary's University have been a great support. Thank you, Paul, Anne-Marie, Magi, Nancie, and Bill. All of the people that I encountered during my studies at Concordia University in Montreal encouraged me to pursue my doctorate. Principally, David Miller has been a long-time friend and mentor. Without his encouragement and advice, in a range of matters, I would certainly not have continued studying religion. Leslie Orr and Sheila McDonough were both helpful along the way and I thank them for all they did.

Two anonymous readers looked at this manuscript when it was first sent to the University of Hawai'i Press. Both clearly took great care and thought in examining it and offered very valuable advice for its revision. I would like to express my deepest appreciation for the assistance of these anonymous reviewers.

The research could not have been done without the financial assistance of the Social Sciences and Humanities Research Council of Canada, the Australian National University, Saint Mary's University, and the logistical support of Professor Phan Huy Lê and the Center for Vietnamese and Intercultural Studies.

Earlier versions of some parts of this book have been published elsewhere. Fragments of Chapter 3 appear in the essays "Masculinities and Buddhist Symbolism in Vietnam," published in *Playing the Man: New Approaches to Masculinity* (Soucy 1999) and in "The Problem with Key Informants," in *Anthropological Forum* (Soucy 2000). Parts of Chapters 4 and 5 appear in "Consuming Lộc— Creating Ơn: Women, Offerings and Symbolic Capital in Vietnam," in the journal *Studies in Religion/Sciences Religieuses* (Soucy 2006), and some of Chapter 9 appears in an essay titled, "Language, Orthodoxy and Performances of Authority in Vietnamese Buddhism," published by *The Journal of the American Academy of Religion* (Soucy 2009).

My family, of course, deserves the biggest thanks. They have been by my side all along, for which I am deeply appreciative. Thank you, Dad and Mom, Terry, Joan, and Jill. An especially big thanks to my wife, Lan, and my children Hiếu and Ái Linh. I love you all very much.

Introduction

It was early morning. Quán Sứ Pagoda, the most important pagoda in Hanoi, was crowded.[1] Because it was the fifteenth day of the lunar month, middle-aged and elderly women were everywhere, wearing the brown robes and the Buddhist prayer beads that marked them as lay Buddhists. In the large main hall there were nearly two hundred devotees sitting on grass mats that flowed out the doors and onto the balcony that surrounded the pagoda. They were waiting for the sutra recital to begin; some of them had been waiting for as long as an hour in order to get a good place, close to the altar. Gently waving their purple fans to cool themselves in the stifling heat, they chatted to their neighbors, or quietly counted on their prayer beads: "*Nam-mô A-Di-Đà Phật... Nam-mô A-Di-Đà Phật... Nam-mô A-Di-Đà Phật....*"[2] Then, as now, women made up the vast majority of people in Hanoi who consider themselves devout Buddhists.

There was also a scattering of men sitting in the first two rows, directly below the large multitiered altar that held gilded statues of the most important figures of the Mahayana Buddhist pantheon. The men, also wearing brown robes, were mostly over sixty years of age, and some of them had long goatees in the fashion of Hồ Chí Minh. Unlike the women, the men did not chat. They sometimes greeted other men who arrived, but they did so in a quick and quiet manner, after which they resumed sitting silently and waiting for the service to begin. They did not come to the pagoda early, because their place in the front was assured. Some of them looked at Chinese characters written on a paper. One of them, younger than the others (perhaps in his mid-fifties), sat with his legs crossed and eyes closed as if in meditation.

These people had assembled for the ritual called the *Sám Nguyện*—the Buddhist version of a penitence ritual—that takes place four times every lunar month.[3] It consists of chanting particular sutras in unison, and was led that day by one of the old men in the front, who used a microphone. Near the end of the ritual an official document in Chinese characters called a *sớ*, printed to look like an imperial petition, was read by another layman who had made himself a religious specialist by studying how to read Chinese characters for ritual purposes. The petition identified the group, the date, and the location, so that the buddhas would know who the supplicants were.

During the chanting, chatting, vying for seats, and making room for friends before the ritual began, there was another activity taking place—not by a group but by individuals acting on their own behest. Mostly young and middle-aged women, they brought offerings of fruit, flowers, and incense; spirit money (*vàng mã*) to be burnt as offerings; and a few small bills of Vietnamese currency that would be left as offerings and donations.[4] After placing the offerings on the altar and praying for the well-being of their families and themselves, or maybe for a special favor, they went to the back of the hall and talked with their friends or waited silently. After about five minutes, they reclaimed their now spiritually charged offerings, called *lộc*. They then left the pagoda and returned home, where they distributed the *lộc* to members of their families and sometimes their friends to pass on the Buddha's blessings.

Outside the main hall, but still in the pagoda compound, there were other activities in progress. In the library there were a few men reading books about Buddhism. In the offices upstairs a team of monks and lay Buddhists were working on the next issue of the magazine published there, *The Research Journal of Buddhist Studies* (*Tạp chí nghiên cứu phật học*). In the store run by the pagoda, there were women buying books and tapes of Buddhist chanting, and in the alcoves and corners of the pagoda complex, still others were engaged in different activities: chanting sutras, counting prayer beads, talking with friends, or bartering with vendors who sold religious books and votive items. Beyond the front gate there were others who passed by, giving no credence to Buddhism or to religion in general.

This book is about all of these people—from the most cynical to the most devout. It explores some of the reasons why they were here on this day, whether or not they were engaged in the different activities. It particularly looks at the way people's life positions—especially age and gender—shape their attitudes towards Buddhism. Their religious practices play an important part in the construction of their identities, and have repercussions that extend well beyond the pagoda walls. Their practices are rooted in their social lives and are integral to their attempts to navigate the vicissitudes of their lives as successfully as possible. Thus, their religious practices also shape their relationships with others.

BUDDHIST IDENTITIES

In Vietnamese Buddhism, there is no systematized, formally imposed, orthodox practice that is required of all devotees. Devotees participate in religious activities that correspond to their social situations, to some extent. Even within one form of practice (e.g., chanting sutras), many interpretations across a wide range are given to its significance and objectives. All of the practices described above, and more, are legitimate ways of interacting with Buddhism, and no one is ever accused of not being Buddhist for lack of participation in a specific activity. These practices are not randomly chosen, however. Rather, they tend to be gender specific, with some activities practiced by women and others by men. The significance of the practices is often interpreted differently by each, though most devotees are women. (Based on my observations of pagodas in northern Vietnam, attendance at most pagoda events is around 80 to 90 percent women.)[5] Implicit in these variations are complex gender dynamics related to the family, age, and historical circumstances of living in Hanoi at the end of the twentieth and beginning of the twenty-first centuries. Thus, the people engaged in their various individual activities at Quán Sứ Pagoda represent complex interplays of gender and religious practice that reverberate through lives and that have an impact on the significant relationships with families and others.

The different ways that people engage with Buddhism presents a challenge to determining who we can call a Buddhist. Many practice without taking part in any formal initiation that categorically distinguishes them as Buddhist. Most approach Buddhism by paying respect to members of the Buddhist pantheon and perhaps asking for assistance when circumstance demands. They usually will give offerings equally to the Buddhist and non-Buddhist supernatural, making little distinction between buddhas and non-Buddhist deities, other than perhaps saying that the buddhas are more potent. Other Hanoi Buddhists will say that these practices and the belief in their efficacy are useless (and potentially dangerous) superstition. They say that the effect of making offerings is only to offer respect to the Buddha and that supplicants should not expect their actions to bring benefit. This doctrinally minded minority, who insist that the Buddha does not have supernatural efficacy, often describes the majority of people who show up to make offerings and ask favors of the buddhas and bodhisattvas as deluded, and not true, Buddhists. Nonetheless, there is an overall tolerance for all activities, even on the part of the most doctrinal individuals, with the reasoning being that misguided actions also may bring about an increased dedication, and perhaps a deeper understanding with time.

People who have encountered Buddhism in the West may well agree with the doctrinal opinion of this minority of religious "elite" who believe that being Buddhist has little to do with making offerings, but instead is about achieving a level of understanding of the nature of existence and living life accordingly. Many Western Buddhists might even believe that being an active Buddhist must necessarily involve meditation. However, in a Vietnamese context, meditation is an exceptional practice that very few people who consider themselves Buddhist actually do, including monastics. Nor is there any consensus in Vietnam over which other activity is essential for Buddhists, other than moral behavior. Most of the fervent devotees chant sutras, but chanting is not perceived as essential, even by those who participate regularly in this activity.

What, then, constitutes appropriate practice for a Buddhist and what must one do to be considered a Buddhist? It has been suggested by Holmes Welch that the criteria for determining whether or not someone is Buddhist should be whether they have taken the Three Refuges or Five Precepts (1973 [1967], 358). In the Vietnamese context, however, such criteria do not usually hold true. The question of what is required for a person to be considered a Buddhist is largely unproblematic and seems to concern scholars and Western Buddhists more than it does Buddhist practitioners in Vietnam. In Vietnam, the equivalent term of "Buddhist" does not even exist in the same sense as the English term. The closest approximate term is "*phật tử*" in Sino-Vietnamese (Hán-Việt), meaning "child of the Buddha." That term is used to designate someone who identifies himself as Buddhist, but self-definition does not need to be ratified by an initiation ritual. More often, people describe themselves as following the Buddha rather than declaring themselves as belonging to a category identified as "Buddhist."

Charles Prebish offers a reasonable solution to the problem of defining who is a Buddhist by stating that we cannot seriously study Buddhism unless we are prepared to accept that if a person makes a recognizable claim to being Buddhist, then that person's claim has to be accepted, regardless of whether their practices and conceptions of Buddhism comply with "orthodoxy" or instead constitute what some have problematically called "syncretism" (Prebish 1979, 188; Prebish 1999, 56).[6] Following his lead, I take Buddhist practice to include any activity that is regarded by practitioners as Buddhist. I do not dwell on the incongruities between these practices and Buddhist texts, but instead look closely at the differences between individual practices and individual conceptions of what these practices mean in order to explore their relations to social positionality. This approach is methodologically imperative in order to take into account conflicting claims of legitimacy and illegitimacy, and to understand the discourses from which such claims emerge.

Many Vietnamese define themselves as Buddhist, but it is not necessarily because they unfailingly participate in Buddhist activities such as chanting sutras. Nor does that self-definition mean that they exclusively engage in Buddhist actions, and that they refuse to interact with spirits outside the Buddhist pantheon, enter into non-Buddhist spaces, or engage in ritual practices that are not regarded as Buddhist from a doctrinal standpoint. It is common in northern Vietnam for people to pray to the buddhas, recite sutras, and listen to Dharma talks at famous pagodas while practicing ancestor worship, consulting fortune-tellers, going to spirit possession rituals, hanging magical paper talismans above their doors, and participating in a host of other activities. In fact, these practices sometimes occur at the same location. Furthermore, most practitioners do not view these various activities as belonging exclusively to one religion or another. Indeed, many of these activities may not even be regarded as "religious," they are so inextricably part of the everyday.

While those who participate fully in this array of activities do not necessarily (or even usually) experience a conflict between the Buddhist and non-Buddhist, those who maintain a doctrinal, "orthodox" understanding of Buddhism see this set of "non-Buddhist" practices as contradicting the teachings of the Buddha. However, both of these views need to be seen as discourses grounded in particular social positions rather than understood as inherently "true" in any sense.

People engage in Buddhist practice at various levels, with some making offerings while not necessarily identifying themselves as Buddhist, and others making Buddhism central to their identity projects. Motivations for engaging in Buddhist practice, therefore, are variable, but can include personal interest, spiritual impulse, a desire to have a certain need met (such as wishing for supernatural assistance to pass an exam), as an activity to alleviate boredom, out of a desire for inclusion and community or conformity to social expectation (or even resistance to social expectation), and as a complement to broader projects of identity construction and performance. These motivations are complicated, particularly because they are not mutually exclusive.

Buddhist practice is more than what goes on inside the pagoda, and cannot be isolated from the overall lives of those who practice. Engagement with Buddhism, and religion in general, provides avenues through which people not only provide meaning, but also wrestle for control of their lives. As Kapferer has stated, religious practice is concerned with "fundamental processes by which human beings construct and transform their life situations" (1997, xii), rather than with abstract philosophies, discrete cosmological systems, or vague soteriological goals.

This book is primarily concerned with gender and Buddhist practice. For reasons mentioned above, though, this subject cannot be discussed without also describing many practices that readers may consider non-Buddhist, because these practices are interconnected. For example, spirit mediumship is not separated from Buddhist practices by most women with whom I spoke and often takes place in Buddhist pagodas. There was no sense that these activities were fundamentally opposed or distinct. Instead, people spoke about them as being complementary and necessary to maintain the spiritual vibrancy of the pagoda, though most male Buddhists would nonetheless avoid participation in them.

KEY INFORMANTS

The gendered nature of religious practice has direct methodological implications, for men's ways of being often lead them to set themselves up in positions of power by assuming (or performing) leadership roles and authoritative positions that resonate with their own worlds.[7] This positioning is tied to the overall hegemonic structure of gender in Vietnam that subjugates women to men by maintaining inherently unequal social structures, which nonetheless appear "natural" to those who participate in their reproduction. The relationship between these structures and religious practice goes two ways: men's authority in the Buddhist space draws on the overall construction of gender in order to maintain power, but the enacting of gendered dispositions in Buddhism also contributes to the overall reproduction of gender structures in Vietnamese society.

The fact that all those who are seen as authoritative within the Buddhist field are men is not incidental, and presents a particular challenge for researching Buddhist practice.[8] Performances of expertise should not be accepted at face value as "truth" because the (male) experts' authority is very much a part of the reproduction of gender hegemony, and therefore need to be regarded as an integral part of social practice. These experts' authority to speak is a manifestation of their cultural capital, which stems partly through signifiers (such as social position, gender, and education level) but also through the way that they present themselves (i.e., their cultural fluency). Key informants or ritual specialists have a vested interest in providing the anthropologist with explanations of ritual symbolism, but the valuing of a particular kind of authoritative knowledge by the anthropologist ignores the social contexts and dynamics from which the explanations emerge. There also are other kinds of knowledge, other interpretations that are not voiced as loudly because of the lack of authority or the lower status of their bearers.

It is not surprising that many anthropologists seek out and rely on ritual specialists. Often in my own research the problem of the existence of "experts" was an obstacle, a situation also noted by other ethnographers (e.g., Ortner 1989, 7–8). People who are not "experts," particularly women, would redirect me to an authoritative figure when I questioned them about the religious practices in which they were engaged. It was not that they did not have their own understanding of their religious practices, but that women were muted by their feelings of inadequacy and lack of authority. As Gal writes, "Some linguistic strategies and genres are more highly valued and carry more authority than others. In a classic case of symbolic domination, even those who do not control these authoritative forms consider them more credible or persuasive" (1991, 177). Those who were considered to be experts (inevitably men) eclipsed others' opinions. Women, however, still framed their practice within their understandings of their worlds, even though they were reluctant to speak of the meanings behind their practice because of a lack of cultural capital that would allow them to do so. Their silence was a statement about the feelings they had regarding their position rather than a statement of ignorance. This study, therefore, will endeavor to give equal credence to these different voices.

RELIGION, RENEWAL, AND THE STATE

The state has always had a close but ambiguous relationship with religion in Vietnam. Keith Taylor (1986) has demonstrated that the Lý Dynasty kings (1009–1225) drew legitimacy from the supernatural. Buddhist monks were close advisors to the king during the Trần period (1225–1400), after which Confucianism took over as the state religion (Ho Tai 1987, 119–128). The southern Nguyễn Lords (1558–1777) turned to Mahayana Buddhism while the northern Vietnamese Trịnh (1545–1787) maintained the primacy of Confucianism (Li Tana 1998, 103). Relying on religion for authority meant that religion also could pose a threat, which is the primary reason for the state repression of religion. The concern about the subversive capacity of religion can be seen in the position that the Communist state took towards religion in Vietnam after independence in 1954. At that time, the state sought to transform Vietnamese society through land reforms, collectivization, and manipulation of the social structure of Vietnam. Religion was targeted as being a vestige of the feudal past that needed to be discouraged, and a threat to the Marxist–Leninist state orthodoxy.

Today, Vietnam is formally a Socialist country founded by Hồ Chí Minh and based on Marxist–Leninist ideas, but is economically and socially capitalist. The country's economic shift towards free-market capitalism has led to a rapid growth of the urban centers, increased industrialization, and expanded international ties. The economic policy under which this transformation has occurred is called the Renovation (Đổi Mới). Since its initiation in 1986, state-owned enterprises have increasingly been privatized, foreign investment has been encouraged, and people have, at least economically, been given free rein. There also has been a substantial decrease in social welfare and subsidies. Control over the economy has been loosened and the Socialist ethic of equality largely abandoned, but the Communist Party still remains in power, and guards its power by controlling the press and repressing dissidents. Concurrent with these economic changes and abandonment of isolationism, the state has adopted a new stance towards religion. While it is still careful not to let religious groups engage in activities that could be politically threatening, the state has largely allowed people to resume their traditional religious practices. It even makes use of some aspects of religion for fostering nationalism and building a national narrative that provides legitimacy.

Religion is now flourishing; new pagodas, temples, and communal houses are being constructed; old buildings are undergoing major rebuilding projects; and increasing numbers of people are filling them. Traditional religious festivals and religious sites are inundated with pilgrims traveling from all parts of Vietnam and abroad. Sites such as the Perfume Pagoda (Chùa Hương) and the Temple for the Lady of the Storehouse (Đền Bà Chúa Kho) in the north and the Shrine for the Lady of the Realm (Đền Bà Chúa Xứ) in the south are seeing more visitors than ever (Marr 1994; Soucy 2003; P. Taylor 2004). Village festivals, centered on their tutelary gods and the village communal houses, are well attended and prospering (Choi 2007; Endres 2001, 71; Malarney 2002). Fortune-tellers, spiritual healers, and geomancy experts service a steady stream of clients. Vendors of religious items such as spirit money and votive objects are evidently doing good business on the streets of Hanoi, with merchandise stacked to the ceiling. Even items for the more controversial spirit possession rituals are openly displayed in shops on Hàng Quạt Street in Hanoi. In fact, without knowing the history of the last fifty years, one would think it had always been this way.

Although the Renovation in Vietnam has brought an improvement in the living standards of most people, it also has produced a sense of uncertainty. The Asian financial crisis that began in 1997 underscored the volatile natures of global economics and business in an open market. Decentralization has removed most of the social safety nets that had existed, leading people to seek out alternative avenues for succor, especially supplication of the supernatural.[9] Conjecture on the tie between religion and economics is not limited to academics, but was also made by some of my informants in Hanoi, who pointed out that business owners are more likely to seek supernatural assistance, through geomancy, fortune-telling, and the burning of spirit money on the first and fifteenth of every lunar month.

Overall, the state still holds a very ambiguous position towards religion, perhaps because the state itself is a social manifestation and is therefore informed by broader discourses in society at the same time that it shapes those discourses. In particular, state attitudes towards religion feed off masculine positions and have an impact on the way that religion is viewed and practiced. The state provides a discursive framing of religious practice and gender in the differentiation between "religion" (*tôn giáo*) and "superstition" (*mê tín di đoan*).[10] While freedom of belief is guaranteed under the Vietnamese constitution, superstition continues to be targeted by the Communist Party as feudal, backwards, and a social evil.[11] What constitutes religion as opposed to religious belief in Vietnam, however, remains unclear. This means that various organs of the state, or even different members of the police in different areas, act on very ambiguous and conflicting criteria, resulting in uneven enforcement. The recent trend to give more freedom to religious practice is legislated to some degree, though there remains a lack of clarity in definitions of what constitutes religion as opposed to superstition, the legislation is not always clear. Media reports on superstition, however, continue to negatively target such activities as expensive weddings and funerals, burning spirit treasure and other votive objects, fortune-telling, séances, spirit possession rituals, and so on.

The differentiation of religious practice from superstition should be seen as a fundamental part of the gender-religion nexus in Vietnam because it is primarily women who are viewed as superstitious. Consequently, women's religious practice is devalued and made illegitimate while male rituals are valorized. This is especially the case in recent years when there has increasingly been a return to valuing Vietnamese culture and tradition, of which men's religious practice is seen as emblematic. I make no claim that religion is a major site of domination, legitimation, or resistance to a political or gender order (although all of these are indeed present in the practice of religion in Vietnam). Instead, religious practice is largely tied to a way of living gender that is enmeshed in, and reproduced through, social practice. The conjuncture of state, gender, and religion is directly relevant to an understanding of how religious practice ties in with the lived experiences of practitioners in Hanoi.

RESEARCH

The summer of 1994 was the first time that I traveled to Vietnam. I had only just finished two years of research in Montreal for my master's thesis on Vietnamese Buddhism, and had gone in search of the homeland of the people I had come to know.[12] During my master's research I noticed the gender discrepancies in attendance and participation at the Montreal pagoda where I had done my work. The Sunday service was typically attended mostly by women, with a few elderly men sitting up front by the statue of Địa Tạng (Kṣitigarbha), the bodhisattva most deeply associated with the cult of the dead in Vietnam. Other men attended only periodically, usually because of a special ritual for a deceased relative, and would not usually go to the pagoda. My travels in 1994 gave me an opportunity to confirm that the preponderance of women was also typical throughout Vietnam. My original intention was to go to Huế to conduct my research, but I instead remained in Hanoi for a number of reasons, not the least of which was meeting my future wife.

The main part of my research took place over a period of eighteen months in Hanoi, from January 1997 to August 1998. I spent another period there from 2000 to 2001 at which time I continued research part time, returning again in 2004 for six weeks of intensive fieldwork, and most recently in 2010 for five weeks to clarify some points for this book. For this study I regularly visited a number of different Buddhist pagodas and participated in the activities there. I also took part in activities that were not located in the pagoda, but that were part of being religious in Vietnam. I went on pilgrimages in dilapidated buses jammed with old women who undertook the excursions not only out of piety, but also because they enjoyed the chance to get out of the house. I went on pseudo-pilgrimages to a variety of religious sites with groups of young people who also had varying purposes, ranging from piety to what participants described as "entertainment." I sat and chanted sutras with the most devout of the pagoda community. I joined the rehearsals of an all-male ritual group, and learned to play the drum rhythms used during the rituals they performed. I sat and studied Chinese characters with the nun of one pagoda and had long discussions with old men about a variety of subjects pertaining to Buddhism and Vietnamese culture. Other religious activities I attended included rites of passage (weddings and funerals), village festivals centered on the communal house, séances, fortune-telling, and spirit possession rituals, in which a succession of spirits enter into a spirit medium who then distributes *lộc*—gifts from the gods. It could be said, then, that while my research focused on Buddhism, I also spent a great deal of effort trying to understand the full range of religious practices in Vietnam.

Hanoi, though not large by Southeast Asian standards, has a substantial population of around 3.4 million.[13] The population density is the highest in Vietnam, with 2,161 people per square kilometer, and with housing space of 1.2 square meters per person in 1992 (Li Tana 1996, 15). However, official figures are notoriously inexact because of the large number of unofficial residents and nonresident migrant workers who come into Hanoi from the surrounding countryside in order to find employment.[14]

The people with whom I worked were mostly permanent residents of

Hanoi. Some of them were from families who had lived in Hanoi for several generations, while a number were more recent migrants. Many of the young people were university educated and currently hold positions in joint-venture companies, state-owned enterprises, or private Vietnamese companies. In terms of the overall population of Vietnam, many of the younger people I met can be understood to be privileged. I also spoke at length with a number of young men who had come to Hanoi as itinerant laborers from villages to find work, who planned eventually to return home to marry and settle down after they had accumulated sufficient capital to do so. They invited me to their home villages on a number of occasions, and I became acquainted with their families and friends. I returned to one particular village in Hà Tây province numerous times, and came to know a few of the inhabitants quite well. I met many of my older informants at pagodas in Hanoi. In general, they were not university educated. Those few who were not yet retired made their living through unskilled labor and petty trade. Many of their children had significant advantages and had been able to receive university educations. Some of the older people with whom I had contact had held middle-management positions and a select few represent the new wealthy minority.

The research for this book was mostly done at two pagodas in Hanoi, though I have visited and chanted sutras in many others throughout Vietnam, as well as Vietnamese pagodas in Canada and Australia. These two pagodas were chosen for specific reasons. Quán Sứ Pagoda, as the pagoda housing the Vietnamese Buddhist Association (*Giáo hội phật giáo Việt Nam*), is politically the most important pagoda in Hanoi. Research at Quán Sứ Pagoda gave me insight into state-sanctioned Buddhism and normative practices and ideas. This pagoda also had the advantage of always being busy, with plenty of people I could observe and with whom I could speak. By contrast, most other pagodas were usually empty, except on specific days and for special rituals.

The second, named "Phúc Lộc Pagoda" (a pseudonym), was located beside a bustling market. It was a peaceful sanctuary from the tumultuous life surrounding it, offering a stark contrast from the world outside its gates. I chose this pagoda because, in contrast to Quán Sứ Pagoda, it was much smaller and attracted only local residents. Because of the smaller scale of Phúc Lộc Pagoda, I was able to get to know a closed group of people from the neighborhood in which I lived, and therefore experienced how the pagoda fit into the community. For this reason, I write as though the information recorded here is specific to Hanoi, though much of it is also applicable throughout the north, in other parts of Vietnam and among the diaspora. Nonetheless, as my data are not sufficient to make this claim, I will be writing specifically of Hanoi throughout the book.

OUTLINE OF THE CHAPTERS

The following chapters are intended to draw out some of the threads of Buddhist practice as they relate to gender and age in Hanoi. They will describe how men and women live as Buddhists in different ways, participating in different activities. As practices differ for men and women so do men's and women's interpretations of what they are doing, reflecting the different ways that men and women construct their identities and negotiate their lives.

Chapter 1 provides background of the Vietnamese religious landscape and different conceptions about how the supernatural relates to people's lives. It starts off with descriptions of some of the ways that people approach religion and religious practice in order to illustrate the widely different interpretations of being religious in Vietnam. It then discusses the Vietnamese religious landscape that I most frequently encountered in the speech and actions of nonspecialist interlocutors with the supernatural. The chapter ends with the opposing, elite view of religion, and how it has played out in recent history.

Chapter 2 looks more closely at the relationship between the state and religion during the last century. It starts with a description of the Buddhist Revival that began in the first part of the twentieth century, and how the state has promoted the view that Buddhist reformers put forward. The way that these state discourses play out on the ground is illustrated through an introduction to the two primary pagodas where I conducted my research: Quán Sứ Pagoda, which is the state-backed representation of Buddhism, and Phúc Lộc Pagoda, which is unremarkable, politically marginal, and architecturally and artistically embodies a more holistic cosmology that recognizes a range of potent and imminent supernatural actors.

The masculine position towards religion is further explored in Chapter 3. Rather than focusing on religious practitioners, it instead focuses on young men, which is the segment of the population most critical of religion. Their skepticism is taken as performance directed towards their masculine gender projects—called "projects" because gender is not a fixed structure, but is constantly being built and changed to suit the environment. It is a part of the way they situate themselves in society and attempt to influence important aspects of their lives. Their attitudes towards religion are in some way a form of religious practice, and need to be taken into account in a discussion of the relationship between Buddhism and gender. In many ways, this chapter is a continuation of the discussion of state power and religion that was started in Chapter 2.

In order to flesh out the holistic way in which the Vietnamese typically interact with the supernatural, Chapter 4 looks specifically at practices and meanings of *lộc*. These supernaturally charged items are part of a practice that is a central activity of all religious expressions, crossing them and uniting them. It starts with a description of the meanings and manifestations of *lộc* before turning to a discussion of the implications of *lộc* for understanding the overall worldview of religious Vietnamese.

Chapter 5 continues with the practice of making offerings and reclaiming *lộc* for distribution to family and friends. It is a practice that is performed especially by women and is by far the most common form of Buddhist engagement. In opposition to the skeptical performances of young men, making offerings is integral to the way that femininity is constructed. This chapter explores the way that young women practice Buddhism as part of an enactment of a sexually desirable femininity that emphasizes qualities such as reliance and weakness.[15] It then looks at how the distribution of *lộc* by married women is also an opportunity to create sentiment and moral debt in the family.

The next two chapters go deeper into the pagoda by looking at the older women who become increasingly engaged in pagoda life. Their practice usually includes supplications and *lộc*, but is intensified through additional activities, such as chanting sutras. Chapter 6 starts by looking at the life changes that bring about this intensification. It then looks at the specific activities of these devout women as part of a religious practice that becomes centrally important to their identity. Chapter 7 looks at a darker side of this increased involvement. While one of the motivations for becoming more involved is the sense of community that involvement in the pagoda provides, there is also competition within the field that manifests itself in what I call "conspicuous devotion." This latter comprises performances of devotion and the collection and display of objects that signify their level of commitment as a way to create distinction and gain status within the group.

Most Buddhist practitioners are women, but there are a small number of older men who become involved at the pagoda. This participation presents something of a dilemma: as I show in Chapter 3, masculinity is partly constructed through performances of skepticism and strength, in opposition to women's reliance. Older men who become involved in Buddhism, therefore, rephrase Buddhist practice in a way that adds to a masculinity more appropriate to older men, and avoids the feminine aspects that are usually associated with Buddhism. The change in perspective towards Buddhist involvement is discussed in Chapter 8 by looking at the way that Buddhist rituals (and practice in general) are interpreted differently by men and women. Chapter 9 looks at how the practice of many male

Buddhists is rooted in a concern for knowledge-based self-cultivation, a pursuit with thoroughly masculine connotations that resonate with Confucian ideals. This chapter focuses on the performative aspects of masculine participation in the Buddhist field that are intended to gain greater status and authority.

A NOTE ON LANGUAGE

A few notes need to be made about language. I have kept all of the diacritics on Vietnamese words. I have done this principally because Vietnamese is a tonal language and dropping the diacritical accent marks may change the meaning of some words. I also maintain diacritics on Sanskrit names and include Chinese characters where applicable for the sake of consistency. I do, however, omit the diacritics on "Ho Chi Minh City," "Hanoi," and on "Vietnam." All other place names do have the proper diacritical marks.

All individuals have been given pseudonyms, with the exception of public figures like Thích Thanh Từ. Furthermore, the name of one of the pagodas where I did my work, "Phúc Lộc" Pagoda, is a pseudonym. I have continued to use the real name for Quán Sứ Pagoda because it is politically important and its stature is relevant to the points being made, and other incidental religious sites, where their inclusion is of no consequence.

Referencing authors is a particularly sticky problem because Vietnamese names are written with the family name first. However, many overseas Vietnamese scholars change their name order to suit their Western environment and some Vietnamese scholars drop the diacritics on their names when publishing in English. I retain the form under which they published. For references, there will be a comma after names that publish using the Western name order (e.g., "C. T. Nguyen, 1995" rather than "Nguyen Tu Cuong 1995"). I also will use the full name in citations for authors who follow the traditional name order (e.g., Ngô Đức Thịnh 2006) and will follow the authors in the use of diacritical markings. Therefore, some Vietnamese names will appear with them and some without. For works written by authors who use the traditional Vietnamese name order, they are listed in the bibliography under their family names (e.g., Ngô Đức Thịnh will be listed under "Ngô").

I use the words "gods" or "goddesses," and "spirits" interchangeably to refer to all supernatural beings except ancestors, ghosts, and members of the Buddhist pantheon (buddhas and bodhisattvas). Thus, tutelary genii and deified national heroes (*thần*), as well as mother goddesses (*thánh mẫu*) will all be called gods and goddesses throughout. Finally, the historical Buddha, Siddhārtha Gautama, who lived and died in India and is credited as the founder of Buddhism, will be referred to as "the Buddha" or in the Vietnamese form as Thích Ca Mâu Ni, or Thích Ca for short. All other buddhas and bodhisattvas will be referred to by name. For the names of buddhas and bodhisattvas, I will use the Vietnamese forms and the index will include both Vietnamese and more common names for reference.

1   Views of the Religious Landscape

For most people in Vietnam religion is lived rather than experienced intellectually. People pray to the buddhas, chant sutras, offer incense to gods, goddesses, or ancestors, and have their fortunes read without, for the most part, pondering the cosmological implications of their actions. Buddhism, as most people approach it, cannot be understood through the philosophical content of religious texts: most people who visit pagodas are unaware of the intricacies of Buddhist philosophy. They do not repeat a creed nor "belong" to a religion. This does not mean that in Vietnam there is one amorphous religion, followed uncritically by all. Rather, there are objectively different aspects, shapes, and contours to the religious expressions that are a part of everyday lives. There is something called "Buddhism," with an institution, corpus of sacred writings, definable rituals, and recognizable religious specialists. At the same time, there are unities and ambiguities that make it artificial to talk about Buddhism divorced from the overall religious landscape. For most practicing Buddhists, what we identify as Buddhism represents only a part of a complex interaction with a supernatural world that is also populated by a variety of other beings that have the power to help or hinder.

The intention of this chapter is to provide descriptions of how the Vietnamese that I knew in Hanoi interact with the supernatural, highlighting the competing views about how to be religious. By introducing some of these people, I hope to show the fluid boundaries between different religious expressions. This will lead into a discussion of the popular view of the beings that populate the supernatural, the ranking that they are accorded, and the characteristics that people attribute to them. While the view I will describe is pervasive, it is politically marginalized by an "elite" view of religion, which also figures in the way that some people (principally men) engage in Buddhism. The chapter, accordingly, will end with a description of this opposing view of religion, and how it has played out in recent history.

DESCRIPTIONS OF THE LANDSCAPE

In Vietnam today there are very few religious practices that are prescribed, with the exception of funerals and ancestor worship. People pick and choose the beliefs and activities that make sense within the context of their own lives. For some, this lack of prescription results in almost total skepticism and avoidance, but religious activities and ideas play a role in the lives of most. The tremendous variance in beliefs and practices means that the supernatural is approached in a multitude of ways. This is especially the case in urban Hanoi, where village-based practices and imperatives are not as prominent, and where people are left to invent ways that religion will be a part of their lives. I first introduce you to four people that I have known in Hanoi. I have remained in contact with three of them since I first met them in 1997—"Mrs. Tu," "Nhung," and "Thầy Linh." I have reinterviewed two as recently as 2010 regarding their religious practices. The fourth person, "Mrs. Thanh," I knew for only a year, in 1997. These four individuals adequately illustrate the variety of ways that people are religious in Hanoi. With the exception of Thầy Linh, they all can be characterized as typical. Though the constellation of their beliefs and practices are idiosyncratic, between them they are also representative examples of the many ways that people approach the supernatural. Their lives bring out the fact that the large choice of possible sites and activities available to those who have a religious inclination makes interactions with the supernatural both personal and varied.

MRS. TU

Mrs. Tu, a religiously active woman in her late fifties when I first met her in 1997, has remained devout. She is a housewife, born in the late 1940s, who never received a high level of education, though her family can be described as middle class. She came from Hà Tây Province and grew up acutely affected by the struggle against French colonialism. Her father had a son and two daughters before his first wife died. He remarried and, with his second wife, conceived Mrs. Tu. When she was still a young child, her father was arrested and executed by the French as a suspected resistance fighter. After her husband's death, and with no support from her husband's family, Mrs. Tu's mother left the village with her daughter, leaving her stepchildren in the care of their paternal family, and went to Hanoi, where she remarried and started a new family. She eventually had two sons and three more daughters. Mrs. Tu, therefore, lives in two families and takes active part in both as the sole offspring of parents who had all of their other children with other spouses. On her father's death day—an important occasion for the commemoration of ancestors—she returns to the village of her father and pays respect to him inside the small pagoda near the place where he was shot. Then she joins with her half-brother and half-sisters to prepare offerings for her father's altar and the feast for the gathered family.

Although she grew up in Hanoi, raised by her mother and her stepfather, she follows tradition in considering the village where she was born—the village of her father—to be her native village. For this reason, she habitually returns to this village not only for the death anniversary of her father, but also for the village festival that centers on the village communal house, where offerings are made to the patron spirit and protector of the village.

The most notable feature about Mrs. Tu's religious life is that she is a devout Buddhist. She chanted sutras regularly at the local pagoda and went to Quán Sứ Pagoda whenever she could in order to listen to dharma talks by well-known monks. When her mother's health failed in 2008, she had to spend time taking care of her until her death in 2010. Now she is busy taking care of an infant grandchild. Nonetheless, while it is difficult for her to go to the pagoda to chant sutras with any regularity, she still chants every day in front of the large altar in her bedroom. She also subscribes to the Buddhist magazines *Enlightenment Weekly Magazine* (*Tuần Báo Giác Ngộ*) and *The Research Journal of Buddhist Studies* (*Tạp Chí Nghiên Cứu Phật Học*), though she seldom reads them. She adorns her house with Buddhist statues, calendars, pictures, and memorabilia from her Buddhist activities. In 2004, she started meditation with Sùng Phúc Thiền Tự, a center that had just been located in Gia Lâm, on the outskirts of Hanoi.[1] At the same time, she is in contact with a Theravada monk in Ho Chi Minh City and regularly sends donations to him, though it is unclear to me whether she draws any difference between Theravada and Mahayana, as distinct traditions.[2]

She also goes on pilgrimages organized by the local pagoda association (*hội phật tử*) to famous religious sites in northern Vietnam, and sometimes farther.[3] In the past few years she has gone to southern Vietnam several times, and once to China. I accompanied her in 1998 on a less ambitious pilgrimage that amply demonstrated the unclear boundaries between Buddhist and non-Buddhist sites and the way in which worship of both Buddhist and non-Buddhist figures is the norm. The bus took the pilgrims to a pagoda and a temple in Hà Tây Province and then to another non-Buddhist temple, Phủ Tây Hồ, in Hanoi on West Lake, before going to the One Pillar Pagoda in Hanoi. Next stop was Hồ Chí Minh's museum and mausoleum, and the stilt house he lived in behind the Presidential Palace.

The visits to the Hồ Chí Minh sites seemed at the time to have as much of a religious feeling as the visits to the temples and pagodas. Historical figures who have contributed to the country, such as General Trần Hưng Đạo and Bà Triệu, have always been venerated in Vietnam. Many of the women not only paid respect to Hồ Chí Minh's embalmed corpse, but also held their hands together in the manner of worship and whispered prayers in the same way they had at the altar of spirits and buddhas throughout the day.

The focus of Mrs. Tu's total religious practice is usually oriented towards bringing immediate benefit for her and her family's health, wealth, and happiness, as it is for most religious people in Vietnam. For example, I accompanied her in the autumn of 1997 to a temple in Gia Lâm dedicated to the goddess Ỷ Lan. Mrs. Tu made an elaborate offering of fruit, flowers, and incense, and, with the palm of her hands pressed together, told the goddess the name and addresses of both her daughter and her daughter's fiancé. She then made wishes for their health, prosperity, happiness, and fertility. While she was there, she also paid a fortune-teller to determine the best time for the wedding.

Mrs. Tu is typical of many women her age in Hanoi. She is an extremely devout Buddhist, but her Buddhist practice is fully integrated into a wider spectrum of religious activities and beliefs. While her self-identity is first and foremost Buddhist, this does not preclude her from visiting non-Buddhist sites and praying to non-Buddhist deities, spirits, and ancestors. It also does not deny her the spiritual resources available for discerning the future and improving her fate and the fate of her family through the supernatural technologies of fortune-telling and geomancy.

NHUNG

Nhung was unhappily single when I first met her in 1997. She was a tailor, so was interested in fashion, and always took great care in the way she dressed. She enjoyed dancing at clubs, shopping, and spending time with friends. However, her single status was a concern for her, and for her family and friends. Young women in Vietnam are expected to be married before the age of thirty, and she was twenty-eight, with no prospects in sight.

Nhung responded to this situation in a number of ways. Her friends actively introduced her to eligible young bachelors. She made herself as attractive as possible and put herself in social situations where her displays of availability would promise maximum benefit. She also altered her behavior to appear less gregarious and more gentle. However, she also enlisted the aid of the supernatural to help her in her quest for a husband. Every month on the first and fifteenth (according to the lunar calendar) she would go to a pagoda or temple and make offerings and wishes to find a husband. Sometimes she went to Phủ Tây Hồ and made offerings to the mother goddesses there, because they have a reputation for granting wishes of this sort. She also would visit famous Buddhist sites in the provinces surrounding Hanoi and would ask for the buddhas to give her a husband. One time, in desperation, she consulted a fortune-teller, who told her that her problem was

that a ghost was attracted to her and the lingering ghost was driving away potential suitors. She underwent a ritual performed by a spirit medium, which was the
spiritual equivalent of a divorce, freeing Nhung to meet with living men. Nhung
was married in 2005 to an overseas Vietnamese living in Prague.

Nhung's religious practice was very pragmatic. She was not particularly
devout, and although she believed in the efficacy of praying for supernatural assistance, she did not make a distinction between the buddhas or other spirits when
seeking assistance. In fact, the reputed potency of a particular supernatural figure
was a more important consideration, and though she would pray to the buddhas,
she did not view herself as Buddhist. Like Mrs. Tu, her religious practice was
aimed at worldly concerns, but she did not have a family, so those concerns rested
mainly with the immediate problem of finding a husband.

Mrs. Thanh

Mrs. Thanh was not a particularly religious woman, either. She was well educated
and made a living as an interpreter, especially for international development organizations working on health issues. She had an ancestor altar in her house, and she
sometimes went to pagodas on the first and fifteenth of the lunar month, but she
did not take part in any group activities, such as chanting sutras. She was religious
in the sense that she had a strong belief in the supernatural, however. This manifested itself primarily in a concern with ghosts, the afterlife, and psychic healing.
She believed that the spirits of the dead were still active in her life and the life
of her family—a belief shared by most Vietnamese.[4] She kept an ancestor altar,
which she kept filled with offerings of fresh fruit and flowers; the ceiling above
the altar had a black spot from the smoke of the incense she lit daily.

Her brother had died in the 1950s, but in the turmoil of those times his
grave had been lost. Out of concern for the fate of her brother's spirit, she had
been on a personal quest for a number of years to locate his remains. She was
intensely concerned that her brother's neglected spirit was hungry for lack of
offerings and lonely for lack of attention. She agonized over the thought that her
brother was suffering from neglect and that he had become a hungry ghost.[5] With
no way to find his remains, she turned to the supernatural with the help of spirit
"callers." However, the many different religious specialists she visited all failed to
give her the location of the grave. In her desperation and faith, her determination
had not waned and she continued to visit spirit callers in the hopes of finding her
brother. Instead of the inability of the spirit callers to find his remains resulting in
disillusionment and doubt over the techniques used, she merely judged some as
fake and others as incompetent.

I went with her once to see a spirit caller in her mid-forties who was holding a séance, or spirit calling (*gọi hồn*).[6] We arrived at the door of an unassuming house in the southern part of Hanoi. The caller's husband ushered us in, and we went up to a medium-sized room that was crowded with people who had come to contact their dead family members. An assistant took the details from Mrs. Thanh about the spirit she wanted to contact and we sat down in the crowd of expectant clients. The scene in the room was emotional, as one by one the clients were reunited with their dead relatives and spouses, channeled through the spirit caller. Conversations with the dead brought tears and provoked offers of comfort and support from those who sat closest. Each client's interactions with their dead presented the crowd with intensely personal vignettes into the sufferings and sorrows of loss that are a part of the human condition.

The most heartbreaking episode came when a mother contacted her dead child. The possessed caller spoke in a childish voice, animating the crowd, most of whom were women, to call out playfully to the child. When the child's spirit asked for candies, some were quickly produced. The scene eventually involved the entire crowd, who laughed when the child was playful and cried when the child expressed the horror of living alone in a land of ghosts.

Eventually Mrs. Thanh's turn came, and we pushed our way through the crowd to the side of the caller, where we sat and waited. She briefly greeted Mrs. Thanh and then gathered herself. After a few moments she became possessed by the spirit of Mrs. Thanh's brother, who wept while relating how he suffered from neglect. He described where he was in vague terms, but was unable to provide details that would aid in the search. Throughout the session the usually strong and stoic Mrs. Thanh cried openly while expressing how she loved and missed him and wanted to find him so that she could care for his soul. I sat near her, feeling slightly embarrassed and uncomfortable while taping the session, at her insistence. After the session, she felt better for communicating with her brother, but was skeptical about the caller's ability and was determined to try another she had heard about.

As with Mrs. Tu and Nhung, Mrs. Thanh's beliefs about the supernatural were not systematic, but she nonetheless held that there were forces at work in our lives. She believed strongly in the power of fortune-tellers—as do most people in Vietnam—and consulted them regularly to determine her fate and to help with major decisions. She believed in the importance of geomancy to ensure that the forces of the world work in her favor rather than against her. She also was interested in the potential of psychic healing and spoke to me often about one master that she particularly favored.

For Mrs. Thanh, the Vietnamese landscape is populated with spirits of the dead, both strangers (ghosts) and family (ancestors) that actively affect the living. Her concern for her brother is representative of how people regard ghosts and ancestors as continuing to have reciprocal relations with the living. Her lack of involvement in most religious rituals at temples and pagodas is not unusual, but cannot be equated with disengagement or disenchantment with religion. Most people believe—and, more importantly, participate—in some aspects of the religious landscape.

Thầy Linh

The most flamboyant monk I ever met, Thầy Linh, let his sideburns grow down the side of his face, extending from the stubble on his shaved head like a Buddhist Elvis. He wore jewelry if he was not going to meet other, higher-ranking, monks. On occasion he would smoke cigarettes, but more often he would chew betel nut—a habit usually reserved for elderly women—which colored his lips a bright red. He was known for having a sharp tongue and a propensity for cursing in the manner stereotypical of a market woman. He was effeminate, flamboyant, and (for a monk) ostentatious, drawing around him a sizeable following of devotees.

I first became acquainted with Thầy Linh on a two-day pilgrimage that was organized by his pagoda community and the community of Phúc Lộc Pagoda. He and Thầy Tâm, the resident nun at Phúc Lộc Pagoda, were good friends at the time. He proved to be an excellent trip leader, always full of good humor and adept at keeping the group entertained and informed. I later found out that Thầy Linh was also a spirit medium when Thầy Tâm arranged for him to perform a spirit possession ritual at Phúc Lộc Pagoda, explaining to me that, though it was not Buddhist, the pagoda had a shrine for the mother goddesses (nhà mẫu) that required service to the goddesses in the form of these rituals.

Thầy Linh was an accomplished bà đồng, exhibiting a high level of artistic skill in the dances and performances that are central to the rituals.[7] As with mediums in the Korean medium rituals, described by Kendall (1985, 1996) and Kendall and Lee (1992), Thầy Linh was chosen by the spirits and so was compelled to fulfill this role. When he was a child, he became ill and his sickness persisted. His parents consulted a fortune-teller and were told that it was his fate to become a medium. As soon as he started apprenticing as a medium, his illness disappeared.

Thầy Linh's story shows the ambiguity between different aspects of the religious landscape of Vietnam. Thầy Linh has achieved the equivalent of a master's degree in Buddhist studies, and is bright, articulate, and charismatic. Although the government and the Buddhist institution do not approve of "superstitious activities" life spirit mediumship, and believe that they are not a part of Buddhism, Thầy Linh does not see a contradiction in being both a monk and a medium. Instead, he feels that the two traditions are complementary and that both are essential. Many Buddhists share the opinion of Thầy Linh in describing the mother goddesses as being complementary to the buddhas, and actively supplicate both as part of their total religious practice.

SPECIALISTS, LOCATIONS, AND PRACTICES

As the above examples show, being religious in Hanoi is varied and multifaceted, leading different people to practice differently. It is mainly their particular concerns that drive them towards one or another form of religious activity and religious space. The way that religion is most often expressed is contextual, through the particularities of specialists, locations, and practices. Thus people speak of having their fortunes read to find the correct date to get married, or become a medium because of a "heavy spirit root" (*nặng căn*), but few would connect these activities and expound in a precise way on the nature of fate (*số phận*) or how it works.

The various activities are usually conducted at specific locations and involve specific specialists, and people usually describe their practices through reference to these. Ancestor worship, for example, is performed primarily by the family at the home altar or at family graves without the help of specialists, other than those needed for siting graves and conducting Buddhist mortuary rites for those who have a stronger affinity with Buddhism. Buddhas are worshipped at pagodas (*chùa*), while spirits are worshipped at temples (*đền*), palaces (*phủ*), or shrines (*miếu*). Individual supplication is the most common interaction with spirits and buddhas, though specific specialists conduct more important rituals at these locations (see Table 1.1).

There are, therefore, a variety of related specialists, locations, and practices active in the Vietnamese religious landscape. However, those who are religious do not usually refer to the groupings of specialists, locations, and practices as separate religions or declare themselves as belonging to a particular religion. Instead, people speak of specific specialists, locations, and practices that play a role in their lives. While specific activities are understood as serving defined purposes, they are nonetheless seen as being part of a whole, like features of a landscape. Thus, Mrs. Tu, though a self-proclaimed and actively practicing Buddhist, did not hesitate to make offerings at locations she fully recognized as non-Buddhist. Likewise, Thầy Linh saw no contradiction between Buddhist practice and the practice

TABLE 1.1
RELIGIOUS ACTIVITIES, LOCATIONS, AND SPECIALISTS

ACTIVITY	LOCATION	SPECIALIST
Worship and make personal offerings (to a variety of supernatural beings)	Any altar, but especially at pagodas and temples	Non-specialist, individuals
Worship the Buddha or buddhas (*lễ Phật*)	Pagoda (*chùa*)	monastic or lay leader (*nhà sư*)
Make official (annual) sacrifices (*tế lễ*)	Communal house (*đình*)	Ceremonial master (*ông tế*) and the community
Fortune-telling (*xem bói*)	Anywhere (but often the fortune-teller's home or on the temple or pagoda grounds)	Fortune-teller (*thầy bói*)
Feng-shui (*phong thủy*)	Home, office, grave	Feng-shui master (no specific term)
Spirit possession ritual (*lên đồng, hầu bóng*)	Temples, shrines, and "palaces" (variously called *đền, phủ, điện, miếu...*)	Spirit medium (*bà/ông đồng*)
Ghost calling or séance (*gọi hồn*)	shrine (*điện*) (usually constructed in the home of the channeler)	Channeler (no specific term)
Ancestor worship	Home or grave	Family
A variety of Buddhist and non-Buddhist rituals (such as making offerings to hungry ghosts to clear the way for a ritual)	Any religious site, usually before rituals	Ritual specialist (*thầy cúng*) or ritual group (*ban cúng*)
Writing petitions to the gods (*sớ*), or talismans (*bùa*)	Usually at the entrance of non-Buddhist religious sites	Scribe (*ông thầy*)
Healing	Home	Physician (*thầy thuốc*) or psychic healer (*nhà truyền cảm*)

Note: This table does not encompass all Vietnamese religious expressions. For instance, it does not incorporate Catholics or agnostics, nor the state-cult, which centers on the figure of Hồ Chí Minh and other national heroes.

of spirit mediumship. Instead, he described the supernatural landscape in a way that included everything. There is a unity to the way that the supernatural world, populated by gods, ghosts, ancestors, and buddhas, is conceived as being a potent force in people's lives. Furthermore, these supernatural entities can be propitiated, through placation, flattery, and gifts, to bring material and soteriological benefit, and to avoid the negative aspects of their supernatural nature. This potency is personalized, so that offerings are most often made to gain support in the worldly affairs of the supplicant. Nonetheless, these beings are not uniform, and are commonly divided into two "sides" in popular speech. Elite discourses, which issue from the state, the academy, and the Buddhist institution, do draw a distinction, though, labeling the former as legitimate, orthodox religion (*chính đạo*) and an acceptable belief (*tín ngưỡng*), and the latter as heterodox (*tà đạo*) and as superstition (*mê tín dị đoan*).

THE BUDDHA SIDE AND THE SPIRIT SIDE

As with Thầy Linh, the most common description that people make of the supernatural landscape draws a distinction between Buddhist and non-Buddhist "sides" (*bên*). The two sides have similarities, in that they are both populated by powerful beings that are regarded as supernatural patrons that can be supplicated with gifts and service, and through invocations of their names for material benefit and protection. Nonetheless, the beings that populate these two sides are not identical, having particular characteristics and proclivities to fulfill specific kinds of requests.

The "Buddha side" (*bên phật*) includes primarily the buddhas (*phật*) and bodhisattvas (*bồ tát*). The Buddhist saints or arhats (*la hán*), usually thought of as followers of the historical Buddha, also are included in the Buddha side. They are honored but do not receive specific prayers, though I was told that these saints or arhats are also buddhas. In the antechambers of most pagodas can be found a pair of martial statues of the dharma guardians (*hộ pháp*) who protect pagodas from evil spirits and are also included in the Buddha side. They, as one nun described them to me, are "the Buddha's people" (*người của Phật*). The Ten Kings of Hell (Diêm Vương) are usually associated with Buddhism in Vietnam, and are traditionally responsible for judging souls for punishment in hell before being reborn. I have also been told that they can be included in the Buddha side (*bên phật*) because they "teach people in hell."

Buddhas and bodhisattvas are believed to intervene in the everyday world, and, like the spirits of the spirit side (*bên thánh*), can aid people with their mundane concerns. Furthermore, there is a sense in which the buddhas and bodhisatt-vas are seen as having specializations. Foremost among these specialized members of the Buddhist pantheon is the Bodhisattva of Mercy, Quan Âm (Ch. Guanyin).[8] She has mercy on those who suffer in this world and is frequently represented as having a thousand eyes and a thousand hands, symbolizing her ability to see our suffering and offer her aid to us. People pray to her for safety, especially those who are at sea. She is also viewed as a figure who will help to conceive children (partic-ularly boys). This ability to aid in conception is especially evident at the Perfume Pagoda in Hà Tây Province, which is dedicated to Quan Âm and renowned for its fertility-granting power. Sometimes she is thought to save souls from hell, though the bodhisattva Địa Tạng (Dizang) is more usually regarded as the bodhisattva specifically dedicated to saving souls that are tormented in hell; he made a vow not to achieve enlightenment until all the hells are emptied. He is frequently seen in pagodas in Vietnam, often to the left of the main altar, wearing a crown and holding a staff that he uses to force open the gates of hell. Once a month at Phúc Lộc Pagoda a sutra is recited for the Medicine Buddha, Dược Sư Phật (Yaoshi Fo), who is seen as particularly potent for curing illness. A Di Đà Phật (Amituo Fo) is also particularly important in the Buddhist pantheon as the central focus of Pure Land Buddhist practice. He has made an oath that anyone who recites his name in faith will be reborn in his Pure Land (Cực Lạc in Vietnamese), a paradise from which enlightenment is guaranteed.

The Buddha side is unique in that it can have the soteriological and escha-tological effects of aiding with reincarnation, teaching souls in hell, and thereby incrementally assisting towards eventual enlightenment. A Di Đà Phật can even assist people to bypass hell and rebirth completely if they recite his name. In this sense, the efficacy of buddhas and bodhisattvas is seen as overriding the cause-and-effect nature of karma, which holds that a person's actions will inevitably result in punishment or reward after death and in the next life. It is in relation to death that Buddhism and the Buddhist pantheon principally distinguish them-selves, though they are also supplicated for material, this-worldly requests.

The "spirit side" (*bên thánh*) refers specifically to gods and goddesses that lie outside the Buddhist pantheon, including immortals or fairies (*tiên*), holy sages or saints (*thánh*) such as the deified hero Trần Hưng Đạo, spirits or genii (*thần*), the complex of mother goddesses (*thánh mẫu*), God or Heaven (*Ông Trời*), the Earth God (*Ông Địa*), the Jade Emperor (*Ngọc Hoàng*), and other figures associ-ated with the Chinese Daoist pantheon (e.g., the Kitchen God—*Ông Táo*) (see Table 1.2). I have even been told that Hồ Chí Minh can be included on the spirit side, though in the following account from a nun he is eventually elevated to the

TABLE 1.2
The Buddha Side (Bên Phật) / The Spirit Side (Bên Thánh)

THE BUDDHA SIDE	THE SPIRIT SIDE
buddhas (*phật*)	holy sages or saints (*thánh*)
bodhisattvas (*bồ tát*)	court installed spirits (*thần*)
Buddhist saints (arhats, *la hán*)*	immortals (*tiên*)
Ten Kings of Hell (Diêm Vương)*	mother goddesses (*thánh mẫu*)
Dharma guardians (Hộ Pháp)*	Earth God (Ông Địa)
	Jade Emperor (Ngọc Hoàng)
	God (Ông Trời)
	The Kitchen God (Ông Táo)
	ancestors (*tổ tiên*)

* These figures are revered but not propitiated to the same extent as the buddhas and bodhisattvas. Although they are especially associated with Buddhism, they have many of the qualities of the spirits.

Portrait of Hồ Chí Minh with portraits of other divinities, for sale on a Hanoi street

level of a buddha or bodhisattva, illustrating that the boundaries between the two sides can be somewhat flexible:

> All of the Vietnamese people pay respect to him. He is a spirit [*thánh*]. Some families make an altar for him and others keep him in their hearts...if they make a wish to him, they make a wish for the country, praying for the country's liberty, peace, for there to be no more foreign invasions and for the north and the south to be peaceful and get along with each other. They also pray to him for everyone to have plenty of food and warm houses. Hồ Chí Minh is perfect. He points out the direction for us. He is also a buddha and he attained complete enlightenment [*giác ngộ hoàn toàn*]. When he died there was nothing left—he was completely rid of greed, anger and ignorance [*bỏ hết tham sân si*], same as the Buddha. He became a bodhisattva, like Quan Âm. (Interview with Thầy Tâm, April 2010, Hanoi.)

Ancestors are not usually included in the division, but they display much the same characteristics, and when questioned about ancestors people will usually say that they belong in the same order as the spirit side. Ancestors have the same dual nature of being both beneficial but potentially punishing, and they eat meat and drink alcohol. The difference is that ancestors are directly related to a particular family, whereas deified heroes such as the Hùng Kings, Trần Hưng Đạo, or even Hồ Chí Minh are considered ancestors of the nation rather than of a particular family.

An essential difference that separates the spirit side from the Buddha side in the eyes of my informants is that the interactions of the gods and goddesses with humans is entirely centered on this world, whereas the buddhas and bodhisattvas, who can also help with the common material issues of this world, are specialists in aiding with the consequences of death and rebirth, as well as with spiritual progress. Thus, when people recite Buddhist sutras, most feel that such recitation will have some effect after they die. When they are supplicated by people on the first and fifteenth of the lunar month, the buddhas are usually approached for things like, in the words of one informant, "peace and health and good for all mankind." On the other hand, the spirits are also approached for issues related to material wealth, and often are approached with requests that are more specific, such as help in examinations, in business, finding a husband, or a cure for illness. One woman in her thirties at Phúc Lộc Pagoda described the objective of her supplications: "I wish for good luck with my clothing sales at the market." The Buddhist pantheon was considered by many of my informants to be above such requests for material benefit, especially when it is obtained by enterprises that involve lying and cheating. The buddhas and bodhisattvas remain somewhat distant, with the possible exception of Quan Âm, who embodies all of the positive but none of the negative attributes of the spirit side.[9]

Another distinguishing feature is that the supernatural beings that populate the spirit side are more dangerous and fickle. The spirits are just as likely to cause problems as they are to help if they feel that they are not properly cared for, or if they believe that they have been insulted. For instance, I was told near the beginning of my research not to point at a statue because the god would get angry and curse me with bad fortune. One nun stressed to me that the spirits punish—something that people never associate with the Buddhist pantheon: "The buddhas will forgive you if you do something wrong and show you how to be a better person, but the spirits will destroy you." Their capricious nature was demonstrated for me once when I went to a séance. At one point in the afternoon's activities the spirit caller, at this point possessed by the main goddess who granted the caller's powers, started to scream at a woman. The story of this woman was then related to me by one of participants of the spirit calling who was nearby:

> That woman has problems because she and her husband didn't obey the spirit. Before she came to see the spirit caller she was deaf, dumb, blind, and paralyzed. After nearly four years of attending the spirit here she was getting better, but then the goddess [through the caller] asked them to devote themselves more fully. They were supposed to be at the service of the goddess for a period of 100 days, but they didn't complete their service. Now, because she and her husband stopped their service prematurely, the woman has been struck blind again. They have today returned to resume their service, but the spirit is very angry at her.

The way in which mediums and spirit callers are chosen by the gods betrays the gods' fickle nature. As in the case of Thầy Linh, mediums become aware that they are called to serve the spirits by experiencing unexplained illness or insanity. Refusing to answer the call will result in the medium's condition worsening.[10]

Buddhas and bodhisattvas are more compassionate than spirits by nature and never punish. Instead, the moral repercussions of karmic cause and effect inevitably lead to causal consequences rather than to direct punishment at the hands of the buddhas. On the other hand, spirits are more likely to punish for neglect than for moral shortcomings of the supplicant. For this reason, goddesses such as the Lady of the Storehouse (Bà Chúa Kho) and the Lady of the Realm (Bà Chúa Xứ) are more likely to be approached by business people, merchants, and petty traders (P. Taylor 2004), whose activities are prone to involving a measure of dishonesty.

The motivations of the two sides are also described differently. The buddhas and bodhisattvas are asked for help, and help is given out of their innate goodness. The spirits, however, are approached in the same manner as human relations. That is, there is always an element of reciprocity associated with the interaction. It can be implied, as in the case of mother goddesses helping those who serve them. It can also be overt, as in the case of people who have to repay "loans" (in spirit money) from the Lady of the Storehouse at the end of the year. However, as with human relations, failure to reciprocate can damage relationships and bring about bad feelings on the part of the spirits, the consequences of which can be dire. Therefore, requests to the spirits are also mostly amoral, in that they are not attached to any requirements of moral rectitude on the part of the supplicant in order for the wish to be fulfilled.

Indicative of the ambiguous nature of the spirits is the line that can be drawn between ancestors and ghosts as two aspects of the same supernatural entity.[11] Someone who dies before his or her time, by unnatural causes, or without heirs to make offerings, will become a hungry ghost, wandering the Earth and making trouble for the living. Ghosts will never help, but if propitiated, one may get by without the ghosts causing trouble. Although people say that ancestors theoretically can help, it is most often their malevolent and vengeful aspects that people are trying to assuage. Special rites are performed not only out of filial piety, but also because ancestors make demands and pose a real threat. In extreme cases, ancestors may require their graves to be relocated. These responses are in reaction to negative circumstances in people's lives, which may be attributed to unhappy ancestors. One family I knew experienced difficulties that were attributed to dissatisfied ancestors. The parents were often fighting physically, one of the daughters was sick, and another was having problems with her husband, who had not come home for three weeks. They went to see a fortune-teller who used betel nuts and leaves to divine the source of the problem. It turned out to be the result of an ancestor who wanted to have a special ritual performed for him. After the ritual was performed, the family's problems seemed to diminish. The possibilities of beneficial or destructive behavior on the part of the dead underlines the ambivalent nature that is inherent in the spirits, whereas this ambiguity is entirely absent from the Buddha side.

Importantly, though, my informants see both the Buddhist and non-Buddhist sides as essential to the whole, while recognizing differences between the two sides. The following explanation, given to me by an old woman when I asked whether it was important to worship the buddhas as well as the gods, clearly illustrates this holistic understanding: "Both [sides are important]. You have to follow the Buddha as well as the mother goddesses. Firstly, the Buddha is higher, and after that the various goddesses are on a lower level. In other words, regarding religion, God [Ông Trời] is highest, after that the Buddha, and then the other [buddhas and spirits]...Like that. It isn't only the Buddha alone, nor is it only the mother goddesses."

Neither "side" is regarded as being irrelevant or dispensable, and this is explicitly recognized in the architecture and statuary of pagodas in northern Vietnam. The most common architectural arrangement has the main shrine in front, and contains the statues of the Buddhist pantheon and sometimes non-Buddhist deities. In a separate building or room, usually situated behind the main shrine, is the shrine for mother goddesses that holds statues of deities associated with their cult. People who come to make offerings at pagodas in Hanoi usually first offer to the buddhas, then go to the other altars to offer incense and money to the spirits. They are seen as being complementary and both have to be addressed for a pagoda visit to be considered complete.

Divisions were made between the two sides, based primarily on the different practices, locations, and religious specialists involved, but at the same time, the various aspects were seen as complementary. For this reason, all but the most doctrinal of Buddhists felt it necessary to worship both the buddhas and the spirits. Nonetheless, these were ranked, with the buddhas usually seen as being more important, if not necessarily more useful, than spirits.

ELITE VIEWS OF RELIGION

While the conceptualization of the supernatural outlined above is overwhelmingly the most common view and the one most often described by my informants, there is also an elite view of religion that is very different. The principal proponents of this view are the state, the academy, and the Buddhist institution represented by the state-controlled Vietnamese Buddhist Association. The elite view was also supported by a number of people in Vietnamese society, most notably by men, whose views reflected those put forward by the masculine institutions.[12] Although there are exceptions, the discourses of religion fall along gender lines, with religious practices and views that are associated with men having authority, and those associated with women marginalized.

When religion is acknowledged by those who uphold the elite view, and in instances when religious practice is enacted by them, what constitutes legitimate "religion" is phrased in a fundamentally different way. Instead of stressing people's connection with a potent supernatural force that can provide material assistance and benefit by engaging in reciprocal relationships, or harm if demands are not fulfilled and precautions taken, the elite view stresses an inert force that needs to be acknowledged, but that lacks potency. In 2010, on the ritual day for the Hùng Kings (the founding dynasty of the Vietnamese people), President Nguyễn Minh Triết made televised offerings in front of the altar to the Hùng Kings. Then, at a dais facing the altar, rather than facing the crowds of high-ranking attendees, he made the following speech:

> In front of the spirits of our Hùng Kings, we, your descendants, with all of our sincere reverence, solemnly show our gratitude to our ancestors who founded and built the Văn Lang country, an independent and sovereign country of ancient Vietnam. At this holy moment, we sincerely and reverently remember and are grateful to our ancestors, our source, past generations of our grandfathers and fathers. We are grateful to President Hồ Chí Minh, all of the veterans and heroic mothers, martyrs and all of the families who contributed to the revolution, all of the remarkable people, and to everyone and all of the heroic soldiers who fought with stamina and a sense of purpose for independence, freedom and for the country and the happiness of the Vietnamese... In front of their spirit we wish [i.e., hope] for peace for our people and for other people in the world to live in peace and to continue to develop.[13]

In this way, the "elite" view stresses honoring and commemorating rather than supplicating for divine favor. Legitimacy is given to world religions, while local practices and beliefs tend to be devalued. The select practices in which the state figures currently choose to participate—primarily commemoration of national heroes—draw on Confucian ideas of correct rituals of remembrance, while denying the possibility of supernatural efficacy.

This view of religion is not new, but has its roots in elite biases against popular religion that has existed historically in China and Vietnam. In imperial China, orthodoxy was defined as "structures of value that valorize order and legitimate existing social institutions and authority" (Sangren 1987, 76). Although orthodoxy incorporated this understanding in Vietnam, the complex relationship that Vietnam had with China and Chinese culture also was important in establishing discourses of legitimacy. Vietnam benefitted from its privileged cultural contact with China relative to its Southeast Asian neighbors, and Chinese cultural products were therefore given a prominent place.[14] In Vietnam, cultural products of China were given a legitimacy that was particularly upheld by the literati, who identified themselves as following the way of the scholars (Nho Giáo, i.e., Confucianism). They relegated Vietnamese indigenous knowledge to a lower status and often were highly critical and even derisive of "the superstitious nature of peasant religion" (Ho Tai 1987, 113). Examples of this discrimination include a bias towards Chinese medical systems over indigenous knowledge (Marr 1987), and the rhetorical predilection towards Zen Buddhism (C. T. Nguyen, 1995, 1997).

Orthodoxy in Vietnam became specifically associated with the elite formulation of three religious traditions of China. This concept of three distinct traditions is called *tam đạo* or *tam giáo,* derived from the Chinese *san jiao.* It literally means three paths or three religions, and refers to Confucianism (Đạo Không or Không Giáo), Daoism (Đạo Lão or Đạo Giáo), and Buddhism (Đạo Phật or Phật Giáo).[15] In China, *san jiao* is a term that is firmly grounded in the textual tradition that stands at the core of Chinese elite culture. It is therefore a view that privileges the elite orthodox view of religion, while discounting the less textual "folk" practices that are prone to be labeled as heterodox.[16]

Elite biases against popular religious views and towards the Three Traditions of China were further reinforced by Western discourses of religion. The Western academic approach to religion in Asia attempted to define clear traditions based on textual understandings. Scholars such as Leopold Cadière consequently grappled with the gap between Buddhist textual discourses and on-the-ground practices, concluding that there were few "real Buddhists" in Vietnam (Cadière 1958, 5–6).

In the colonial period, critiques by male Vietnamese urban elites were directed against religious excesses and focused especially on village ritual—where approximately 10 to 15 percent of household budgets were given over for such purposes (Malarney 1993, 281). These polemics seem primarily motivated by the question of how Vietnam was taken over so easily by the French, how the Vietnamese could modernize society so as to eventually gain independence (Marr 1981, 344–346), and how they assumed a largely Western secular view.

When the Communists consolidated power in northern Vietnam, they carried with them the elite view of popular religion as socially destabilizing and outside the boundaries of what had been defined as "religion." This view was further fuelled by the Marxist discourse against religion. Aspects of religious practice that the state felt posed a potential threat were curtailed. Communal houses, for example, that had housed the local tutelary deity and were the seat of the village power structure, were dismantled and desacrilized (Malarney 1993, 2002). During the post-1954 period, the discourse focused on "superstitious" beliefs and practices as being reactionary or antirevolutionary. The effervescent, but diffused, popular religious cults and practices were strictly curtailed (Choi 2007, 103–104; Larsson and Endres 2006, 152–154; Malarney 2002, 80–85; P. Taylor 2007, 13). The practices specifically banned as superstitious were those in which women were mostly engaged, including séances, spirit possession rituals, the burning of votive objects and spirit money, the use of protective amulets, divination, and fortune-telling (Malarney 2002, 81).[17]

The institutionalized religions—Buddhism and Christianity—were officially recognized as legitimate, though significant pressure was brought to bear on them as well. Fearing Communist repression, many Catholics fled to the south after the 1954 partition of Vietnam along the 17th parallel. Vatican authority was not recognized, and a new government-controlled organization took control of the Catholic Church in Vietnam. The Catholic Solidarity Committee fell under the purview of the umbrella organization that controlled all associations and societies (the Fatherland Front; Ramsay 2007, 384–387). Similarly, the Vietnamese Buddhist Association was eventually formed to impose control over Buddhists and Buddhist ideology.

Vietnam underwent a series of drastic reforms in the late 1980s, opening itself to the world and moving from a state-run to a market-driven economy in a process called the Renovation (Đổi Mới). At the same time, some social restrictions were eased. Although legal shifts have been minimal, there was an on-the-ground relaxation of enforcement that amounted to tacit permission for the resumption of religious practices of all kinds, and this has contributed to the effervescence of religious activity. Since then, ancestor altars, which some of my informants said they had hidden during less-permissive years, have been reinstated in prominent places in most homes. Other nonsanctioned religious activities, such as spirit possession rituals and séances, also have become popular again. Devotee traffic at pagodas has increased significantly, and donations are driving the renovation of old pagodas and the construction of new ones. Throughout the Hanoi area, there are large-scale reconstruction projects on Buddhist pagodas and other religious sites.

Despite the religious resurgence, there is a continued bias against popular religious practices and ideas. The "three religions" still hold some currency among scholars in Vietnam, though this explanation of the religious landscape is not commonly encountered in popular discourse.[18] Furthermore, there is a persistent legitimacy given to religions that came from China (Daoism, Confucianism, and Mahayana Buddhism), giving them the designation of religions (*tôn giáo*), rather than some other label. Anything that falls outside the parameters of these world religions is termed popular belief (*tín ngưỡng*), tradition (*truyền thống*), or custom (*phong tục*), all of which are still acceptable. The idea of some religious expressions being heterodox and unacceptable, however, is maintained through the labeling of certain practices as superstitions (*mê tín dị đoan*).[19]

The prevailing attitude now is that there are some religious expressions that hold value for society, especially those that are useful for fostering patriotism (Endres 1998, 6). These religious expressions include the cults of Hai Bà Trưng and Trần Hưng Đạo, national heroes who fought against the Chinese (Phạm Quỳnh Phương 2006, 50–51, 2007); the veneration of the war dead (Jellema 2007, 61; Malarney 2001, 2002, chap. 6); and ancestor worship and village rituals (Choi 2007, 91; Malarney 2002, chap. 7).[20]

Thus, the "elite" view tends to deny the popular understanding that sees the supernatural as consisting of powerful forces, and instead gives legitimacy to textual traditions, especially favoring the so-called world religions. The prejudice against popular religious practices has a long history and is persistent, being successively adopted by Confucian officials, Vietnamese reformers, Marxist revolutionaries, and bureaucrats; and by the post-Renovation state, academy, and Buddhist institutions.

CONCLUSION

The religious landscape of Vietnam is sprawling, with a vast and rich profusion of life, as Cadière famously described in 1958. There are numerous religious expressions that have been transmitted from elsewhere and absorbed into the Vietnamese view of the supernatural. Without effective systems of authoritative control, the view of the supernatural remains relatively unsystematized. Nonetheless, both popular and elite understandings exist side by side. Furthermore, the view of the latter is, with some historical exceptions, not so much imposed on those who hold the popular view as it is used by the elite to create distinctions.

The popular view sees the supernatural as potent and omnipresent. The supernatural can assist in the vagaries of life, but also can cause great misfortune if not dealt with carefully. Furthermore, the supernatural is not uniform, but is inhabited by different kinds of beings that are ranked and that have different characteristics and roles. The primary distinction is drawn between the Buddha side and the spirit side; the popular view sees these two sides as being complementary rather than exclusive. Thus, at the popular level people see no contradiction in chanting sutras in front of the Buddhist altar and then making offerings to the mother goddesses. This popular view is pervasive and is held by the majority of practitioners, who are women. The "elite" view, on the other hand, is expressed mostly in print and in media, is upheld by the institutions of power in Vietnam, and is tacitly supported by men. The supernatural, in this view, lacks both potency and imminence.

The different ways that the supernatural realm is conceptualized in Vietnam has important implications for identity, personal and political legitimation, the exercise of state power, and gender hegemony. The distinctions between these views are also crucial for understanding the choices people make regarding their participation in certain religious activities and the significance that regular and elite practitioners attribute to their choices. It is not mere coincidence that religious practices in which most women are engaged have been labeled as "superstition," consistently targeted for ridicule by the press, or that women have nonetheless continued to follow these practices under the threat of institutionalized violence.[21] Many of the Buddhist practices and perceptions—and all of the religious actors—that will be discussed in this book have been deeply and continually affected by the discourses surrounding religion.

2 Space and the Ranking of Buddhisms

At the foot of the steps of Quán Sứ Pagoda, where I first started research in 1997, there was a notice board that warned, "Do not commit the offense of bringing spirit money into the pagoda to worship." As I stood in front of this notice board, I found it difficult to reconcile the dictate, given that this practice is an important part of the way Buddhism is practiced by most people in northern Vietnam. However, Quán Sứ Pagoda is politically the most important pagoda in northern Vietnam, as headquarters of the state-controlled Buddhist organization, and therefore stands as representative of state and Buddhist orthodoxies.

By contrast, my other main field site, Phúc Lộc Pagoda, holds an annual ritual for the non-Buddhist saint whose statue sits in the entrance area of the pagoda. I attended this ritual on the third day of the third (lunar) month of 2010. The ritual was performed by the volunteer ritual group of the pagoda along with a non-Buddhist ritual master called a *thầy cúng*. In contrast to the prohibition of Quán Sứ Pagoda, an important element of the ritual was burning spirit money. The resident nun at Phúc Lộc Pagoda, Thầy Tâm, had made arrangements for the service, but did not take part in it. That evening, I went with Thầy Tâm to the pagoda of Thầy Linh to watch him take on his role as a spirit medium and allow himself to be possessed by the spirits of the Four Palaces. Spirit money was an important element in this ritual, also.

Neither of these views on popular practices—one discouraging and the other encouraging—can be dismissed. Both are part of Buddhist practice in Vietnam, though they hold very different positions in the elite hierarchies of religion. On the one side stands the politically legitimized form of Buddhism that has the full weight of authority of the only legally recognized and state-backed Buddhist organization in Vietnam, the Vietnamese Buddhist Association. It controls the education of members of the *sangha* (the Buddhist monastic order) and has on its side the most notable and visible monks at a national level. Theirs is the national voice of Buddhism, presented at a national level in publications related to Buddhism, including all the magazines available to Buddhists. Its position on popular practices such as burning spirit money is reinforced by the Buddhist magazines published in Vietnam. For example, the weekly Buddhist magazine published by the Buddhist Association of Ho Chi Minh City included an article in its December 9 issue titled "Superstition and Waste in the Vu Lan Season." This article explicitly condemned the burning of spirit money as an "outdated custom" and of no use for aiding fathers and mothers in the afterlife—as commendable and understandable as the sentiment might be.[1] The article suggested that people save the money wasted from activities such as burning spirit money and releasing birds, and instead give it to charity (Diệu 2010, 28–29).

Nonetheless, and while the importance of the institutional form of Buddhism is undeniable, Buddhism is practiced and understood quite differently by most Buddhists at the local level from the institutional view. Most local pagodas are involved with the spirit world as well as with the buddhas, and see practices such as burning spirit money as an essential element of reciprocity for maintaining relationships with the supernatural (including the buddhas). Salvation is nominally a goal, but it is overshadowed by the more immediate goals of personal and familial happiness. Notoriety, at least at a local level, is gained by some monks (such as Thầy Linh) by reputation of how well they perform various rituals, including funerary rites that involve burning spirit money and spirit goods, rather than through official rank or publications.

THE BUDDHIST REVIVAL AND CREATION OF TWO BUDDHISMS

Buddhism in Vietnam underwent a revival that began in the 1920s and accelerated in the 1930s, as one of a number of competing ideologies that sought to address the issue of Vietnam's colonial situation (McHale 2004, chap. 5). Although Woodside has written that the Buddhist Revival had limited impact at the time (1976, 194), its long-term effects have continued to reverberate through the development of Buddhism in Vietnam today (DeVido 2007, 281–284). The momentum of this Revival movement in the north was interrupted and then coopted by the state, but the seeds proved to be both powerful and volatile in the south during the war with the United States (Topmiller 2002), and are continuing today to have an impact on Vietnamese Buddhism as it is practiced throughout Vietnam and overseas.

In Vietnam, the occurrence of the Buddhist Revival is a result of a historical juncture between several factors related to the Vietnamese colonial situation, and to Buddhist developments that were taking place throughout Asia at the end of the nineteenth and opening decades of the twentieth centuries (Đỗ 1998, 6–7). These Buddhist reform movements, in countries such as Ceylon (Sri Lanka), China, and Japan, sought to answer colonial, and Christian, critiques of their societies by purifying Buddhism of "superstitious," local, elements. At the same time, the pan-Asian reenchantment with Buddhism was fed by Western interest in Eastern philosophies from the likes of theosophist Colonel Olcott, which provided legitimacy to Buddhism as a "world religion" that could equal those of the West. The transformations in print culture spurred it on by making scriptures, commentaries, and translations of sacred texts more available than ever before (McHale 2004, 170).

The Revival movement also was strengthened by the institutional linkage of Buddhists in Vietnam that were taking place for the first time. A national Buddhist leadership arose out of a need for direction in the anticolonial struggle. The organizations formed only a limited unity at first because they were greatly impeded by French suppression, competition from Christian missionaries, the nascent Communist Party, and by entrenched Buddhist conservativism. In 1935, the Tonkin Buddhist Association could only claim around two thousand monks and nuns and ten thousand lay members. Even with this limited number, "its membership lacked even a modicum of ideological discipline and participatory zeal" (Woodside 1976, 193).

One of the central concerns of the Revival movement was to return to the original and authentic Buddhism while disengaging from the aspects that were particularly Vietnamese. The movement favored an interpretation of Buddhism that accentuated the life of the historical Buddha and his teachings at the expense of local buddhisms and devotional beliefs and practices (Bechert and Vu 1976, 192; DeVido 2007, 267; Soucy 2007, 344). Humanistic Buddhism in the vein of the Chinese Buddhist reformer Taixu, in which Buddhism refocused on relieving suffering in this world instead of being concerned entirely with the next, was also important (DeVido 2007, 257–258). Meanwhile, practices related with the spirit side became equated by elite discourses with superstition; women in particular were implicated as the source of its perpetuation.

Finally, there was a privileging of a Zen narrative that had always been most popular among the elite. The Vietnamese elite have, at least since the Trần dynasty (1225 to 1400), attempted to associate Vietnamese Buddhism with Zen by assuming a narrative that mimicked those of the Chinese Ch'an lineages— another example of elite bias towards Chinese cultural forms. The basis of this assertion in the twentieth century is a text titled the *Thiền Uyển Tập Anh* (Compendium of outstanding figures of the Zen garden), discovered, translated, and published in French by Trần Văn Giáp in the early 1930s, at a time when the Buddhist Revival movement in Vietnam was gaining steam (see Trần Văn Giáp 1932). The Vietnamese text was written in the fourteenth century and records the biographies of famous Zen monks in Vietnam from the sixth to thirteenth centuries in the manner of Chinese "transmission of the lamp" texts. Since Trần Văn Giáp translated the text, it has thereafter been used uncritically by scholars as the single authoritative piece of evidence to argue that the core of Vietnamese Buddhism is Zen. However, after careful analysis, Cuong Tu Nguyen has persuasively argued that the *Thiền Uyển Tập Anh* (Compendium of outstanding figures of the Zen garden) merely takes on the external form of a Chinese Ch'an text in order to lend legitimacy to Buddhism in Vietnam (C. T. Nguyen, 1995, 1997).[2]

The reformulations of the Buddhist Revival in Vietnam are highly problematic in that they do not reflect the religious lives of most practitioners. Instead, the historical Buddha is still regarded as important, but only as one of several buddhas and bodhisattvas who are part of a host of potent supernatural beings. Buddhism in Vietnam continues to be largely devotional; despite claims that Vietnamese Buddhism has a Zen core, there are very few who engage in any meditation, even among monastics.

Nonetheless, the Buddhist Revival has had a lasting impact. The idea of unifying Buddhist organizations led to the formation of the Unified Buddhist Church in South Vietnam that actively protested in the 1960s against religious persecution at the hands of Ngô Đình Diệm, against American intervention, and against the war. In the north, the state took control over the Buddhist organization by creating the Vietnamese Buddhist Association, under the umbrella of the Fatherland Front. This institution has since controlled all aspects of the official face of Buddhism and has provided some unity by training monastics and by publishing Buddhist magazines and books. Other measures that were put in place included refusing permission for draft-aged males to be ordained as either Catholic or Buddhist clergy, confiscating property, and assuming responsibility for schools and orphanages (Ho Tai 1987, 144).

The close connection between the Buddhist Revival and the later state view of Buddhism can be seen by the fact that the headquarters of the Vietnamese Buddhist Association was established at Quán Sứ Pagoda, where the earlier reformist Tonkin Buddhist Association had been located. The views that had been propagated by the reformers must have fit closely with state intentions and elite views, because they are largely those that continue to be perpetuated today by the Buddhist institution. These views have the weight of authority and continue to impact Buddhism as it is presented at a national level through the Buddhist and regular media. Nonetheless, while people draw on the legitimacy that association with this central institution continues to convey, most people still practice Buddhism in a way that does not conform with the intentions of the reformers.

FIELD SITES AND DISCOURSES

The proliferation of books, starting in the early 1990s, that discuss pagodas in Vietnam attests to the importance of pagodas as sites of contested religious practice and discourses of legitimacy. Many of these books come in a glossy coffee-table format, and most are bilingual (English and Vietnamese) or trilingual (English, French, and Vietnamese); at least one volume includes Chinese.[3] Others have fewer pictures, are more cheaply produced, and are only in Vietnamese, and are clearly intended for Vietnamese readers who are interested in exploring their cultural heritage.[4]

The high regard for the architectural representations of "culture" and "tradition" as embodied in pagodas in Vietnam has led to ever-increasing numbers of pagodas being given the status of "historical and cultural relic" by the ministry of culture. The certificates declaring this status are usually framed and prominently displayed in the pagodas. Nguyễn Thế Long and Phạm Mai Hùng (1997, 307–311) list 130 pagodas that have been given the status of historical and cultural relic in Hanoi alone.

The emphasis on art and architecture indicates that interest lies not in religious activity (with the possible exception of village festivals), in Buddhist lives, or in the acknowledgment of the power of the deity enshrined, but in external forms, such as art and architecture, whose symbolic meaning is more easily manipulated and less likely to be contested. By highlighting the relatively static and symbolically malleable architectural objects as representative of Vietnamese culture and tradition, the more problematic issues of belief and practice are avoided. The state attempts to use religion, as represented through these objects, as a symbol of Vietnamese tradition while maintaining a program of eradicating "superstitious beliefs" and "feudalism." State intentions are mirrored in most writings on Buddhism, which focus on either art and architecture or historical narratives that center on Zen or national heroes. Perhaps inadvertently, the state has thereby become complicit in supporting a modernist movement within Buddhism that has its roots in colonialist apologetics.

At the same time, the Buddhist institution has benefitted by conformity to the view held by the state. Whereas in the past there was no real unity between different Buddhist pagodas and different monastics, the imposition of a state organization has allowed certain monks to gain national prominence and take control over a unified "religion," though this unity at times remains superficial. Furthermore, individual Buddhists may profit by association with the formal institutional structure. For example, a woman I know, "Mrs. Bình," works at

Quán Sứ Pagoda, and therefore has access to important monks. She is able to maintain a wide circle of acquaintances (mostly older Buddhist women) by virtue of her ability to capitalize on her connections at Quán Sứ Pagoda, despite her difficult character (she has a tendency to be duplicitous for personal gain). Her acquaintances, in return, gain in prestige amongst their peers by having met important monks and having their pictures taken standing with them—pictures that are then usually displayed prominently in their homes.

Describing the structures and activities at these two very different Buddhist sites will help illustrate how state discourses on religion are given expression through architectural elements of pagodas in Hanoi. I will start with the politically powerful and central Quán Sứ Pagoda, and then follow with a description of Phúc Lộc Pagoda, a local pagoda that is not particularly notable or politically connected, but that is representative of the average pagoda in Hanoi. The juxtaposition serves two purposes: first, it highlights how the elite hierarchies of religion play themselves out in a physical and practical sense in Hanoian pagodas, and second, it provides a description of the physical setting of my main field sites for subsequent chapters.

QUÁN SỨ PAGODA

The political importance of Quán Sứ Pagoda is unmistakable. Its centrality is attested to by the fact that the abbot of the pagoda, the Most Venerable Thích Thanh Tứ, is politically one of the most important and visible monks in Vietnam as the standing vice president of the Central Committee of the Vietnamese Buddhist Association. He was born as Trần Văn Long in 1923 in Hưng Yên province, and his mother died when he was three. Once while he was at the local pagoda praying he told his father that he felt destined to become a monk, so his father, who was a devout Buddhist, sent him to live at the pagoda at the age of six. He later joined revolutionaries in Hưng Yên province as a Buddhist, fighting against the Japanese and the French, and covertly training the village militia.[5] Someone, under torture, revealed his activities, and Thích Thanh Tứ was eventually sent to Hỏa Lò Prison. When Vietnam was liberated from the French in 1954, he became a representative in the National Assembly, and today sees himself as a bridge between the people and the government (Nguyễn Đình Cần 2010, 5–7). His prominence, and that of Quán Sứ Pagoda along with him, is attested to by the photographs of him with various dignitaries hanging on the walls all around the pagoda: Thích Thanh Tứ with current Vietnamese President Nguyễn Minh Triết, Thích Thanh Tứ with former Prime Minister and Secretary-General of the Communist Party Đỗ Mười, Thích Thanh Tứ with international Buddhist leader Thích Nhất Hạnh, and so on.

The pagoda has been politically central for much of its existence. It was built during the fourteenth or fifteenth century and was used to accommodate visiting dignitaries from neighboring Buddhist countries (Nguyễn Thế Long and Phạm Mai Hùng 1997, 227; Võ Văn Tường 1993, 460), hence the name, which literally means "Ambassador's Pagoda." The structure was restored in 1855, to be used for prayer by soldiers of a nearby garrison. After the soldiers left, it was turned over to the local villagers and the resident monk, Thanh Phương, who made additions, including colonnades, colored statues, and bells. In 1934, the Tonkin Buddhist Association, established its headquarters at Quán Sứ Pagoda under the leadership of the Buddhist reformer Trí Hải (DeVido 2007, 266–267, Hà Văn Tấn, Nguyễn Văn Kự, and Phạm Ngọc Long 1993, 306). As a center of reform, a school for monks was established in 1934 and a school for nuns in 1941; the association's journal *Torch of Wisdom* (*Đuốc Tuệ*) was published there until 1945 (DeVido 2007, 266–267). In 1941, the pagoda was repaired and rebuilt according to the architectural designs of Nguyễn Ngọc Ngoạn and Nguyễn Xuân Tùng (Hà Văn Tấn et al. 1993, 306). The front gate, with its unusual inscription in Romanized Vietnamese script (*quốc ngữ*), rather than the more usual inscription in Chinese characters, indicates how involved it was in the reform project to modernize Buddhism along rationalist and nationalist lines.[6]

It is not surprising, then, that Quán Sứ Pagoda became the headquarters for the Buddhist organization, put in place by the Communist government after independence was achieved in 1954 as a means to centralize control of all Buddhist activities and pagodas. It also capitalized on the pagoda's already important role and usurped the power and aura of authority of the Tonkin Buddhist Association. The Vietnamese Buddhist Association became the only official Buddhist organization in Vietnam and remains a member of the Fatherland Front.[7]

Quán Sứ Pagoda has been at the center of pan-Asian Buddhist conversations, giving it a uniquely international outlook and representative importance for a modern, rationalized Buddhism. It also has been a part of efforts by the Vietnamese Buddhist Association to represent Vietnamese Buddhists on an international stage. It was here that in 1951 the international Buddhist flag was first flown in Vietnam (Võ Văn Tường and Huỳnh Như Phương 1995, 39). More recently, the 2008 international celebration of the United Nations Day of Vesak was hosted in Hanoi and at this time Quán Sứ Pagoda was visited by many international Buddhist figures, such as Thích Nhất Hạnh, and it marked an important engagement with Buddhism internationally.

Quán Sứ Pagoda's status as headquarters for the state-regulated Vietnamese Buddhist Association means that much of the pagoda complex is taken up with

The front gate of Quán Sứ Pagoda with Romanized inscriptions

offices for various administrative bodies. These offices include the two administrative branches of the Association, which direct the institution internally: the
office of the Central Management Council and the office for the Sangha Council.
Quán Sứ Pagoda is also the main branch for the Vietnamese Buddhist Research
Institute, and from 1981 was the headquarters for the Vietnamese Institute of
Buddhist Studies, where Buddhist monks were trained until recently.[8] The role
that the pagoda plays as central to the Vietnamese Buddhist Association means
that Quán Sứ Pagoda holds the only Buddhist library in Hanoi. The library is
open daily to the public; books can be borrowed on a short-term basis.

Some books and a magazine are published in a top-floor room of the pagoda.
That magazine, *The Research Journal of Buddhist Studies*, is one of the two most
prominent Buddhist magazines published in Vietnam; the other, *Enlightenment
Weekly Magazine,* is published in Ho Chi Minh City. However, few books come
out of Quán Sứ Pagoda compared to the enormous numbers that are published in
the south. The books that are published at Quán Sứ Pagoda appear to be mainly

concerned with the proceedings of congresses that decide the future direction of the Vietnamese Buddhist Association rather than with teaching Buddhist doctrine, history, and culture.

The pagoda also has a small store run by women of late middle age, facing out onto the street with a side door to the main courtyard. The store sells books, the latest Buddhist magazines, and paraphernalia (porcelain statues, prayer beads, Buddhist robes, and so on). In 1997–1998, this shop was the only place in Hanoi where a Buddhist could purchase many of these books and objects. By 2010, there was a line of stores across the street that sold these books as well as a greater variety of Buddhist ritual supplies and statues. Nonetheless, the pagoda's bookstore continues to be crowded on the first and fifteenth of the lunar month.

Quán Sứ Pagoda is not an attractive structure, being more monumental and less graceful than other famous pagodas in the Hanoi region. It is tall, square, and blocky, hemmed in on all sides by the offices that are required to fulfill its official functions. By contrast, other pagodas tend to be low-lying one-story structures with broad, sweeping roofs that curve gracefully at the eaves. Its architecture does not distinctly conform to the style of most other northern pagodas. The arrangement of space at Quán Sứ Pagoda instead reflects the modernist intentions of the reformers who rebuilt the pagoda. With the exception of the main shrine and the front gate, it has a striking resemblance to a government office.

There is, as in other pagodas, a shrine dedicated to the patriarchs of the pagoda that is the monastic equivalent of an ancestral hall. The most unusual feature here is the large murals of the Buddhist saints (arhats) that run along the periphery of the room. This juxtaposition of the pagoda patriarchs with the saints of Buddhism again suggests an attempt to tie Vietnamese Buddhism, as well as the pagoda's own lineage, specifically to the historical Buddha and his followers— that is, with what is perceived as the "pure," original Buddhism. It is not uncommon to have statues or images of the arhats in pagodas of the north. However, the juxtaposition of the arhats and the pagoda patriarchs is unusual.

In keeping with the political nature of the pagoda and the reformed Buddhism that it attempts to portray, there are several iconic elements that are missing from Quán Sứ Pagoda. The usual statues of the dharma guardians of the pagoda that protect it from malevolent spirits, are conspicuously absent, as are statues of the Ten Kings of Hell. To the left and the right of the main sanctuary, in the antechamber, are statues of Địa Tạng (Dizang) and Quan Âm (Guanyin). These statues are usually not in such prominent spaces in other pagodas. This arrangement, with these two bodhisattvas in line with the main altar, is reminiscent of the placement more commonly seen in pagodas of southern and central

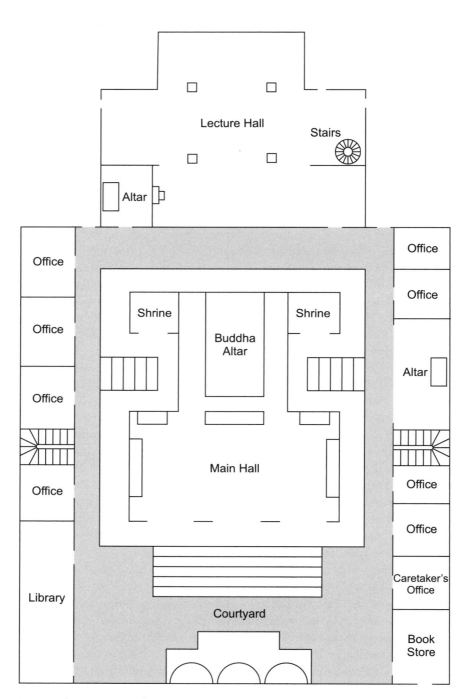

Layout of Quán Sứ Pagoda

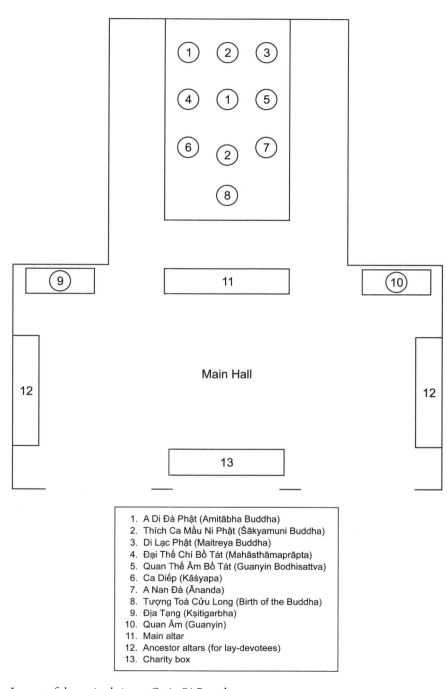

1. A Di Đà Phật (Amitābha Buddha)
2. Thích Ca Mầu Ni Phật (Śākyamuni Buddha)
3. Di Lạc Phật (Maitreya Buddha)
4. Đại Thế Chí Bồ Tát (Mahāsthāmaprāpta)
5. Quan Thế Âm Bồ Tát (Guanyin Bodhisattva)
6. Ca Diếp (Kāśyapa)
7. A Nan Đà (Ānanda)
8. Tượng Toà Cửu Long (Birth of the Buddha)
9. Địa Tạng (Kṣitigarbha)
10. Quan Âm (Guanyin)
11. Main altar
12. Ancestor altars (for lay-devotees)
13. Charity box

Layout of the main shrine at Quán Sứ Pagoda

Vietnam. There is a significant absence of a mother goddess shrine, in which the mother goddesses of the spirit side are displayed and worshipped. In fact, statues of non-Buddhist deities are missing entirely from the pagoda. By contrast, most other pagodas have at least some representations of mother goddesses, even if they do not have a shrine for mother goddesses as part of their architectural structure.

The iconography at Quán Sứ Pagoda bears witness to the almost self-conscious cleansing that this pagoda has undergone of the symbolic elements of what Đỗ Thiện calls "the grassroots level of a locally based, adaptive Buddhism" (1998, 7). There are references that remain to mark it as being a Mahayana pagoda—statues of bodhisattvas, for instance—but the accent on early Buddhism is much more prominent than it is in other pagodas of northern Vietnam. Rather than the more usual statues of bodhisattvas such as Văn Thù Sư Lợi (Mañjuśrī) and Phổ Hiền Bồ Tát (Samantabhadra) on the main altar, there are paired statues of the important followers of the Buddha, Ca Diếp (Kāśyapa) and A Nan Đà (Ānanda). These arhat statues are not unusual, but they again stress the historical Buddha.

The modernist discourse, which links Vietnamese Buddhism to a global Buddhist movement and has been a part of Quán Sứ Pagoda since the 1930s, was also evident in 1998. In an alcove that houses a statue of Quan Âm there was a display of photographs that depicted monastic delegates from countries such as Japan and the Republic of China (Taiwan), a delegation of German Buddhists, and the prince of Thailand. In 2007, there were many more displays showing notable events, visits by politically powerful figures, and activities of the monastic students. By 2010, there were also photographs of the international celebration of the 2008 United Nations Day of Vesak, which was hosted in Hanoi.

Despite the general lack of success that the Buddhist reform movement has had in the everyday religious practice of northern Vietnamese, the state favored their view of Buddhism because it reflected the rationalist discourse that distances religion from superstition and most easily fit with the materialist ideology of the Communist state. Quán Sứ Pagoda continues to reflect this reformed Buddhism in its valorizing of the historical Buddha, in its institution-wide portrayal of a pointedly un-Vietnamese Buddhism, and in the practices and opinions of many in its community.

A librarian at Quán Sứ Pagoda, Mr. Đức, was a perfect fit for the pagoda. His version of Buddhism was among the most text-based of the interpretations I have encountered: he always spoke of Buddhism in a way that primarily drew on understandings of what the historical Buddha taught, especially the Four Noble Truths and the Eightfold Path. The book that he insisted I read for an understanding of Buddhism was a Vietnamese translation of Walpola Rahula's *What the Buddha Taught* (1974 [1959]), itself noted by Gimello as being a product of Buddhist modernism (Gimello 2004, pp. 240–241). Mr. Đức tended to stress the Buddha's teachings while de-emphasizing Buddhism's Vietnamese particularities. He was among the most critical of my informants when speaking of popular practices, such as the burning of spirit money, dismissing them as superstition. We once had a long discussion on images of hell (*địa ngục*) that I had recently seen at Trăm Gian Pagoda, a famous pagoda in Hà Tây province. In typical fashion, he lectured me in French:

Mr. Đức: "*Địa*" means Earth; the stratum below the Earth. "*Ngục*" means "prison." In this world there are "prisons." But…according to the sutras they say that after people die there is also a world for the dead. In the world of the dead those who do evil also go to prison, as in this world. However, according to the Buddha, it is only symbolic—it is not based in reality at all—these symbols are only to teach people that when they are living they have to do good things. However, those who believe too much that hell is below are not correct at all. If you do evil, do bad, then you also will have to endure bad things. It is done that way to teach people not to do wicked things. And now, science asks us, Can you prove whether hell exists or not? We can't do that because no one has ever seen hell. No one can see hell. However, the hell that is mentioned in the sutras is only symbolic to teach people that if your heart is bad you will be punished in this way, and therefore you better avoid doing bad things.

Me: But, in your opinion, do the majority of people who go to pagodas know that hell is not real, or do they think that it is real?

Mr. Đức: Many people who go to pagodas think that it is true because their level of education is low. That is called superstition. They burn fake money and gold. What are immolative objects? They are things made of paper: bicycles and motorcycles [and so on] made of paper. They are burned to send down to hell [for souls] to spend. [Practices] like this are not correct.

Me: Making immolative offerings is not correct?

Mr. Đức: It doesn't do anything. Modern ideology, modern science, and Buddhism proves that doing this isn't correct. Śākyamuni Buddha acknowledged that we should only cultivate ourselves. To cultivate yourself is the main thing in order to become good, not worshipping. [Making offerings] is only intended for showing your respect.

The authority of Quán Sứ Pagoda is widely recognized and serves to attract a large number of devotees: despite its somewhat ungainly appearance, it is by far the most active pagoda in Hanoi. Its appeal is not aesthetic, but is a result of its prestige, as articulated by one woman who regularly went there: "I go to Quán Sứ Pagoda because I like it. It is more credible. It isn't beautiful, but there are monastics with a high level of culture, a high level of Buddhism. At other pagodas the monastics have simply been assigned to the place to take care of it."

Despite (or perhaps because of) it being unique in both architecture and function, this pagoda is billed as a showcase example of a Hanoi pagoda. This is attested to by a brass descriptive plaque that was donated by the Canadian government in 1997 as part of a development project intended to boost tourism. In another part of Hanoi, I once visited a small pagoda where I was told by an old, tourist-weary nun that if I only wanted to visit a pagoda for sightseeing then I should go to Quán Sứ Pagoda.[9]

The formality of Quán Sứ Pagoda led people to act in particular ways. Women at Quán Sứ Pagoda were more concerned with form and appearance. They were more apt to point out how things should be done correctly. There appeared to be more intrigue and attempts at social positioning.

The political nature of Quán Sứ Pagoda also led to more reticence on the part of some. In a strange and short conversation I had with one old laywoman at the pagoda, the concern over speaking with me was particularly clear:

Old woman: Sit here.
Me: Yes. Do you have the time to speak with me for a bit?
Old woman: Where?
Me: Here.
Old woman: OK…except, only one thing, the guard may say something not nice, but we can prove that there is nothing. Everybody makes mistakes, but if I make a mistake it needs to be pointed out. If they kick us out, then we will go [laughs]. Let's go to the library to talk.
Me: [Not really understanding her meaning] I don't have anything to do at the library.
Old woman: OK. Now. Because of that…today we won't talk. Talking is not useful. Even until now we still don't know what kind of mis-

take we are making. Then I go to talk with foreigners, and then maybe I make an even bigger mistake. So, we should delay. [She shakes my hand and leaves.]

Quán Sứ Pagoda does not reflect popular conceptions and practices, yet it remains important as the central political pagoda in northern Vietnam. It is seen as being authoritative because it represents the reformed Buddhism that holds hegemonic sway over other understandings and practices. Furthermore, it represents rationalist discourses of how Buddhism fits into today's world, in a way that is acceptable to the state, and accepted by almost all as being legitimate, despite the incongruities with popular Buddhist conceptions and practices.

It is difficult to say whether the state directs the Buddhist institution, whether the Buddhist institution reflects the desires of the state for benefit, or whether they are both embroiled in a similar discourse of modernity and secularity. What can be claimed with certainty is that it is mutually beneficial that the state and the Buddhist institution collude in this worldview. The state benefits because the Buddhist institution, which represents, at least officially, a large number of Vietnamese, upholds an ideological order that underpins the state's right to rule. The Buddhist institution benefits in that it avoids confrontation with the state, and instead is able to gain legitimacy by standing within the aura of state authority.

PHÚC LỘC PAGODA

Phúc Lộc Pagoda is similar to dozens of other pagodas in Hanoi that are not mentioned in the coffee-table books on Buddhist pagodas in Vietnam. It is not regarded as being historically or architecturally important, although having been built in the Lý dynasty (1009–1225) its age would make it old enough to merit recognition. As one of the many pagodas that dot Hanoi, most holding similar pedigrees, it could be said to be typical, unimportant, and anonymous. Such pagodas are plentiful, but most are well hidden down small alleys, lost in the city that has grown up around them. [10] Small doors on side streets will let you into a different world if you know how to look for the signs that indicate the presence of a pagoda.

Phúc Lộc Pagoda is in the vicinity of one of the markets in Hanoi. Outside the front gate, market women haggle with prospective buyers, bicycle rickshaw and motorcycle taxi drivers wait around and shout at overburdened shoppers in the hopes of getting a customer, and policemen survey the scene with cynical grimaces. The large front triple gate that once announced the presence of the pagoda is now crowded by market stalls selling merchandise. I lived around the corner for months before realizing that behind that portico was a living pagoda, camouflaged by the piles of wares wrapped in brown paper and straw and stored under the archway by vendors.

As is true of many pagodas in Hanoi, Phúc Lộc Pagoda is quiet and unobtrusive. There are occasional visitors who come to make offerings at the various altars, but unless it is the first or fifteenth of the lunar month, such visitors are so rare that the lights in the main hall are usually switched off. The only monastic there, Thầy Tâm, is a constant presence, however. Unlike Thích Thanh Tứ, Thầy Tâm is a nun, and therefore has no status or notability beyond the pagoda. She is capable of fulfilling her ritual responsibilities and she takes care of her pagoda well, but she is not acknowledged—and she does not see herself—as being an expert. She is likeable, and people are always happy to sit and chat with her in the reception area. Monks like Thầy Linh can draw followers, so that it is always crowded on days when he recites sutras or performs a spirit possession ritual. People come to Phúc Lộc Pagoda, however, because it is the local pagoda. One woman, Mrs. Xuân, takes a lead amongst the old women at the pagoda, traveling an hour in each direction to take part in the Sám Nguyện (the penitence ritual, which is performed four times each lunar month). However, she only does it because she considers it her home pagoda, "the pagoda of my ancestors," and the one she always went to before she moved from the neighborhood in 2009. All of the other old women come because it is the closest.

Thầy Tâm was born in 1956 in a village across the river from Hanoi. When she was in her early twenties she wanted to become a nun. On the advice of her aunt she consulted an astrological book, which told that such a life would be appropriate for her. She decided to go to Phúc Lộc Pagoda because the nun at her village pagoda knew that the old nun there needed a novice. When Thầy Tâm went to see the old nun at Phúc Lộc Pagoda, the latter agreed to take her in, and she taught her ritual procedures until the nun's death seven years later. Thầy Tâm has managed the ritual and functional affairs of the pagoda ever since, though at first she found the burden of responsibility overwhelming. When I first met her she had finished studying college-level courses for monastics at Bà Đá Pagoda, and was studying in the university-level monastic training program at Quán Sứ Pagoda. Since then, she has continued to manage the affairs of the pagoda, periodically meeting other nuns and monks. Though sometimes the relationship is rocky, she has shared a friendship with Thầy Linh for many years; she almost always calls on him to do the spirit possession ritual in the pagoda's mother goddess shrine.

Although Phúc Lộc Pagoda is usually very quiet, there was a small commu nity of people who were continuously active there. In 1997 a group of old men got together twice a week to practice drumming and chanting sutras for the rituals held at the pagoda, and a Tai Chi group met daily in the front courtyard. This had changed somewhat by 2010. The death of the leader of the Tai Chi group brought this activity to an end, and the ritual group had stopped meeting because they had learned all they needed to know and there were no new members.[11] One old man who was central to the group continued to come for these rituals, despite the fact that he had moved to a new house an hour away from the pagoda.

There is a monthly ritual calendar with days on which activity spikes. The first of the lunar month is the biggest day, and sees a steady stream of people coming in to make offerings and wishes to the buddhas and to the spirits. On this day, the ritual group of old men and the ritual master meet to perform rituals that are intended to invite the buddhas to the altar. Following this they recite the Bhaiṣajyaguru Sūtra. The second biggest day is the fifteenth of the lunar month, which again sees a stream of visitors to supplicate both sides of the supernatural world. On this day, the ritual group again performs a cúng (a particular kind of ritual), followed by a recital of the Universal Door Sutra (the twenty-fifth sutra in the Lotus Sutra, describing the attributes of Quan Âm Bodhisattva). The most devout women gather for the penitence ritual on the eighth, fourteenth, twenty-third, and twenty-ninth days of the lunar month, completing the monthly ritual calendar.

The annual ritual calendar is indicative of the way that the ritual life of Phúc Lộc Pagoda acknowledges the potency and importance of both the Buddha side and the spirit side. For example, on the third day of the third month there is a ritual to worship the main spirit of the pagoda (Lễ Hội Tế Tế Đức X).[12] Another important ritual in the annual calendar is the first of the fourth month, when the Ritual for the Opening of Summer (Lễ Vào Hè Cầu Mát) is held to wish for cool weather and no illness. The largest celebration in the ritual calendar is the ritual Lễ Giỗ Tổ, commemorating the former monastics of the pagoda, which is followed by a community feast. In addition to the monthly and seasonal rituals, there are also occasional rituals that are performed as needed. These include funerary rites and special rituals to commemorate the dead. People also occasionally sponsor rituals for specific purposes such as bringing good luck to a new business. For example, the sister of the director of the local market organized a special ritual on his behalf when he first took up the position in order to bring him luck in his appointment. Once a year, Thầy Tâm arranges for a spirit possession ritual to be held in front of the mother goddess altar.

At Phúc Lộc Pagoda, much of the ritual activity is directed towards the spirits rather than the buddhas. Partly because of Thầy Tâm's lack of expertise, there are a variety of actors that perform at this pagoda. On most special occasions a ritual master is paid to help with the ritual. The ritual group is usually called upon for major rituals as well. There are also other occasional actors. For example, in 2010, after the worship ritual that was held in honor of the pagoda's spirit on the third day of the third month, a retired singer who has long been part of the pagoda community, though she did not chant sutras, came to sing for the spirit.

There are a number of lay Buddhists who also volunteer regularly to dust the statues on the altars, clean the floors, and cook the meals for Thầy Tâm. In the thirteen years that I have been going to this pagoda, the cast of helpers has changed somewhat. Thầy Tâm's mother was frequently there in 1997–1998, and a number of other women from the neighborhood helped with the chores. Several years later, there was a young man who came from a neighboring rural province who lived at the pagoda. For a while he thought that he might renounce and become a monk when he finished school, but he decided against it and started a career in business instead. He was still living at the pagoda in 2010, and would help out on busy days. In 2010, a young niece of Thầy Tâm was also living at the pagoda. She had come in from her village to study accounting, but because her classes were in the evenings she spent a good part of each day cleaning the pagoda and preparing meals. Two old ladies who lived nearby would still come to help on busy days.

There was a family who lived next to the pagoda, and they came in and out of the pagoda almost daily since their one-room apartment was cramped. The father raised birds in the pagoda, hanging the cages from the pagoda eaves, so that pleasant chirping filled the quiet air. The family's daughter spent more time inside the pagoda than in her home. As a high school student in 2010 she still came daily, often eating lunch there. In many ways, Thầy Tâm was like an aunt to her. Though they were a part of the community, members of this family never took part in any of the rituals.

Phúc Lộc Pagoda is not a political pagoda; it is not under the gaze of the state, though, like all pagodas, it receives an occasional glance. It does not receive a wide variety of visitors, only people from the surrounding neighborhood and people who work in the market, and they only go there because it is the closest pagoda. Unlike Quán Sứ Pagoda, it does not have a bookstore, a research center, a lecture hall, a library, or a training institute. There are no talks given by monastics to the Buddhist laity, and there are no classes. The nun is not really comfortable teaching people about Buddhism because she believes she does not really understand well enough herself. In response to my questions, which must have seemed simplistic to her, she once said that me asking her for explanations about

Buddhism was "like two idiots talking together." She said that I should be asking monks who knew more about the symbolism of Buddhist rituals.

All of these lacks at Phúc Lộc Pagoda only add to its beauty and peaceful-ness. There is no weighty feel of state or institutional presence. No signs mark rooms such as the offices in a government building. There is no presentation of orthodoxy or conformity to political dictates. There seems to be less competition and dissimulation amongst the community of the pagoda. People at this pagoda are more willing to talk to me about their religious activities and beliefs without worry of expressing a view considered incorrect (unlike Quán Sứ Pagoda, where people would frequently ask if I had written permission for my research). There is an informal and unhurried atmosphere at Phúc Lộc Pagoda.

Phúc Lộc Pagoda's architecture, statuary, and rituals incorporate the Bud-dha side / spirit side cosmology in a way that is more common to Buddhist pago-das in northern Vietnam than is the elite view embodied by Quán Sứ Pagoda. In both architecture and practices the Buddhism practiced at Phúc Lộc Pagoda reflects the nondoctrinal, grassroots, adaptive, local approach to Buddhism that views the spirits and buddhas as both having a place in their ritual repertoire.

Similar to Quán Sứ Pagoda, Phúc Lộc Pagoda has a main hall dedicated to the various buddhas and bodhisattvas of the Mahayana pantheon. The main altar holds statues that represent the Buddhas of the Past, Present and Future (consist-ing of A Di Đà Phật [Amitābha Buddha], Thích Ca Mâu Ni Phật [the historical Buddha], and Di Lặc Phật [Maitreya Buddha]), standard for all pagoda altars; immediately below is a statue of Amitābha Buddha, flanked on either side by his helpers Quan Âm and Đại Thế Chí Bồ Tát (Mahāsthāmaprāpta Bodhisattva); below is a statue of Thích Ca Mâu Ni Phật Buddha flanked by Văn Thù Sư Lợi (Mañjuśri Bodhisattva) and Phổ Hiền Bồ Tát (Samantabhadra Bodhisattva).[13] Below them, and on the last level, is a statue depicting the Buddha's birth (depict-ing the baby Buddha surrounded by nine dragons. A statue of Di Lặc Phật is on the right of the Buddha's birth, and a statue of Thích Ca Mâu Ni Phật fasting in the Himalayas before he became a Buddha on his left. There is also a shrine for the patriarchs of the pagoda in a separate building, differing little from the one in Quán Sứ Pagoda other than in the absence of imagery representing the arhats.

Where the statuary starts to differ from Quán Sứ Pagoda is in the rows of statues of the Ten Kings of Hell that line either side of the main hall. In addition, in front of the main Buddha altar that is the focal point of the pagoda, straddling the divide between the main sanctuary and the antechamber, is a large statue of the main spirit of the pagoda. In the antechamber there are also a number of stat-ues that are not part of the canonical Buddhist pantheon.

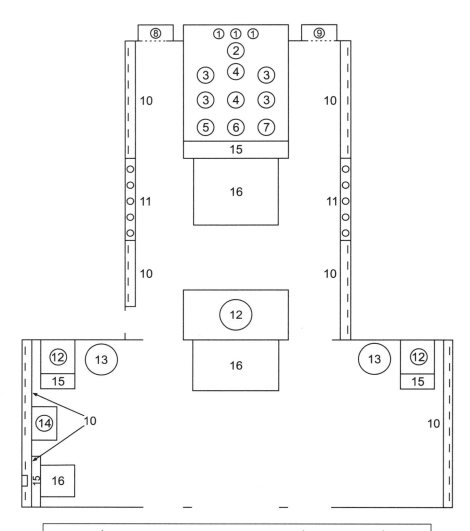

1. Tam thế phật (Buddhas of the Past, Present, and Future)
2. A Di Đà Phật (Amitābha Buddha)
3. Bốn Vị Bồ Tát (Four bodhisattvas)
4. Thích Ca Mầu Ni Phật (Śākyamuni Buddha)
5. Di Lạc Phật (Maitreya Buddha)
6. Tượng Toà Cửu Long (Birth of the Buddha)
7. Tượng tuyết sơn (Śākyamuni fasting in the Himalayas)
8. Nghìn Mắt Nghìn Tay Quan Âm (Thousand eyes and hands Guanyin)
9. Quan Âm Thị Kính (Thị Kính Guanyin)
10. Ancestor tablets
11. Diêm Vương (Ten Kings of Hell)
12. Non-Buddhist spirits
13. Hộ pháp (Dharma guardians)
14. Địa Tạng (Kṣitigarbha)
15. Altar
16. Dais

Layout of the Main Hall of a Typical Pagoda in Hanoi

However, the biggest difference between this pagoda and Quán Sứ Pagoda is the large amount of pagoda space given over to altars dedicated to the mother goddesses and other spirits. Though mother goddess shrines are never central to pagoda architecture, they are a distinguishing feature of Vietnamese pagodas in the north, indicating the integration of Buddhism to the broader religious landscape.[14] There is an expression concerning the construction of pagodas that goes, "The Buddha in front, the saint/spirit behind," which holds true at Phúc Lộc Pagoda (Hà Văn Tấn et al. 1993, 24). Directly behind the main sanctuary that holds the Buddhist statues is a model of a green mountain festooned with small statues of spirits and animals, at which offerings of meat and alcohol are made (something that would never be done at a Buddhist altar). Behind this mountain is a statue of a spirit titled Great Uniting Mandarin, flanked by two small statues of the female and male child-deities Little Princess and Little Prince, both of which are incarnated in spirit possession rituals.

The shrine for mother goddesses has a number of statues. Rather than representing a cult dedicated to a specific figure (as with the cult of Liễu Hạnh, for example), this shrine is dedicated to the holistic cosmological concept, known as either the Three Palaces or the Four Palaces. The altars in this shrine hold the statues of the Lady of the Market, Five Guardians of the Goddess, Three Thrones of the Queen Mother, and the Five Lords. There is also a statue of the Great Virtuous King and one to the Five Tigers situated on the floor below the center altar.[15]

The shrine for mother goddesses is an important religious space within Phúc Lộc Pagoda. Almost everyone who goes into the pagoda to make an offering to the buddhas also makes offerings and wishes in the mother goddess shrine. At Quán Sứ Pagoda, many people told me that belief in the spirits was superstition, or at least that the spirits are lower than the buddhas and therefore inconsequential. At Phúc Lộc Pagoda, it is accepted by everyone with whom I spoke that although the buddhas may be more important, the gods and saints cannot be neglected, as illustrated by Thầy Tâm's sponsorship of a spirit possession ritual. Thầy Tâm, like most of the women who regularly attend rituals at the pagoda, did not see a clear difference between Buddhism and what the state calls superstition.

Ritually, the two pagodas also are very different. There are never funerary or commemorative rites taking place at Quán Sứ Pagoda. Instead, I have only ever seen groups chanting sutras there. There are no worship rituals done for the spirits. At Phúc Lộc Pagoda, by contrast, there are rituals performed for both sides, and two sets of ritual specialists. Thầy Tâm is responsible for taking care of the Buddha side, but she says that she does not serve the spirits by acting as a medium or by performing *cúng* (which only men do, she says). Instead, she serves the spir-

Mother goddess shrine (*nhà mẫu*) in a local Buddhist pagoda

its by sweeping out and maintaining their space and by welcoming supplicants. It is men who perform the various functions related to the spirits. The ritual master and the ritual group take care of the *cúng* on the first and fifteenth, on special holidays and when people sponsor rituals, and Thầy Linh serves as the spirit medium for the mother goddesses by performing the correct possession rituals.

CONCLUSION

For the elite, the secular state, and the Buddhist reformers, the spirits and the buddhas are equally disempowered. They are no longer potent spirits: they are ancestors worthy of respect, in the former case, and figures that lead by example but have no power to grant salvation, in the latter. Within the Buddhist context, the spirits are safely and actively ignored because they represent a presecular, premodern understanding of the cosmos and are seen as inherently opposed to the imaginings of the historical Buddha and his teachings of morality and self-perfection, in the eyes of Buddhist modernists. Quán Sứ Pagoda continues to project this modern view of Buddhism in a way that corresponds with the general disenchanted view of world as secular.[16]

However, outside this particular pagoda's gates there is a reenchantment taking place, as Philip Taylor points out (2007). In pagodas around northern Vietnam—pagodas such as Phúc Lộc Pagoda—people continue to perceive themselves as embedded in a world that is actively influenced by supernatural elements that can be both dangerous and beneficial, and to have resumed ritual actions that reflect this view. Phúc Lộc Pagoda, in other words, more closely adheres to the Buddha side / spirit side cosmology in its architecture and statuary, and in the practices that take place there. It is politically marginalized, served only by a single nun, but it is largely left alone by the state.

This is not to say that the secularized view of Buddhism that is put forward by the Buddhist institution is wholly ignored, but it is not grasped in the way that is perhaps intended. Quán Sứ Pagoda is the focal point of many lay Buddhists' religious activities because it holds authority that transfers to individual prestige. However, engaging in the power of this legitimizing space requires performances that diverge from common religious practice. The people at Quán Sứ Pagoda tend to speak about Buddhism in ways that reflect the views of the Buddhist Revival. Those who do not have the cultural and linguistic capacity to speak in this way, like the woman at Quán Sứ Pagoda mentioned above, are made mute by their concern with correctness.

3 Masculinities and Performances of Skepticism

Minh was twenty-two years old when I first met him in 1997. He was in charge of the guesthouse where I lived for most of my first year in Vietnam. He was bright, thoughtful, and had a good sense of humor; we quickly became good friends. Minh came from a poor family in a village one hour west of Hanoi, in Hà Tây province. His father died when he was a baby and his mother, brother, and sister had to struggle to survive. He regretted that he was only ever able to attend a couple of grades of elementary school. Circumstances were not in his favor as a child: instead of going to school he had to gather firewood to sell in the nearest large town, and to care for the family's cow.

Like many other young men from the surrounding rural areas, Minh came to Hanoi to find a job and make some money. The guesthouse was owned by a distant relative, who took advantage of her country relations for cheap and reliable labor. This relative put him in charge of the guesthouse after a couple of years because of his hard work there and his facility with English, which he had learned on the job. He returned to his village and married in 2000, had a son after a year, then returned to Hanoi to continue earning money to support his family. By 2009, he had saved enough to buy a car and so started working as a taxi driver, going to his home village to visit his wife and child once a week.

Minh is typical of most young men I know in northern Vietnam in terms of his involvement with religion. He visits pagoda grounds only when sightseeing with friends, and that is infrequent. When he does visit, he never makes offerings, lights incense, or brings his hands together in a gesture of reverence. He went with me to some religious sites in the vicinity of his village in 1997, and at that time showed me around without being able to say much about the religious or historical significance of the temple, and never approached the altars. He holds the view that all religion is superstition. Frequently his skepticism turns into joking mockery, as when he emphatically makes the point that people who believe there are supernatural agencies that will assist them in their lives are foolishly deceiving themselves and wasting time and money. In one conversation, he bluntly stated this opinion:

Me: What do you think happens to you after you die?
Minh: Death is the end.
Me: What does burning immolative money do?
Minh: Nothing at all. It is literally burning money!

He tried to make sure that his mother did not waste the family's scant resources on religious practice, and believed that she was "stupid" and superstitious for doing so. On one occasion in 1998 he returned to his village to find that his mother was holding a séance at their house to contact his dead father. Flying into a rage, he assaulted the medium and forced everyone out of the house. He told me later that he then told his mother that if she was only going to waste the money that he gave her, he would stop giving it to her.

Following the experience I had with Mrs. Thanh trying to find the grave of her dead brother with the help of a spirit caller (described in Chapter 1), I returned to the guesthouse, opened a bottle of beer, and sat in the shade on the front steps, looking out at the bustle of Hanoi and contemplating what I had seen. Minh joined me and I related my experience to him, playing him a section of the recording I had made of the medium possessed by the spirit of the dead boy. The spirit, at one point, giggled and asked for candy with an infant's pronunciation. Minh laughed hard when he heard this and made reference to the state prohibition of such activities, by joking, "And if the police showed up, I bet the ghost would run faster than a motorcycle!"

In his view, women are more prone to engage in religious activities than are men because of what he described as their feminine nature. He points out that strength and self-reliance are important features for men; turning to the supernatural for help is not only misguided, but also betrayed weakness and an unmanly inability to take care of oneself. In short, he believes that being religious is feminine and it puts men's masculinity in question because it indicates that they are neither self-reliant nor strong. His views of religion and his humorous dismissals of religious beliefs and practices—that is, his performances of skepticism—are intricately tied to his views of masculinity and the construction of his own identity as a man.

The depth of his conviction of the uselessness and wastefulness of all religious practices arises from the cultural and historical circumstances of Vietnam, which has resulted in performances of skepticism being particularly tied to the construction of masculinity. Minh's concern with waste is certainly heightened by his poverty, but he unknowingly participates in the discourses against religion that are tied to the masculine state's historical alignment of secularism and modernity. These antireligious sentiments are, therefore, not unique to Minh, but are the most typical responses that men in general, and young men in particular, gave to me when we spoke of religion. The continued association of skepticism with "elite" male culture suggests strong links between these views and avenues of male power and authority.

SKEPTICISM AS RELIGIOUS EXPRESSION

It may seem strange to write about skepticism in a book that is ostensibly about Buddhism. However, male statements of skepticism make up one end of a continuum that covers the way that gender and religion interact in Vietnam. In its simplest form, this continuum has masculinity aligned with state secularity and skepticism at one end, and femininity aligned with religiosity and belief in the Buddha side / spirit side worldview at the other.

Male performances of skepticism are seen with regularity in Hanoi. These performances draw on the stance of the secular Communist state. In doing so, they reflect a Western-inspired disenchantment with a traditional worldview that acknowledges the potency of supernatural forces embedded in the world. These performances embrace a rationalist, scientific, view where religion is no longer a process of engagement with these forces, but is secularized to express respect and gratitude to ancestors, to regard the Buddha as only a teacher, and to take as its guiding principle personal and moral cultivation. Performances of skepticism can be seen through actions (usually actions of avoidance) as well as rhetorical utterances that dismiss the potency of the supernatural and the authenticity of religious experts. Two more examples will suffice to show that Minh's opinion is not anomalous.

In 2010, I was at the house of a family that I have known for a long time. A young woman who lived in the neighborhood had recently discovered her ability to call spirits of the dead. The family's daughter, Hạnh, decided to visit this spirit caller and persuaded her husband to go along. Her intention was to contact her brother, who had tragically died ten years before without a wife or children. Because of his lack of descendants, Hạnh was concerned that he was suffering in the afterlife. She returned later very pleased with the results. She described how her brother had said that all was well, but that he wished his mother would offer cigarettes for him, as he had enjoyed smoking during his life.[1] She also made a point of describing how the spirit caller had identified things in her house that Hạnh believed she could not have known. Hạnh, an accountant in her thirties who describes herself as very religious, firmly believed that she had been speaking with her brother. Her husband, a businessman named Nam, was less sure, though he had witnessed it with Hạnh. He said, "What the woman said about our house was true, and she could not have known. So, I am not sure how she knew."

Mr. Thiện, Hạnh's father, had not attended and did not share his son-in-law's ambivalence. He had been born an only child into a rich village family in Hà Tây province. Mr. Thiện's father had been killed during the land reforms of 1954, because he had been an official who had worked with the French. Mr. Thiện, denied further education and access to all but menial jobs, educated himself and was able to work his way up to a managerial position in a state-owned enterprise by dint of his intelligence and gentle manner, which had brought recognition and goodwill from the company's director. When his daughter told him about her experience with the spirit caller, he stated that he did not believe it, and then insisted on explaining some of the ways that the spirit caller could know—she was a neighbor, after all. In a later discussion with him, he explained to me his feelings about the possibility of communicating with the dead: "In my opinion, when you are dead you don't know anything more. When my mother was still alive, my mother said to me that I didn't need to do anything for her after she was dead. I replied to her, 'If, after you die, you return to me and you say that you are still conscious I will certainly do rituals for you and send you money,' but since she died I have never heard one little word from her. Even though I really wish that she would return to speak with me, she never has."

A pseudo-pilgrimage I took with a group of young people to Thầy Pagoda also demonstrated male ambivalence towards religion.[2] The group was made up of Nhung (discussed in Chapter 1), my wife and I, a young man, and two other couples. The group, therefore, consisted of eight people, equally divided between men and women, most below thirty in age. When we reached the pagoda, the women promptly arranged the bags of edible offerings onto a few trays that pagodas always supply for this purpose. The women went in to make offerings and wishes at the various altars in the pagoda complex. The men of the group, meanwhile, took a cursory look around the pagoda, and then went to stand around in the courtyard while they waited for the women to finish their business. They smoked and chatted while they waited, making derogatory jokes among themselves about people who believed in the efficacy of religious practice.

As with Minh, Nam, and Mr. Thiện, these men expressed a great deal of ambivalence about religious practice. They were willing to travel to the spot with their wives and girlfriends. They also were willing to acknowledge the significance of the sites as culturally important. However, they were unwilling to take the least religious action. They went in and looked, but made it very clear that they did not believe in the potency of the buddhas and spirits by paying no respect and making no prayers or offerings. Performances of skepticism such as these are not exceptional, but are instead the most common male interaction with religion.

IMPOVERISHMENT OF RITUALS OF SKEPTICISM

As a type of religious action, we therefore have men most commonly expressing disengagement towards religion, denying the possibility of the supernatural world being entangled with this one. They typically avoid religious spaces and maintain a tight refusal to participate in any way. They are frequently dismissive of women's religious practices, which they call superstition, and imply that the activities are ineffectual and a waste of both time and money. These performances, consisting of total avoidance, off-the-cuff disparaging remarks, and curt dismissals, are also rituals of a sort, in being repetitive, symbolic, and scripted actions. However, in comparison with women's elaborate explanations of the efficacy of the spirits and the buddhas and ritually involved engagements with the supernatural, men's "rituals" of skepticism are sparse and impoverished. Men make use of standardized phrasing such as Minh's comment "death is the end" (chết là hết), or perform accentuated avoidance, or have rituals performed by proxy while they affect condescension.

In northern Vietnam after 1954, the secular view became more than just an elite view, but was adopted and enforced by the state, so that many common religious practices became forbidden. Especially targeted were spaces and practices that perpetuated ideologies that challenged the power of the centralized state, such as village communal houses and family rituals. However, an additional target was practices with which women were particularly associated, such as spirit possession rituals. Reactions to government reform policies concerning religion were not uniform, with some people (particularly men) buying in to state rhetoric while others continuing clandestine Buddhist and spirit possession rituals. Old women did not give up their everyday religious practices, and the unofficial Elderly Women's Buddhist Association continued to exist throughout the revolutionary period (Luong 1992, 183).

Men were far more restricted because of the closer ties that many had with the Communist Party, which at that time was the only avenue for social mobility. Many young men became zealously antireligious in the 1950s; though the wide-scale destruction that was wrought in China during the Cultural Revolution did not occur in Vietnam, many ritual objects were destroyed, and the performance of rituals curtailed (Endres 2001, 84). Nam, Hạnh's husband, came from a village in

Gia Lâm, on the outskirts of Hanoi. He related to me how his village's communal house, spirit temple, and Buddhist pagoda, along with all of the statues and ritual items, were destroyed by young men in the village in 1954. The village partially rebuilt them in the early 1990s and the work still continues twenty years later. He also told me, "All of those involved in destroying these buildings died an early death. I can't explain why or how, but I know that they all died young. There are many instances of this happening."

As the male attitude towards religion, and particularly women's practices, are part of a discourse that is perpetuated by the state, it follows that attacks on practices associated with the Buddha side / spirit side cosmology are national in scope. So, Philip Taylor's study in southern Vietnam of the translocal cult of the Lady of the Realm (Bà Chúa Xứ) shows that it is especially the marginalized female petty traders that form the core group of pilgrims to the site. The cultural commentators most likely to label their activities as superstition, on the other hand, "can be located with relative geo-social precision as urban-based, educated, white-collar professionals, the majority of them male" (P. Taylor 2004, 12).

Men's lack of engagement in religious practice and performances of skepticism may be partly due to the political ramifications and social stigma of participating in something that has been consistently condemned by the state. This prohibitive force emanating from the state was certainly a major determinant before the Renovation, when declarations of religiosity would stand in the way of social advancement. However, the skepticism that is expressed by the state is so closely associated with men, and has been maintained so resolutely for such a long time, that performances of skepticism are certainly something more than artifacts of a militantly secular ideological past. In fact, men and women relate so entirely differently to religion in Vietnam that it is clear that religiosity is closely tied to the construction of gender. It is because structures of gender are remarkably durable and uniform throughout Vietnam, and across class lines, that gendered discourses of religion have persevered with such ease.

As these discourses are so hegemonically powerful and backed by the authority of the state that there is no need for a sustained ritual that matches women's in intensity and commitment. Men's speech acts and avoidances are shorthand ways of evoking the authority of these discourses (which are themselves masculine in nature). Men are able to access the power of these discourses through simple comments and relatively impoverished rituals of avoidance, through selective and conspicuously minimal participation, and through rephrasings of significance. It is, therefore, enough for Mr. Thiện to say, "My thinking is like this: I think that you light incense at the grave of your father, mother, grandfather, grandmother, and that you have to always do it. But burning spirit money, clothes, and other things is just superstition." In engaging in this kind of speech act, he has not only made a personal statement of opinion, but has also evoked a trope that reifies his status as a man in relation to an understanding of women's religious practice.

RELIGIOSITY AND GENDER STRUCTURES

The underlying assumptions that tied performances of skepticism to masculine gender projects in the explanations of my informants went something like this: (1) Women are religious and men are not. (2) The reason for this is that women are inherently weak and need to lean on others for assistance in their lives. (3) In this world, it is their fathers, husbands, and sons on which women rely, but because dependence is an essential part of their nature, women also turn to the supernatural for assistance with their lives. As a result, (4) men should believe in their own ability and rely on themselves—not on other people and certainly not on the supernatural—in order to be masculine.

This pervasive and constant expression of women's weakness and reliance on others as the root of their religiosity was seen, for example, in responses to a question included in a questionnaire I developed and carried out about why women go to pagodas and temples overwhelmingly more than men. Women responded in this way: "Because women wish for so many things but don't know how to achieve them" (twenty-year-old female student), "Because women have more time and are weaker than men" (fifty-two-year-old housewife), and "Because they are women, they have to ask for help, for their health and for wealth" (eighty-one-year-old housewife). Men responded to the same question in this way: "They are easily influenced by others and don't believe in themselves" (thirty-five-year-old male driver), "Women are weak and they don't believe in themselves" (fifty-year-old male retiree), and "Because their character is to believe in themselves less than men" (fifty-eight-year-old male white-collar worker).[3]

Women are seen (and mostly see themselves) as not only physically weaker, but also technically less skilled. Many people, both men and women, explained that there are fewer women in leadership roles in business and in scientific research because women are intellectually inferior and less rational. They are also seen as morally weaker, less able to control their emotions, and karmically inferior. As Peletz (1995, 1996) has written of Malay society, men and women are attributed the respective characteristics of reason and passion, a dichotomy that also informs a great deal of the gender discourse in Vietnam. One woman at Quán Sứ Pagoda described women's involvement in religion in precisely these terms: "The Buddha taught us how to live morally and to live properly. In a word, women have a heavier karmic burden (*nặng nghiệp hơn*) than men. Therefore, they have to go to pagodas to repent (*sám hối*)—and women have really bad karma. In previous lives, a long time ago, they did very bad things, so now they have to pay for it." The caretaker at Quán Sứ Pagoda also pointed to women's weakness as the main cause for women going to pagodas: "Women go to pagodas more because they are the weaker sex, weaker than men. Men are stronger and women are weaker, so they go to pagodas more. Because they are weaker they need to go to pagodas to get the protection of the Buddha, while men don't need the Buddha's help as much."

Young men, especially, view religious practice as a feminine activity antithetical to masculine characteristics of self-reliance and self-confidence. This is commonly phrased in ways that are reminiscent of the Confucian Three Submissions, which dictate that women are supposed to rely first on fathers, then on husbands, and finally on sons. The fact that it is largely rhetorical—and that many men rely heavily on the income of their wives, and on being taken care of by women—does not diminish the effect that it has on the overall construction of femininity and masculinity.

Religiosity and irreligiosity are therefore seen as traits of femininity and masculinity, deeply enmeshed in ways of being. They are expressions that, as much as they are religious acts, are also performances of gender identity. All actions in some way go towards the construction of gendered identities, but religious acts are particularly relevant to these gender projects. In fact, religious practice was referenced so often in relation to gendered behavioral expectations that it might not be too bold to say that religion is one of the primary referents in the construction of gender stereotypes in Vietnam.

HEGEMONIC MASCULINITY AND THE MARGINALIZATION OF RELIGIOUS MEN

On an individual level, people are constantly constructing their identities, identities that are rooted in a number of key components, including class, group identity (i.e., ethnicity, nationality, region, family or clan, and so on), age, gender, and so on. These other identity markers are of varying importance, but gender identity is perhaps one of the foremost in importance in that it is so completely implicated in virtually all aspects of a person's identity. The dynamic nature of the construction of gender identity makes the term "gender projects" an appropriate one, because it accentuates that gender identity is an ongoing process that continues throughout a person's life (Connell 1987). These projects, at a personal level, are part of the construction of overall identities, and serve the practical goal of creating and maintaining social relations. At a societal level, such performances fit into the larger reproduction of the gender structures that result in the overall subordination of women to men.[4]

While in some cases performances that constitute the gender projects of individuals are conscious (for example, men avoiding religious behavior that is perceived as feminine), these projects often are unconsciously lived and embodied (for example, through speech utterances that occur spontaneously in conversation). They are part of what Bourdieu identifies as the *habitus:* "The system of structured, structuring dispositions...which is constituted in practice and is always oriented towards practical functions" (1990, 52). These "structuring structures" are acquired and embodied over time, starting with early childhood, and are constantly acted out in such a way that the rules seem sensible, natural, believable, and even beyond question within the context of the field (Bourdieu 1990, 66–67).

In Vietnam, hegemonic masculinity is constructed in relation to a subordinated femininity as the "other," with the main purpose being the dominance of men over women.[5] Hegemonic masculinity is assumed and reiterated as part of the *habitus* of men through myriad actions. Hegemonic masculinity, as a dominant ideal, works as a persuasive instrument to convince men to conform to a particular way of being that results in men's overall power relative to women. However, it is clear that few men live up to the hegemonic ideal (Connell 1987, 185). As well as demanding conformity (at the risk of ridicule, ostracism, and denial of power, money, and social advancement), the hegemonic model also creates the self-realizing illusion of male power, which institutionalizes men's dominance. Usually this conformity takes the form of performing token acts that reify the ideal rather than actually living the ideal in its totality.

Hegemonic masculinity is successful, overall, in establishing and maintaining male ascendancy by subordinating women and demanding complicity in a way that is embodied and assumed rather than questioned or debated, at the same time by marginalizing those who do not conform. While hegemony, subordination, and complicity are internal to the gender order, marginalization involves the interplay of gender with other structures, such as class and race. Marginalization occurs in the relationship between the masculinities of dominant and subordinate groups, with the hegemonic masculinity of the dominant group being legitimated and the subordinate being marginalized.

Men, particularly young and middle-aged ones, who contravene gender expectations of avoiding religious practice, risk the possibility of drawing criticism of being like a woman or effeminate. This opinion was clearly shown by a middle-aged businessman who told me, "If a man goes to a pagoda to pray, he might as well wear a skirt." Such acts of marginalization are fairly common. So, for example, a middle-aged woman described a man who exhibited a form of religiosity that was regarded as too feminine:

> I work with one thirty-year-old man who is too feminine in the way that he carries out his religious practice. Usually when men go to the pagoda, they will only bow to the Buddha three times, and that will be the extent of their practice. However, he liked to prepare flowers and arrange trays of fruit and offerings. He felt that if he made an extra effort to make beautiful offerings then he would get more luck in return. He would enter the pagoda with the tray of offerings on his head in the most supplicative manner. The result was that the other men in his company would call him *đồng cô*—effeminate—his friends to his face, but many others behind his back.

The man in the office did not conform to the hegemonic ideal in other ways as well. There was a yoga class given for company employees and there were nine women, but only this one man who took the class. Sometimes the students in the class would go out together to buy clothes and silk and he went with them to buy new clothes ("silk underwear," my informant remarked). The women in the yoga class, as well as the men in the company, would often say that he was like a woman, and both men and women would make subtle jokes at his expense. For instance, they would ask him to come and peel and cut fruit for his colleagues, because this is understood as being women's work. The women in the company enjoyed being with him, but the men thought he was a bit strange and their wives did not want them to go out with him because they had the opinion that there was something wrong with him.

A young woman at Phúc Lộc Pagoda pointed out in 2010 that there are an increasing number of men going to famous and efficacious locations to make offerings and wishes. However, their activities are mostly limited to making wishes for good luck. Only a very few would chant sutras at the pagoda. Furthermore, she said that this kind of participation was so unusual that it would draw comments even from fervent Buddhists. "The other women that chant sutras with them will, to their face, praise them for being so devout, but even those women will also say behind their backs that they are a little like old women."

There is also a common view in northern Vietnam that Buddhist monks are feminine in nature; they are frequently described using the pejorative term "*đồng cô*," or effeminate. By renouncing socially sanctioned family life and joining the *sangha* (the Buddhist monastic order), they have bowed out of the most potent symbol of masculinity—the patrilineage. They also have shirked the most important duty of sons, which is to respect and care for parents both in old age and after death through participation in the ancestor cult. For this reason, Thầy Tâm at Phúc Lộc Pagoda attributes the shrinking numbers of young men willing to become monks to her belief that people, especially those in the city, are having fewer children, and are therefore less willing to let a child leave secular life and their families.

The term *đồng cô* itself, used in a derogatory way to describe effeminate men, underlines the close connection between women's behavior, femininity, and "superstitious" practice. *Đồng cô* literally refers to a female spirit medium, but has been appropriated to more commonly refer to men who do not conform to norms of hegemonic masculinity.[6] The fact that the most common Vietnamese slang for overly effeminate behavior is borrowed from religious terminology points to the close association between femininity and religiosity.

In an example of how religiosity and sexuality are often conflated, Nam also told me that he thought most monks were homosexual:

Nam: Very many monks are gay. Even my friend [who is a monk] is gay. Almost all of them are like that.

Me: Why?

Nam: Because they are not normal, and so they are scared.

Me: Scared of what?

Nam: They can't come out. They are afraid that society will be against them. My friend is also probably like this. But I don't know....In Vietnam gays are very scared, so they really like to go to pagodas, where they are more accepted. If they like it, that's fine. These gay men, they don't like women, so women are happy with that [because it makes pagodas safe for them].

Sexuality is also a significant aspect of male performances of skepticism. Men seek women who are weak, considering it an appealing characteristic in potential girlfriends and wives, while women perform (and embody) weakness in order to make themselves more attractive. Masculinity, on the other hand, is constructed in opposition to this weakness; therefore, eschewing religious practice becomes integral to performances that are a part of their gender projects. While men expressed sexual preference for soft-spoken and outwardly compliant women, the women I spoke with expressed a marked preference for men who were strong and self-assured. Some even told me of physical revulsion when they see a man act in an effeminate (*đồng cô*) manner.

Whereas men who enact a religiosity that does not conform to hegemonic ideals are marginalized, women who are religious are merely subordinated. I rarely heard men ridicule specific women for going to pagodas and making wishes, instead tending to speak of women and superstition in a general way. They did not discourage women from engaging in religious practice, except in cases where their mothers' or wives' religious fervor became overly extravagant and came to be seen as excessively wasteful. Instead, religious behavior on the part of women is passively supported as something expected of women. Young men often can be seen escorting wives and girlfriends to make offerings on the first and fifteenth of the lunar month. They also readily share in the supernaturally charged offerings (*lộc*) that are produced at these visits. Yet they will maintain a skeptical stance despite their tacit involvement. When speaking of women's practice, men's tone is usually patronizing, in the same way that they talk about children's behavior as something negative, or even humorous, but nonetheless expected and therefore accepted. Conversely, men directly ridicule other men who make offerings at pagodas and display too overt a belief in the supernatural. At an individual level, men receive dividends for this masculine behavior in the form of peer approval and the possibility of attracting a mate, while at the societal level it contributes to the overall dominance of men over women.

CHANGES IN MEN'S RELIGIOUS EXPRESSION

The construction of masculinity, and the way that religious practice has been equated with "retrograde" superstition, the practice of which is especially associated with women, has been moderated to some degree since the beginning of the Renovation. Whereas pagodas and temples are still overwhelmingly attended by women, as of 2010 men are going to pagodas in greater numbers, though it is by no means an activity in which most men are willing to involve themselves. Statements of skepticism are less emphatic today than they were when I started my research in 1997, and men's avoidance is less absolute. As one monk I visited in Hanoi put it, "There are more men who go to the pagoda now, though it is still just a few." While most men still avoid religious spaces entirely, there are some young urbanites that are starting to go to pagodas on the first and fifteenth of the lunar month. In 2010, for example, staff from the nearby market (in their late twenties to early thirties) would come as a group to Phúc Lộc Pagoda to pray in front of the altars of both the buddhas and spirits (though they may have been influenced by the director of the market who either came to make offerings fairly regularly or who had his sister do it on his behalf). Aside from this group, there were also a few young businessmen who would come in briefly to make wishes for success in their business ventures.

It appears that it is primarily those engaged in business that are turning to religion to improve their chances. Hạnh, the employee of a pharmaceutical company, told me that her director regularly gave donations to pagodas when he was undertaking important activities such as buying a house or a car. When a large office tower and shopping complex was recently built on Bà Triệu Street, a neighboring pagoda was purportedly given a large donation by the developers for it to be completely renovated and repainted. The demographic locations of these new male practitioners are very specific, as is the intention of their religious practice. Whereas women usually speak about going to pagodas for their families, businessmen engage in religious practice specifically for luck in their businesses and their careers, as described to me by one woman in her thirties:

> Some women like to go to the pagoda for fun and to have peace in their souls, but most men think that if they go they will be luckier and earn more money. Even some of the leaders of Vietnam, like the prime minister or the president, go to pray very often, and they allow statues or relics to be brought from India, because they want to do something good for the country. Women pray mostly for their children's health and success in school, though they also pray for money and maybe for work. But men mostly pray for money and their business, and only after that for their families. They especially go to pagodas when they prepare to do something big in their business and they need the confidence to make sure they are successful. For example, when my husband is about to buy or sell a piece of land, he likes to go to the pagoda to pray.

Nam (Hạnh's husband), himself a businessman, has a statue of Ông Địa in his home office to which he regularly makes offerings. While long popular in the south, these floor altars are new in the north, but, he told me, they have become very popular with businessmen. They can be seen in virtually every store and business around Hanoi today. In 2010, on the night before he was about to close a business deal that he was not confident would happen, Nam bought a large durian fruit (which are expensive) and offered it to Ông Địa to enlist his aid. He also makes offerings at pagodas and temples on the first of the lunar month and at the beginning of the year. He believes that it is specifically businessmen rather

Nam's altar to Ông Địa (the Earth God) on the floor of his office

than people in other lines of work that have become more religious in recent years because of the risk involved in doing business: "People who don't have money don't need to make offerings. They don't have anything to lose." He thought that a big reason why rich people, especially businessmen and government officials, were increasingly making offerings at pagodas was to counteract the effects of the immoral acts that were an inevitable requirement of the accumulation of wealth.

The reasons for the increased engagement in religious behavior by some men in recent years are not entirely clear. One factor is certainly that the state itself has been less strident in its statements of skepticism. This change has decreased the negative associations of religion with feudalism and backwards ignorance. A monk with whom I spoke made a strong connection between Vietnam's recovery from colonialism and war, and an increased interest in Buddhism: "Women have a heavier karmic burden, but it is not because of this that men don't go to pagodas. Men go to pagodas less because it takes a lot of time and men are busier than women. Also, Vietnam was dominated for a long time. This affected the people, but Buddhism was not completely lost. Now it is starting to come back; men are participating again."

It is significant that it is particularly businessmen, including the wealthy and the powerful, who are most involved in the male reenchantment with religion. This makes it unlikely that male religiosity is a counterculture expression or act of resistance by a marginal group, as Philip Taylor found was the case with many engaged in goddess worship in the south (2004). Instead, a more reasonable explanation would follow Weller's observations of religious practice in Taiwan (Weller 1994, 1996): that the riskiness of doing business in a liberal trade environment brings out a Malinowskian desire to turn to the supernatural when all worldly efforts have been exhausted to ensure success and avoid danger. Certainly, this explanation is echoed in the reasons I heard most often from businessmen themselves. In various forms, the way that it was phrased was that, although they may not believe completely, religious practice at least helped to calm their nerves, and might actually help. Nam put it this way: "I only believe a certain percentage—not 100 percent. But if I make offerings to Ông Địa I feel more relaxed when I work."

Men, especially businessmen, can be seen in small numbers at pagodas today, but this does not mean that they replicate women's supplicative practices. Indeed, strong distinctions continue to be made by men both rhetorically and in their practice. The rhetorical expression is given not as much through statements of skepticism, but rather in an ambiguity that seems to permeate expressions of religiosity. Nam's explanations of religious practice, for example, tended to be as ambiguous as was his interpretation of what had happened at the spirit calling, described above. After telling me that businessmen are going to pagodas to pray for good luck, he also said, "People go to pagodas because they lack education. They go because they think that they will get material boons." He continued,

> Nam: For pagodas, mainly it is women who go, though some men
> go.... In general, men hesitate to go to pagodas because they
> can't be relaxed. They cannot eat, drink alcohol, talk loudly, so
> men are very hesitant. It is not because they think that going to
> the pagoda is not good. When you go to pagodas you mainly
> have to eat vegetarian, but men don't like to eat vegetarian.
>
> Me: Women like it more? Why?
> Nam: It is more suitable for them.
> Me: Why is it more suitable for women?
> Nam: Because women don't drink beer or alcohol very much.

Me: And when you drink beer and alcohol you have to eat meat…
Nam: Yes.

Thus, while Nam conceded that men, especially businessmen like himself, were engaging in religious activities much more than they used to (he estimates that things started to change around 2000), he still tends to see religious activity as women's labor. He takes care that offerings are made to Ông Địa in his own office, and he occasionally goes to buy fruit for offerings, and will light incense himself, but it is his wife who takes out a prayer book and recites a passage to Ông Địa before praying audibly for good luck for her husband's business and the fortune of the family.

The ambiguity of religious practice for men is often seen in half-hearted participation—a standoffishness expressed through restrained hand gestures and semiparticipations. So, though Nam is religious to some extent, he cannot bring himself to express full faith in his offerings or in the authority of the spirit caller. This is typical of businessmen who engage in some religious practice. In April 2010, I met a number of people who pooled funds for a memorial ritual at Phúc Lộc Pagoda for their dead relatives. There were fifty souls in all that were given offerings of food, paper houses, and money to improve their condition in the afterlife. Among the sponsors of this group ritual were several young men. One that I spoke with in the reception area of the pagoda had recently returned from Russia, after working there for several years as a trader. He told me that he had decided to come back because life in Russia was getting too dangerous due to the recent spree of terrorist attacks in Moscow. He said that he was taking part in this ritual for his mother's spirit as the sole representative from his family. There were a few other men there as well. However, while they clearly had enough religious conviction to pay for the ritual and help organize the offerings, their behavior was different from the female participants. The women stayed seated behind the monk, the ritual master, and the few old men from the ritual group (who had all been invited to perform the ritual), with their hands clasped together during the whole ritual. The young men, on the other hand, stayed for only a few minutes in the pagoda and then left to wait out in the courtyard or in the reception area, where they smoked, drank tea, and spoke on their cell phones.

At the end of April 2010, I attended a pagoda ancestor feast (Lễ Giỗ Tổ) at Vẽ Pagoda, in the northern part of Hanoi. It was a large event and the pagoda area was a sea of old women in brown robes and prayer beads. There were a few old men and a few young men who were there as well. The ritual and sutra chanting that took place inside the pagoda drew crowds of women. Some sat and tolled prayer beads while others stood behind them and offered short prayers. Many could be seen clutching fistfuls of money, which they would place on the altars or tuck into various spaces (such as the raised hand of a white statue of Quan Âm Bodhisattva). The young men, on the other hand, might pass by the front of the pagoda, but only long enough to put their hands together briefly in supplication, and then would wander off. Again, while young men were present more than I had seen in the past—and it was still proportionally an extremely small number—their behavior was nonetheless conspicuously nondevotional and seemed to be aimed at drawing a distinction between their engagement and that of the women who were present.

On a number of occasions I have gone with men to visit pagodas, and their behavior has consistently been different from women's. In 2010, I visited Dâu Pagoda—an important pagoda at the heart of Vietnamese Buddhism's most ancient center, twenty-four kilometers outside Hanoi—with a monk and two men from the region who had interest in the historical and archaeological relics of the area. When we visited the main altar of the pagoda, the two men walked in front of the altar, apparently without intention of paying respect to the buddhas and spirits. However, when they saw that the monk and I had both paused to bring our hands together and bow, they too briefly brought their hands together, but without commitment and without bowing, looking clumsy and uncomfortable. Even the few men who go to pagodas on their own, and must therefore have some belief in the efficacy of the buddhas, do not exhibit the same investment in their supplicative performances as do women. Bows are minimal, the time spent in front of an altar is much shorter, and they do not tend to audibly mumble prayers as do women. Where offerings are made at all, it is usually only a stick of incense and maybe some money.

At a spirit possession ritual I attended in 2010, in which Thây Linh was the medium, men were taking a greater role than I had ever seen before, but they still acted differently from the female devotees. Aside from the male helpers and musicians, who had previously told me they were homosexual, the few men there sat outside the shrine and chatted on cell phones while the ritual took place. A woman who was not involved with the group and was not present described the difference in men's and women's participation in this way:

> Now men and women go to possession rituals, but when the men go they don't have to prepare anything. They just sit and drink alcohol with the monk. For example, at the pagoda of one monk, there are people who go to help as devotees, but in general men don't need to prepare a lot. They

don't need to do anything, but the women have to do a lot. In general, the more you do, the better it is, but most of the preparations are women's work. Men don't have to do anything to prepare for the offerings. They don't have to buy fruit, don't have to prepare a lot, they just have to come and drink tea with the monk and afterwards go and listen to sutras being recited and go to bow three times. But women have to go buy and arrange the flowers, cook and clean dishes, sweep and clean the pagoda. They have to do a lot of work to have fulfilled their duties. That is what people think. Men don't have to do anything except sit there, while the monk does the ritual.

Though male participation in religion has increased, most men avoid the kinds of activities that relate to a view of the supernatural as being responsive. Even businessmen who have been more visibly active at pagodas in recent years continue to express ambivalence about their involvement. Men, however, are willing to engage in activities such as paying respect to ancestors, both national and familial, by making offerings and taking part in feasts on the death days of ancestors. Renewed village communal house rites and ancestor worship (especially when reinterpreted as respect for national heroes) also involve men to a much greater extent than they did before the Renovation. Within Buddhism, as we will see later, men are particularly drawn to activities that are farthest removed from so-called "folk" practices and that have official sanction as representing "true" Buddhism. It is notable that a greater proportion of men can be seen at Quán Sứ Pagoda than at other pagodas, which is directly due to its status as an "orthodox" and state-approved site.

CONCLUSION

Young men in Hanoi generally equated all religious practice with superstition, and superstition with women's practice. Given that young men also have their share of troubles and anxieties, and one need not have complete faith in order to be assured that offerings will be efficacious, why are young men largely not involved in making offerings?

Minh and Nhung represent two different points of view regarding religious practice, though both draw on structuring dispositions that play a role in maintaining the gender order. In fact, men and women may hold a variety of beliefs, but behavioral patterns will often override more thoughtful reflections, so that some men may express respect towards Buddhism, but avoid practice, and women may express skepticism but nonetheless find themselves making offerings to buddhas or spirits during times of stress. In a broad sense, however, the variance in these two distinct attitudes towards religious practice holds true. The number of men who define themselves as religious is relatively small, as is the number of women who do not practice at all. Moreover, the ways that men and women either practice or disparage religion are distinct. Though there are some businessmen who go to pagodas on the first and fifteenth, these same men also retain an ambivalent attitude towards their own practices, which may be manifest in actions and statements that are contradictory.

Interactions with religious practice, whether as statements of belief or disbelief, are not merely expressions of personal preference. Instead, they are interactions with ways of being in the world that have very specific connotations in relation to the gender projects of individuals, and they partake in broader hegemonic gender structures that subordinate women to men. The reasons for the variations in religious practices of men and women were most commonly explained as being rooted in women's fundamental weakness and men's inherent strength and self-reliance. These constructions, while serving an explanatory function, also reassert underlying assumptions of gender (through sexual preference, labor, politics, media imagery, family dynamics, and so on) to maintain men's hegemonic position.

Nonetheless, gender structures are not solid and unchanging, but are recreated, altered, and negotiated at the individual and societal levels. Individuals draw on, reject, and reinterpret these structures in their daily lives. Just as religious choice in urban Hanoi is made from an overall repertoire from which people choose individual preference, people also draw on a gender repertoire that may reinterpret religious practice differently and insert alternative understandings. While there is an overall discourse of male abstinence from religious practice, there are men who do engage with religion generally and Buddhism specifically. In doing so, however, they often assert important differences in the way they engage and the significance with which they invest their actions.

4 Offerings and Blessings

The fifteenth day of the lunar month had arrived, one of the two days each month when offerings are believed to be most efficacious and when most devotees make an effort to visit a pagoda. My wife called up and reminded me that she wanted to go to the pagoda that afternoon. On our way to the pagoda we stopped to buy things from street vendors to offer at the pagoda. By the time we arrived at the front gate of Chân Tiên Pagoda on Bà Triệu Street, her basket held nine oranges, a bunch of bananas, a wad of votive spirit money, a large bundle of incense sticks, three cones of compressed sweet bean flour (*oản*), and five red roses.[1]

The main shrine hung with a cloud of incense smoke that had been accumulating with the day's steady stream of devotees who came to pay their respects to the buddhas and bodhisattvas, make offerings, and wish for good fortune, happiness, and prosperity for their families. We arranged the offerings on three trays provided by the pagoda and put the trays on the main altar. We put three sticks of incense in the incense holder, and then went to the front of the altar and stood shoulder to shoulder with palms pressed together in prayer. After we finished making our wishes and identifying ourselves to the buddhas, we repeated the process at the two altars on either side.

We then went out to wait for the offerings to soak in the buddhas' blessings, joining the elderly nun in her regular position on a platform close to the entrance. She greeted us, served us tea in small stained cups, and offered us some fruit to eat. As we sat and talked with her, another woman emerged from the small side door of the main sanctuary holding a bag of fruit she had offered on the altars. She approached us, took some of the fruit offerings from her bag, and gave them as a gift to the nun. In return, the nun handed her some of the fruit that had been accumulating in front of her all day as gifts from other devotees who had come to make their bimonthly offerings and wishes.

My wife and I then reentered the main sanctuary and retrieved the trays of offerings we had previously set on the altars, leaving behind the roses, which we had already put into a vase sitting on the main altar. We took the spirit money to the furnace in the courtyard, where I burned it. Meanwhile, my wife talked with

A young woman
making an offer-
ing to wish for a
husband

another woman who was busy pushing her spirit money bit by bit into the furnace, making sure that it burned entirely, so that it would be fully effective.

The spirit money burned, we went back out to the old nun and gave her
a portion of our retrieved offerings, now transformed into *lộc*—the reclaimed
offerings that embody the buddhas' blessings and, more concretely, hold spiritual
potency to bring good luck. The nun, in return, offered some items from her pile
of the pagoda's *lộc*, for which we respectfully thanked her before putting them in
our bags and walking down the path and out the gate. We paid the motorcycle
keeper, climbed onto my wife's Honda, and weaved our way back through the
crowded streets of Hanoi to our house, believing that we had done what we could
to protect ourselves against misfortune for the next two weeks. Most of the *lộc*

we had brought home with us we took to her parents' house the next day to share with her family.

The most common form of religious practice that takes place at Buddhist pagodas in Hanoi is the process of making wishes and offerings, and reclaiming them as *lộc*. This practice is especially done on the first and fifteenth of each lunar month. It involves presenting offerings to the buddhas, which are then reclaimed as "the buddhas' blessings"—being objects that have the ability to bring luck or happiness to the person who possesses or consumes them. While these practices are central to the majority of people who go to pagodas, they are not exclusively Buddhist, and the same practices occur on the same days at non-Buddhist shrines as well, including those of gods, goddesses, spirits, and ancestors.

The practice of making offerings and then reclaiming them as talismans is performed almost exclusively by women, and is not restricted to age groups, as are other practices, such as chanting sutras at Buddhist pagodas. In most instances, the practice of making offerings and reclaiming them is both personal in nature, and has implicit interrelational connections through their distribution (*phát lộc*). These items serve in a very important way to cement relational bonds within families and between friends. The logic of this practice was explained to me as being a way of improving merit (*đức*) through the act of giving.[2] For this reason, *lộc* reaches out beyond the confines of strictly religious practice, even affecting the lives of men who remain skeptical about religion, or who express derogatory comments about it, and whose practice is negligible.

MEANINGS AND MANIFESTATIONS OF *LỘC*

The richness of practice associated with *lộc* has meant that it has been particularly difficult to translate or define. The term *lộc* is a Sino-Vietnamese word, and the Chinese and Sino-Vietnamese words literally mean "the salary of a mandarin." In China, *lu* (祿, V. *lộc*) is closely associated with the words *fu* (福, V. *phúc*), meaning luck, happiness, or fecundity, and *shou* (壽, V. *thọ*), meaning longevity. This triad of concepts is present in Vietnam as well as in China. Pham Van Bich refers to *phúc, lộc,* and *thọ* as meaning, respectively, "to have (1) many children, (2) a great many gifts and benefits from the gods, and (3) longevity" (Pham Van Bich 1999, 183).

It is from the literal meaning of *lộc* as prosperity from high rank that the French scholar Paul Giran rendered *lộc* as *bonheur* (happiness) (1912, 279), but the abstraction of this translation does not acknowledge the connection it has with the intricate and diverse practices that are associated with the objects.

Maurice Durand, another French scholar, later translated it as *porte-bonheur* (talisman) (1959, 13n), a rendering that stresses its practical use, but again misses nuances and fails to convey the value of these objects as material signifiers of supernatural benevolence. Another translation renders *lộc* as "gift from the gods" (Bùi Phụng 1993, 783), which, though clumsy, may come a little closer in capturing the essence of its meaning in most, though not all, circumstances. More recently, contributors to the book *Possessed by the Spirits* have collectively rendered *lộc* as "blessed gift," though they admit that the translation was not arrived at without some dispute (Fjelstad and Nguyen 2006b, 11). Kirsten Endres, one of the contributors to the book, has separately called *lộc* a "divine gift" (2007, 202).

The variety of translations for *lộc* indicates that it is a concept not easily defined because of the crosscultural etymology and multiple manifestations of it in practice. *Lộc,* as I understand it, combines the above translations to a certain extent, with Endres' "divine gift" perhaps being the best. However, a simple translation fails to capture the full meaning of *lộc:* the essence of *lộc,* that it is also a gift given to the supernatural that is transformed, returned, and then distributed, entails a reciprocity that informs both divine and human relations. *Lộc,* rather than being translated, would probably be best explained and then left in its original form, because it is only through a description of the contexts in which *lộc* is used that the multivalance of the term can be fully appreciated.

THE FIRST *LỘC* OF THE YEAR

The most important day in the Vietnamese calendar is the Lunar New Year (Tết Nguyên Đán). Tết is infused with symbolism related to luck and prosperity. Good luck trees (usually plum or mandarin trees) are planted in containers in people's houses. Special foods such as *bánh chưng* (a square glutinous rice cake stuffed with fatty pieces of pork and mung bean and wrapped with *dong* leaves—a kind of plant related to arrowroot) are eaten or given as gifts. Business dealings are completed, debts are paid, and houses are cleaned.

Lộc appears in a number of instances in relation to Tết customs. During customary visits to close friends or relatives, one usually gives a red envelope containing a small amount of money, in new bills if possible, that people sometimes call *lộc.* The intended meaning is to wish for them an increase in wealth (Toan Ánh 1996, vol. 2, 333). This money is also called *mừng tuổi*—literally congratulations on your age—because in Vietnam, as in China, age is not reckoned on the date of birth, but on New Year's Day (Trần Ngọc Thêm 1997, 149).[3] With this sort of *lộc* there is a strong link between money, luck, and happiness.

This association also can be seen in another practice associated with business. In this case, the money is called *mở hàng,* meaning "to be the first customer in a shop" and "to start a sale" (Bùi Phụng 1993, 863–864; Toan Ánh 1996, vol. 2, 333), but the literal meaning is to open (*mở*) a store (*hàng*). In this context, *mở hàng* is the money received from the first customer of the new year. This money is also said to be *lộc,* able to bring good luck to the business for the entire year. On a daily basis, the first sale is also significant for the same reason. Thus, often sellers are willing to discount prices for the first customer of the day or of the year.

In another Tết tradition, branches with new leaves, especially from trees on the grounds of communal houses, pagodas, and other remarkable scenic locations, are torn off and presented to friends and family members on New Year's Eve. In this case, the branches are considered lucky, able to bring fortune in the new year (Tân Việt 1996, 142). In a process that Victor Turner described as "homonymy" (1995 [1969], 64), which allows meanings to carry between words that have a similar sound, the word for bud (*lộc*) takes on the meaning of prosperity (*lộc*). The meaning of *lộc* as a new shoot is extended so that the shoot itself is viewed as a physical manifestation of *lộc* as happiness, good fortune, or prosperity, and thereby becomes a talisman. At the same time, the freshness of a new branch is used as a metaphor to indicate the start of a new year, and the potential growth that the new year holds. *Lộc* as a talisman, in this case, has the properties of sympathetic magic, extending power through the law of similarity.

All of these forms of *lộc* that are associated with Tết hold a commonality in that they are strongly linked to luck and happiness in the form of future wealth. *Lộc* is revealed, particularly in these applications, as being intensely materialistic and directed entirely towards prosperity in this world rather than towards soteriological or eschatological goals. Giran's translation as *bonheur* (happiness) fits nicely with this sense of *lộc*. Durand's translation into French as *porte-bonheur* (talisman or lucky charm) also seems particularly suitable because the term holds the implication of portable happiness, reflecting an important aspect of *lộc,* particularly at Tết. However, *lộc* in other contexts also has a dimension of sacredness that these glosses do not convey.

LỘC, PILGRIMAGES, AND PLEASURE TRIPS

Pilgrimages and pleasure trips to pagodas such as the Perfume Pagoda in Hà Tây Province, or other religious sites such as the temple dedicated to the Lady of the Storehouse in Hà Bắc Province, usually take place in the first lunar month and have become increasingly popular since the Renovation. These trips may have varying degrees of religious intent, ranging from youths going to a scenic spot that includes a famous pagoda and entering briefly to make offerings, to buses of elderly women whose main purpose is to visit important religious sites and obtain blessings from the buddhas and spirits (Soucy 2003; P. Taylor 2004, 165–166). No matter the degree of religious intent, however, *lộc* remains a constant factor— even for the most skeptical. It can augment picnics and be eaten as a snack, it is bought as souvenirs, and in some cases is the focal point of pilgrimages.

The process of offering part, or all, of the picnic on one of these trips is common practice. As an offering, it becomes a talisman—good fortune to be consumed. Only "sweet offerings" (usually fruit) are supposed to be offered to buddhas, while gods are given "salty offerings," such as meat and alcohol. The offerings at Buddhist pagodas can consist of biscuits and fruit and therefore become snacks. At temples, a more substantial meal will be offered and consumed as *lộc,* including meat, rice wine, beer, and sticky rice. Perhaps for this reason, seldom did I go on a pilgrimage where both Buddhist and non-Buddhist sites were not visited and offerings made. The food offered and consumed on these pilgrimages or trips is seen as integral to the pagoda experience, and is part of the mechanism by which the blessings of the gods and buddhas are transferred to the participants.[4]

Trinkets, mostly plastic necklaces with images of Guanyin or other divinities, are often sold at religious sites, especially those that attract Vietnamese tourists and pilgrims. They are bought and taken home to be given to friends and family, and are also called *lộc.* When the trip is to a religious site rather than to an area that is solely for tourism, the small gift that is brought back is usually religious in nature. However, whether or not it is a religious item, because it was obtained on a trip or pilgrimage to a religiously special place, the item is called *lộc.* In this case, the *lộc* does double duty as a souvenir. Though it is called *lộc* it is thought of both as a religious and a secular artifact. As a souvenir, this object on the one hand expresses the emotional bond of a relationship, as with any gift, and on the other is a public declaration of having made a pilgrimage. These souvenirs are also bought for oneself and kept. In these cases, people often wear the *lộc* during the outing. When they return home, it may be hung up in the house in a conspicuous place or given to someone.

Lộc, as an object that is brought home and kept for continuing good fortune, can be the principal focus of pilgrimages, such as in the practices associated with the Temple for the Lady of the Storehouse. The shrine is non-Buddhist and has special implications for *lộc:* its popularity is based almost entirely on the potency of its *lộc.* It is dedicated to an anonymous queen of one of the Lý kings who purportedly made agricultural reforms and built storehouses to supply the army resisting the Chinese, thereby bringing prosperity to the region (Khánh

Lộc vendor at Thầy Pagoda

Duyên 1994, 19–21). Although there is some doubt whether there is any historical truth to the legend (Phan Huy Đông 1998, 7–9), the spirit's potency serves to attract devotees, especially at the beginning and end of the lunar year.

The Temple for the Lady of the Storehouse is popular with entrepreneurs and petty traders who go there to borrow from the spirit for their businesses. The currency is spirit treasure and votive paper objects that are brought home and put on one's altar for the year. The borrowed spirit capital is called *lộc,* and is thought to bring good luck to one's business ventures. A middle-aged woman who engages in entrepreneurial activities describes the practice:

> I have also gone to borrow money from the Lady of the Storehouse. When you worship the Lady of the Storehouse you borrow spirit money. But it isn't the same spirit money you use at pagodas: it is a special kind just for the Lady of the Storehouse. It is more special. So when you worship you say, "My name is such and such, I want to borrow a little from you." And

at the end of the year you go and return the money to her. The money you borrow is spirit money, it isn't real money, but it will help you get real money. So, for example, if I was starting a new business but was having trouble borrowing from the bank, I would first go to the Lady of the Storehouse and borrow some money from her, then I would be able to go to the bank and have more luck with them lending me real money. This is a true example. At the end of the year I have to go back to do a ritual using spirit money to return it to the Lady of the Storehouse.... You burn most of the spirit money that you get from the Lady of the Storehouse, but you ask her to give you a little bit to take home as "*lộc*" for your home altar (*xin lại một ít cho mình để làm lộc thờ ở nhà, bàn thờ nhà mình*).

Lộc, therefore, is the main focus of the shrine and the main reason for its popularity. The *lộc* in this case consists of paper bricks of gold, paper coins, and paper branches with metallic green leaves representing jade (again, the branches are homonyms for *lộc*). At the end of the year they are repaid to the Lady of the Storehouse, and burned along with the "balance" of interest accrued. To not return the debt is said to bring divine punishment as might be expected from any moneylender. The centrality of money to the practices associated with the shrine is underlined by the fact that it has become especially popular since the late 1980s, when the state started to condone a free-market economy (Marr 1994, 15).

Whereas *lộc* associated with Tết can be seen as a talisman that lacks any direct connection with the spirits or buddhas, it is definitive of the *lộc* that surrounds pilgrimages. The power of the object is, in the case of pilgrimages, attained through the spirits or buddhas receiving the object and then returning it to the supplicant as a "gift from the gods." *Lộc* in association with pilgrimages are inherently part of human-supernatural and human-human relationships, evoking both sentiment (*tình cảm*) and mutual obligation (*ơn*).

Lên Đồng—*Lộc* as the Manifestation of the Spirits' Benevolence

Spirit possession rituals have now received thorough academic attention relative to other aspects of the religious landscape of Vietnam (e.g., Durand 1959; Fjelstad and Nguyen 2006a; Simon and Simon-Barouh 1973, 1996). We now have very good studies that describe the ritual process (Nguyễn Minh San, Ngô Đức Thịnh, and Đoàn Lâm 1999), the main spirits that possess the mediums (Ngô Đức Thịnh 1996a, 1996b, 1999, 2006), the unique music that accompanies the ritual (Bùi Đình Thảo and Nguyễn Quang Hải 1996; Ngô Đức Thịnh 1992;

Norton 2000a, 2000b, 2002, 2004, 2009; Thanh Hà 1996), the therapeutic aspects of performing *lên đồng* (Fjelstad and Maiffret 2006; Nguyen Thi Hien 2002), transnational aspects of *lên đồng* (Simon and Simon-Barouh 1996; Fjelstad 2006), explorations of the mediums themselves, including gender and sexuality (Norton 2006), their construction of identity (Endres 2006, 2008), power struggles and rivalries between master mediums (Larsson and Endres 2006), and the growing prominence of Trần Hưng Đạo in spirit possession rituals (Phạm Qùynh Phương, 2006, 2007, 2009). Nonetheless, the role of *lộc* has been largely overlooked, with Nguyen Thi Hien's article "A Bit of a Spirit Favor Is Equal to a Load of Mundane Gifts" being the only study to discuss *lộc* in a more substantial way (2006, 131–132). Although the ritual is made unique by the music, the costumes, and the ways in which the spirits' different characters are displayed, the ritual's main purpose is to communicate with the spirits and receive their blessings, primarily through *lộc*. It is therefore surprising that *lộc*, which is centrally important as the material manifestation of the spirits' blessings, is given only passing reference in the literature.

Spirit possession rituals involve the possession of the spirit medium by a succession of male and female spirits that are part of a pantheon that inhabit the Three Palaces or Four Palaces of the universe (Sky, Earth, Water, Mountains, and Forests) (Fjelstad and Nguyen 2006b, 7). The female spirits are dressed primarily in clothing of mountain minorities, and male spirits are dressed in martial dress and act in the style of Sino-Vietnamese Confucian mandarins. While possessed, the medium dancer drinks tea and alcohol, chews betel nut or smokes, listens to songs recounting his or her life, and then gives advice and dispenses offerings that the spirit has blessed (i.e., *lộc*).

The *lộc* in spirit possession rituals are of two types. The first is the offerings that are prepared on trays and arranged on the altar in front of the medium, and are presented to the spirits when they possess the medium. After these offerings have been offered to the spirit, they are distributed to the devotees. These are paid for by the medium or by the sponsor of the ritual, depending on the context. This *lộc* is more varied than in most other religious practices. *Lộc* in the form of food— such as fruit, cookies, cucumbers, chili peppers, and drinks such as beer, rice alcohol, tea, and soft drinks—are given out along with nonedible *lộc*, such as combs and mirrors, notebooks and pens, towels and handkerchiefs, and intoxicants such as cigarettes and betel (areca) nuts. These offerings are prepared in advance and are arranged spectacularly on trays on the altar. They are often color-coded, so that the packaging or color of the offering matches the color of the costume worn by a particular spirit. For example, in 1998 I participated in one *lên đồng* where the spirit Cô Bơ, dressed in white and associated with water, was presented with a tray piled high with small satchels of white monosodium glutamate (MSG), which she blessed and distributed to the crowd of devotees.

The other kind of offerings comes directly from the devotees who sit around the dais, to the back and the sides of the medium. These are offered to particular spirits (embodied in the medium) in a practice called *xin lộc,* meaning to ask or beg for *lộc.* Money is the most usual form of offerings—in new, crisp bills of small denominations. They are arranged in a fan pattern on a plate and are passed up to the possessing spirit. The spirit then takes the plate and throws two coins (termed *âm dương,* the Vietnamese for *yin* and *yang*), the combination determining whether or not they are accepted by the spirit. If it is not accepted, the plate is passed back to the person who offered. If it is accepted, some of the money from the plate is taken by the spirit and some money that is in a pile on the altar is put back on to the plate and given to the person who made the offering. The money accepted is transformed into *lộc*—not only through contact with the spirit, but also from the spirit's will to bless his or her devotees.

The distribution of *lộc (phát lộc)* is not uniform in the *lên đồng.* Variations occur according to the spirit and the recipient. The people who play the largest role in the *lên đồng* receive more than the rest. The sponsor, the four helpers that attend the spirits, and the musicians who provide accompaniment receive the most *lộc.* If the musicians are successful in pleasing the spirit by singing improvised flattery, the spirit will give extra money to them, sometimes several times during one performance. The crowd of devotees receives *lộc* (both in the form of money and other objects) in lesser quantity and as a group, usually distributed by a helper rather than by the medium directly.

An important aspect of *lộc* from *lên đồng* is that its potency is relative to the rank of the spirit. The spirits incarnate in order of importance, with the highest in stature arriving first. The highest-level spirits who make an appearance are usually mandarins or kings, and the *lộc* that they give reflects their high position: they only distribute selectively to the most important players in the possession ritual (the musicians, the helpers, the sponsor) and they only give money in higher denominations. As the ritual continues, the spirits become more frivolous and the general atmosphere of the crowd becomes less solemn. The *lộc* distributed reflects this gradual change in atmosphere. By the time of the last incarnation, a child prince (Cậu Bé), everyone is laughing. He plays with the crowd, dancing, joking, and clowning. The money given out at this stage is in small denominations, but there is much more of it. Frequently, the spirit will throw the money and the crowd will frantically grab at it as the bills flutter through the air, trying to catch as much as they can, laughing and tumbling over one another in their attempts. Cookies and beverages are then passed out as *lộc*.

The Vietnamese see the supernatural as being intimately connected by reciprocal relationships and present in the daily workings of the world rather than distant and removed. As such, they are primarily interested in the processes of this world rather than other celestial realms or attaining particular states. Spirit possession rituals are a clear example of this interest, but the idea extends through most interactions with the supernatural, and is even carried over into conceptions of how the Buddhist pantheon interacts with the human world.

THE QUALITIES OF *LỘC*

As we have seen above, the practices of *lộc* are as pervasive and crosscutting as are the subtleties of meaning associated with it. There are, nonetheless, a number of features that weave through the different variations. All instances of *lộc* contain the following elements: (1) Attached to *lộc* is a hope of happiness for the future, through prosperity, good fortune, and imminent benefit (i.e., *lộc* is never regarded as bringing transcendent, spiritual, or soteriological benefit), making it *world affirming* in its orientation. (2) *Lộc* is innately powerful, and its efficacy *is not contingent on the faith* of either the giver or the receiver. (3) *Lộc* is something that is given, either from the buddhas or gods to a devotee or from one person to another, or both, and the potency is therefore *transferable*. (4) Finally, *lộc*, while involving hierarchies because it tends to flow downwards, also represents the *reciprocal* element of relationships. It is worthwhile elaborating on each of these points: I contend that the qualities of *lộc* also represent the religious aspirations of most Vietnamese, regardless of whether the form of practice is Buddhist or non-Buddhist.

WORLD AFFIRMATION

Vietnamese religion, as a general characteristic, embraces the mundane, revels in money and business, and affirms an essential goodness of material wealth and success, as well as valuing longevity, health, and happy families with many descendants. In other words, Vietnamese religious sentiment and the goals of most religious practice are focused unabashedly on this world rather than the next, and rarely touch on soteriological goals. This general supposition applies as much to Buddhism, as it is practiced by the majority in Hanoi, as to any other religious expression. One might presume that the more ascetic tendencies of Buddhism would in some way have filtered out and permeated Vietnamese culture with temperance for the enthusiasm with which material wealth is embraced. However, with the exception of only the most rigorous of monastics and a very small number of laity, this is not the case. I am not arguing in any way that what the Vietnamese practice is therefore not Buddhism. The elite, Confucian, censure of overt displays and waste of wealth in ritual, weddings, and funerals do not appear to have had any effect on the general population of religious practitioners; this is not surprising, given that elite attempts at control of popular religion were largely unsuccessful even in China, where the Confucian tradition had a deeper impact (e.g., Weller 1987). The Communist government similarly has had limited success (Luong 1993; Malarney 2002, 126–127, 164–162).

Rarely has anyone described to me the goal of their Buddhist practice as being aimed at becoming enlightened, achieving nirvana, becoming a bodhisattva, or even achieving the Pure Land. More often, people describe the central aim of Buddhism in moral terms, saying that Buddhism was meant to teach us how to act correctly. Some people described it to me as having compassion. However, the most dominant theme in explanations of the purpose of Buddhist practice was that of bringing good luck and wealth to the practitioners and their families.

The Vietnamese world view is diametrically opposed to asceticism or worldly asceticism, a term that Weber (1948 [1930]) employed to describe Protestantism, where the individual is to act in the world, and undertake worldly activities (such as business) while remaining detached from the rewards of his labor. Weber's statement about China, that "In no other civilized country has material welfare ever been so exalted as the supreme good" (1964 [1951], 237), rings true for Vietnam as well.

The attainment of material benefit is a goal that is openly and unabashedly pursued, and wealth is seen as virtually synonymous with happiness. Everyone I spoke with (rich and poor, rural and urban) spoke of wealth positively, even enthusiastically, and supplication to the supernatural was seen as a legitimate avenue for the pursuit of wealth. It is very often the major reason for going to pagodas, as well as temples, for only with the blessing of the buddhas, gods, and ancestors can this wealth—and by extension, happiness—be reached. Conversely, good fortune and material wealth are signs of supernatural blessing. The close connection between wealth and religion as embodied in lộc were clearly seen in the cases of lên đồng as well as in the case of the shrine for the Lady of the Storehouse. In both instances, the function of the gods and spirits were seen to be solely directed towards assisting in the most material and immediate of ways.

The contrast with doctrinal Buddhism is notable, where everything in the world is insubstantial, and attachment to it is the cause for the suffering of all sentient beings. However, a transformation that makes Buddhism world affirming rather than world negating is not isolated to Vietnam or even to the Mahayana cultures of East Asia. For example, Spiro (1982) notes of Burma that there are different kinds of Buddhism, each with specific goals, eschewing lofty soteriological aims. Similarly, Tambiah contrasts Buddhist monasticism with the process of merit-making to secure the best and fastest rebirth possible (1970, 55). Both Spiro's and Tambiah's observations are important in that they recognize that, whereas the goal of world renunciation may be the ideal, worldly success is an important aspect of Buddhist practice for the majority of people in most Buddhist countries, and likely always has been.

FAITH

Another important aspect of *lộc* is that it is in no way seen as dependent on the faith of either the person who makes the offering or the one that consumes the *lộc*. It is particularly striking that many participants in practices associated with *lộc* are not entirely convinced of its efficacy, but do it "just in case." Nam, for instance, gave an offering of durian fruit to the Ông Địa despite his ambivalent feelings about it. In another example, one woman returned home with the fruits of her offerings (*lộc*) from a local pagoda and gave them to her family. When I asked her whether she thought that *lộc* would have a positive and active effect even if her family did not believe in its efficacy, she replied that *lộc* itself has intrinsic supernatural power, not related to whether people believe or not. Another woman I knew routinely went to pagodas and made offerings and wishes and then collected the *lộc*, though she also insisted to me that she did not really believe that it would work. She said that she did it because she just wanted to be sure, and that it made her feel more at ease for going through the motions. Another middle-aged woman brought up an expression: "If you pray, have the supernatural and avoid dangerous things, you will have happiness."[5] She then went on to explain her interpretation: "Like me. I don't believe that praying to Quan Âm will help anything, but I have a statue and I pray to it for important matters, and offer incense, and this makes me feel calm."

Those who embark on pilgrimages and make offerings often claim that they do not fully believe that their wishes will come true. Instead, they explain their motives by stressing the possibility that it *might* be true. Faith, in these instances, is often explained in terms of percentages:

Me: Do you think that making offerings on the first and fifteenth of
        every lunar month will help you in your life?
Young man: I am not sure. I believe 50 percent.

Me: So then, do you go to pagodas to make offerings?
Young man: Sometimes. When I have time.
Me: If you only believe 50 percent, why do you bother to go?
Young man: Just to be sure. It can't hurt.

To be sure, some degree of faith, it could be argued, must underlie these actions as a precondition to their undertaking, or they would not take place at all. Needham (1972) had good reason to question the validity of belief as an anthropologically useful concept, because social analysis does not have the tools to evaluate the mental states of individuals, and nor do statements of belief necessarily constitute the actual state. My point here is not to argue that the practitioners of *lộc* experience, or do not experience, faith. Rather, it is to show that the descriptions of *lộc* from all my informants demonstrated that they believed that their commitment was not a precondition for supernatural assistance or for *lộc*'s potency. They told me that whether or not the person believed in the power of the buddhas or spirits, the act of making the offering was sufficient to imbue that object with power. Thus, I am not claiming that the participants had no faith, but that they believed that faith was not important to the potency of the *lộc*.

The distinction is an important one because the distribution of *lộc* to skeptical husbands would have no meaning if its potency relied on the faith of the husband rather than in the efficacy of the object, spirit, or buddha. Men whose gender projects are antithetical to religious practice can therefore take part in materially beneficial religious activity while maintaining the skepticism that is important for the maintenance of their identity. Thus, in 1998 I knew the director of a company who paid for offerings twice a month, at the supposed insistence of his female employees, while he simultaneously mocked the practice. Nonetheless, he was ultimately "willing to go along," saying that it would do no harm and just *maybe* would help. One of the vice directors at the company also had his doubts about the efficacy of the practice, but said that it certainly did not hurt to make the offerings, and if it did help, then it would be best to make the offerings. Besides, everyone in the office was happy to have an excuse to sit around all afternoon chatting and eating fruit.

There is also a common belief that benefit will be accrued—not only regardless of faith in the efficacy of the *lộc*, but also regardless of other actions (moral or immoral) that take place outside of the pagoda. For this reason, *lộc* received by offerings to gods or buddhas on the first and fifteenth of the lunar month need not be part of a more comprehensive religious life or moral striving for it to be efficacious.

Transferability

A fundamental implication of the practices associated with *lộc* is that good fortune or happiness is transferable, and the potency of *lộc* is given to another along with the object. However, opinions vary regarding the extent to which transferability is believed to take place. Some say that making the offerings itself will give merit, but in most instances people believe that it is the object, as a talisman, that has the power to affect one's life. *Lộc* that is produced through making offerings is seen as specially designed to pass on to others, but it is usually given to people with whom one shares a close relationship and with whom one shares bonds of sentiment (i.e., close friends and, especially, family). Thus, distributing *lộc* is believed by many to be an act of self-sacrifice and to be symbolic of a close relationship.

There are some instances in which people believe that a person can lose good fortune by indiscriminate distribution of *lộc*. Thus, if *lộc* at a spirit possession ritual has been given directly and specifically to you by the spirit, then to give this *lộc* to someone else means that you will lose your good fortune. Similarly, I was told by one woman that if I give money or *lộc* to a beggar at a pagoda after I have made my offerings, I will lose the good fortune to the advantage of the beggar.

Doctrinal Buddhism places a strong emphasis on giving as one of the few actions open to the laity to improve their chances for a good rebirth. In Theravada countries, the accumulation of merit through making donations is central to Buddhist lay practice as a way to influence one's future rebirths. Giving gifts to the *sangha* is an especially important, if not crucial, part of lay Buddhist practice in the Theravada tradition (Spiro 1982, 92–113). In the Mahayana tradition, a greater range of possibilities for religious practice is open to the laity. Nonetheless, the act of giving is still regarded as a moral act of central importance to lay practice.[6] By exchanging *lộc* with the elderly woman at the entrance of the pagoda, for example, karmic merit is increased.

However, the process is distinctly different in Vietnam than it is in Theravadin countries. Tambiah describes merit-making for Thailand as having eschatological consequences of "immunizing the consequences of death and ensuring a prosperous rebirth," while at the same time having the effect in this life of "producing a happy and virtuous state of mind" (1970, 53–54). It is thought to have these effects in Vietnam, but at the same time it is believed that although merit is accrued through making offerings, possessing *lộc* will immediately influence this life more directly. Therefore, *lộc* is removed from the abstraction of rebirth and has a direct effect on relationships and life circumstances on a day-to-day basis.

It is commonly held that going to a pagoda to make offerings on the first and fifteenth of the lunar month will have a number of good effects. The first is that by performing such a moral act you will offset some of the bad things that you have done when it comes time to be judged in hell. The second effect is that by making offerings there will be an immediate reward. The most common presupposition is that this action will bring one's family happiness and good fortune.[7] Thus, an important aspect of *lộc*—and by extension, of religious practice in general—is that the positive effects of one person's practices can be transferred to another, regardless of the other's beliefs. This transferability is most concretely expressed through the distribution of *lộc*.

RECIPROCITY AND FLOW

An important aspect of *lộc* is that there is a tendency for it to flow downwards. The original definition of *lộc* as a mandarin's salary connotes this aspect, as a reward given to servants by the emperor. In a similar way, the buddhas and spirits receive the offerings from devotees (or ancestors from descendants), consume the essence of the objects, and then transform them into *lộc* for the benefit of those who are below them. *Lộc* represents in a tangible way the potency of the supernatural, as objects that have been derived by contact with the divine, making them "divine gifts," as Endres describes them (2007, 202). The flow downwards continues to some degree in that it is usually mothers or grandmothers who bring it back and give it to families, particularly to children and grandchildren. This downward flow can also be seen in the *lộc* money that is given to children at the beginning of the new year. Some of the potency of *lộc* can be attributed to the fact that it is given from higher to lower, thereby passing on fortune and longevity by association.[8]

The transfer of properties in this way is a common element in Vietnamese beliefs. Thus, a baby boy who is laid on a wedding bed can help bring a newly married couple a baby boy of their own. It is thought that the first person to enter a house on New Year's Day will affect the household, so it is hoped that a rich and successful person will be the first to enter. This power of association to influence is part of the potency of *lộc*, but in the case of most *lộc* it is the ultrapotent power of the spirits that lends power to the item itself. In this way, *lộc* also serves to reify cultural and cosmic hierarchies.

At the same time, the transferability of *lộc* means that it can be given as a gift, and especially a gift that is actively passed on. That is, *lộc* is actively circulated, between people and the supernatural and between people and other people. The circulation starts at the pagoda, where some *lộc* is usually given to the pagoda and the pagoda's *lộc* is returned, and is continued at the home or office. *Lộc* by its very nature is something that is distributed rather than selfishly hoarded, so that one of its principal functions is to create bonds and reify the power of the group in a Durkheimian sense.

However, inherent in this sharing are dynamics of reciprocity that are a part of all relationships. This aspect is perhaps most obvious in the practice of "borrowing" capital from the Lady of the Storehouse, where the transactional aspect is overt, with the supplicant agreeing to pay back the loan, with interest determined by the success of the venture for which the capital was employed. As one businesswoman told me, "The amount that you give back depends on your success for that year—whether you were able to earn a lot of money. If you earned a lot, you give a lot. There are people who give back five times as much as they borrowed, while others may only give back three times." The same principle also holds for ancestors, where descendants give offerings from which the spirits of ancestors are able to subsist and thrive in the afterlife; in return, they assist in the lives of their descendants. The power of the object is derived through the exchange, and this power is continued through its distribution. As we will see in the following chapter, this reciprocity also has very real repercussions for social relations.

CONCLUSION

Lộc, because of the multiple practices and forms associated with it, evades a simple definition. Although "talisman" in some instances might be the closest translation, there are serious drawbacks to this definition. The effect of *lộc* is that it always brings happiness in the form of good fortune, most commonly framed in terms of wealth. However, a definition that centers on this function does not address the relationships and feelings intrinsic to the object. The relationship that *lộc* expresses is in some cases between individuals—for instance, between family members or between friends—but it can be understood more broadly to include the relationships between the supernatural and the recipient. In all cases, *lộc* is a gift, and as Mauss (1969 [1950]) and others have pointed out, gifts bind relations, bringing them closer through understandings of obligatory reciprocation. Relationships with the supernatural in Vietnam are considered to involve the same process of reciprocity, emotion, and obligation as human relationships. In much the same manner as outlined by Arthur Wolf of Taiwan (1978), devotion to the supernatural in Vietnam depends on the spirits' and buddhas' continued ability to fulfill the wishes of their supplicants. In this light, *lộc* can be understood as a material representation of the bond between two agents, supernatural or otherwise. *Lộc* is part of a larger social process of reciprocity and relationship construction, of which the building of emotional linkages is very important—a critical point that will receive more discussion in Chapter 5.

It is women who are at the center of this reciprocal transaction between the supernatural and the human worlds. This female transaction ensures the ongoing support of the spirits and buddhas and protection of the living; women are therefore essential for the reproduction of this supernatural reciprocity. Men have the luxury of standing on the sidelines and mocking the practice, but they are linked to this chain of relations and also benefit from it.

5 Women, Offerings, and Symbolic Capital

When I met Thảo in 1997, she was a thoroughly modern, urban, twenty-five-year-old woman who came into frequent contact with foreigners because of her job in a joint venture company. She wore fashionable clothing, was well educated and multilingual, and viewed many Vietnamese traditional attitudes towards women as outdated and unreasonable in today's society. Despite her career and her education, which marked her as one of the emerging middle class, marriage and children remained the central goals in her life.

At the same time, she defined herself as being religious, even "superstitious," though that label is usually used in a condescending way by men towards women, saying unabashedly, "I admit I believe in all superstitions." She was conscious of the rhetoric against her beliefs, but confident enough not to be daunted by it. In an interview, she stated at first that her whole family was religious, but later qualified this by indicating that, while her father believed in Buddhism, he did not generally practice. In their house they had an altar that held various statues of the Buddhist pantheon, where sutras were recited by the women of the family. It was her grandmother who erected the altar where, until her death the previous year, she had recited the sutras daily. Her mother (and sometimes Thảo) had then taken over the responsibility for maintaining the altar and reciting the sutras.

Thảo visited pagodas when she could to make offerings and wish for her family's health and success, and that she might soon find a husband. On the first and fifteenth of every lunar month she made a point of going to the pagoda and bringing lộc home for her family. She was not alone in doing this. In the first month of every lunar year, on the first and fifteenth of every lunar month, and at special times such as during exam period, young women can be seen in large numbers making offerings at pagodas and temples in and around Hanoi. Phủ Tây Hồ, a prominent temple on Hanoi's scenic West Lake, becomes especially crowded with people, including throngs of young women going to wish good luck and health for themselves and their families, success in school and in new careers, and to make wishes to find a husband.

The crosscutting aspects of lộc outlined in the last chapter—that the practices surrounding it are world-affirming, that faith of the recipient is not necessary for it to be effective, and that *lộc's* power is transferable and involves reciprocity—makes *lộc* particularly potent for women's religious practice, which is centrally concerned with the construction of identity and reproduction of social relationships. There is always sentiment attached to the material object—between the supplicant and the supernatural being (buddhas or spirits) and between the distributor and beneficiary of *lộc*—which calls into play obligations formed through the demands of social reciprocity that are an inherent part of gift exchange.

It is usually women who make offerings and distribute *lộc*, though both old and young make these offerings in similar ways. Unlike older women, however, making offerings is typically the central religious activity for young women, to the virtual exclusion of all other practices. For older women, making offerings is often only part of a more involved repertoire of practice, which we will look at in coming chapters.

The pervasiveness of *lộc* as an element of religious practice points to the complex role that it plays as an object that simultaneously expresses sentiment and holds meaning related to the construction of feminine gender identity. One of the principal determinants for differentiating between variable significances of *lộc* is age, or life-stage. For younger women, the act of making offerings can be framed as the complementary opposite of men's expressions of skepticism, in that it constitutes performances of femininity that accentuate weakness, compliance, and sexual receptivity. For women with families, *lộc* is emblematic of salient aspects of femininity (such as being reliant), but its practices also can be seen as involvement in a symbolic economy where capital is raised through the tangible and demonstrable representations of women's caring and ritual action on behalf of others, primarily members of the family. As with other forms of gift giving, distributing *lộc* generates obligation and feelings of moral debt (*ơn*). As a generator of symbolic capital, the distribution of *lộc* can therefore be understood as gift giving, employing the same rules of reciprocity. By participating in these same rules of reciprocity, the practices associated with *lộc* can elevate relative social position and power beyond what the hard structure of patriarchy would suggest. This is not to say that the importance of *lộc* can be reduced merely to its social function, but rather that the social aspects that form a part of a more comprehensive religious expression are significant.

A nagging question that I had while doing my research was why, despite men's derogatory remarks regarding religious practice, young women begin to go to pagodas regularly to make offerings and collect *lộc*. I concluded that there are connections between women's involvement in making offerings and the experience of being a woman in Hanoi. These connections partially explain why women are perceived as being more religious than men, and correspondingly why they participate in religious activity to a greater extent, despite the way their practices may be marginalized by men. The intent of this chapter is to examine how religious practice—especially the practice of making offerings and distributing *lộc*—relates to the femininities of premarried and married women.

STRUCTURES OF GENDER

The wishes that are made by young women at temples and pagodas are an expression of their central concerns: finding a husband, maintaining (or achieving) familial health and wealth, and—for the middle class—passing exams. The importance that these religious activities have for enabling young women to deal with the emotional pressures and strains that are placed on them, to express their aspirations, and to actively do something to achieve them by enlisting the aid of the supernatural cannot be underestimated. This function of religious activities becomes particularly important because the expression of inner feelings is not usually encouraged in Vietnam, and there is considerable reluctance to divulge too much information about oneself, even to close friends.

At the same time, the entire process of making offerings and reclaiming them as *lộc* that is then distributed has an element of social performance, integral to the gender projects of participants. Ultimately, these performances, taken as a whole, serve to reinforce hegemonic gender structures, whereby men are able to maintain power within the society as a whole. There are three interwoven structures that make up the overall structure of gender relations (Connell 1995, 73–75): first, the division of labor, which organizes, values, and compensates women's and men's work differently; second, the structure of power, which involves authority, control and coercion, hierarchies, symbolic and actual violence, domestic authority, and so on; and third, cathexis, which refers to the patterning of sexual desire and object choice. These interwoven structures appear unrelated in daily life to most people, and can even seem contradictory at times, but they nonetheless are mutually supportive. The gender structures in Vietnam provide men the balance of advantage and greater resources, allows them to assert hegemony, and to "set the terms in which events are understood and issues discussed" (Connell 1987, 107). The overall flexibility and resilience of these structures makes the patterns of gender relations surprisingly difficult to alter. Thus, in the Vietnamese context there have been significant cultural changes in the past one hundred years, but this has not meant that gender relations have substantially changed. Despite a Communist revolution and the toppling of a Confucian system that rigidly and overtly gave authority and power to men, and contrary to Jayawardena's optimistic pronouncement on the eve of the Renovation that women in Vietnam have "achieved equality with men in education and in the economic and social spheres" (1986, 212), the situation of women has not, in practical terms, changed to the same degree as have other aspects of society (Soucy 2001).

There is an undeniable and persistent expectation that men are the authority in the family. Thus, for example, one old woman I knew wanted to go to exercise with the Women's Club, but her husband told her she could not, so she stayed home. This woman also liked going to the local pagoda but her husband again told her to stay home. In response, she did not confront him, but instead sneaked out occasionally. In another example, a fifty-year-old man went overseas to work, and wanted to use the money he earned to buy land. Because he was overseas, he thought that it was prudent not to buy in his own name. His wife wanted to put her name on the deed, but he did not agree, so he had his parents use their name instead of his wife's name on the deed. We also see examples of male ascendancy within the pagoda. One can be found in the Buddhist stricture, still followed today, that nuns must always be subservient to monks whenever they meet, regardless of relative seniority. As a final example of how Vietnamese norms accord power to men, in Phúc Lộc Pagoda, seats in the reception area (two benches facing each other with a table between them, on which a heavily used teapot and cups are found) are always relinquished by women to men, regardless of relative age.

This is not to say that women are powerless, as there are alternative discourses of women's predominance in the family. Women are commonly said to be "generals of the interior," whereas men's actions lie primarily in the public sphere. Furthermore, women in Vietnam often have more power within certain contexts than would initially be thought if the rhetoric of men's power were fully believed. Women can have great influence in family decision making, often control the household finances, and certainly have more practical control over children. Nonetheless, women's power in the family is not structural, but depends on ability to maneuver and manipulate structures that are primarily patriarchal. While women make most day-to-day decisions, the major decisions, such as substantial expenditures, are made by the husband, or jointly. Furthermore, being a "general of the interior" reinforces (or at least does not contradict) a public/private dichotomy where the outside is accorded more prestige then the inside. Thus, when men grant that women are the generals of the interior—and it is usually men, not women, who invoke this phrase, in my experience—the implication is that they are happy to let women do all the work at home, so they accord women some power within that domain. However, the final say in any decisions is usually reserved for the husband.

Changes do, of course, take place over time, and there are instances of resistance, but overall these structures have so far persisted, though the internal dynamics have changed somewhat in the past century. Religious practice is not separate from broader social structures, and is therefore deeply influenced by gender discourses, while simultaneously it reinforces and reproduces the dominant gender discourse.

THE RELIGIOUS PRACTICE OF YOUNG WOMEN

I first met Yến, a friend of my wife, at a party in 1997. At the time she impressed me as unique by her lack of conformity to the pervasive ideas of appropriate feminine behavior. She helped to prepare the food for the party along with the other women in the group, while the men sat around the TV and talked, but when the eating began she joined the men in teasing me and drinking beer while the other women drank soft drinks and behaved with more restraint. She joked about relationships and teased me about becoming her "English teacher," with a measure of innuendo.

During most of the time that I knew her, she did not have a boyfriend, whereas most of the other women in her group of friends were already married or were in long-standing relationships. In university, Yến dated an older man who was quite wealthy, but not for long. She told me that she had to end the relationship with him because he asked her to try to be more gentle and feminine. She made an effort, but found it too difficult to hide her personality and to act weak and dependent. She expressed her frustration to me once by saying that Vietnamese men only wanted women who are weak and compliant, but that she cannot act that way because she believes that she is equal to men.

She was well liked by all, fun to be with—the life of the party—but always single. By the time of her twenty-eighth birthday party, a year after we had first met, she had stopped drinking beer with the men and refrained from teasing me. I imagined it was difficult for her to do this because she had always derived a lot of amusement out of trying to make me say something incorrect (or inappropriate) in Vietnamese. She explained to me in response to my questions regarding the change of behavior that she was now "acting like a lady." One of her friends later explained that the sudden change in Yến was because she was getting worried about finding a husband. The social pressure to marry before the age of thirty in Vietnam is immense, and is a constant concern for most young women. She eventually married and had two children, but her friends say that she is not the same as she used to be—she has settled down completely.

Another young woman described for me a friend who was in a similar situation, in that she needed to alter her behavior in order to appear more attractive to men:

> My friend Minh Anh was twenty-seven at the time [2005]. She liked to drink beer and alcohol, which women aren't supposed to do. At that age she should have been on her way to being married, so she was concerned and tried to find ways to improve the situation. She felt a lot of pressure from her family, especially her mother, to behave more feminine so that she could find someone to marry. She was worried, too. She went to pagodas to make offerings and wishes to find a husband. She also tried to change her behavior. One time I was at a party with her. She was there with her new boyfriend, who I hadn't met before. I remember how she changed her behavior completely for her boyfriend and tried to be like a completely different person. She tried hard to be more gentle and ladylike. When she was asked if she wanted some beer she acted very softly and exaggeratedly feminine, saying [with head tilted slightly and smiling sweetly], "I don't know how to drink." This was completely not true!

In addition to their attempts to enact a kind of femininity that was intended to increase their sexual desirability, both Yến and Minh Anh also sought a religious solution to their dilemmas by making offerings at pagodas and temples on the first and fifteenth of the lunar month. It is in the twenties that engagement in religion typically starts for women, and continues to develop as a reaction to the stress felt regarding marriage. Young women, both single and married, tend to focus their practice on making offerings and wishes, despite the fact that it is exactly this sort of practice that is lampooned in the media in association with antisuperstition discourses. Religious practice can be understood as part of the process of building and performing a feminine gender identity. It is therefore worthwhile discussing femininity in more depth in order to better understand the religious practices of women.

The kind of femininity that stands in opposition to what I described in an earlier chapter as hegemonic masculinity can be called "emphasized femininity." There are two main tropes that form the core of femininity in Vietnam, occurring in relation to life stages. The first is fragility and sexual receptivity for young, unmarried, women, and the second is motherhood for married women. Although these tropes are distinct to some degree, they also interact with each other, so that young women are rewarded for behavior that emphasizes subordination, particularly to men, at the same time that they are expected to orient their lives towards eventual marriage and to exhibit the self-sacrificial attitude that is seen as the ideal of motherhood. Similarly, appropriate behavior for married women centers on the creation and maintenance of the "happy family" (*gia đình hạnh phúc*), but also on submissive behavior towards husbands and competence at serving their needs (e.g., cooking, cleaning, and assuming childcare duties to provide men with more free time).[1]

Emphasized femininity is a version of femininity that acts to order views and behaviors at the societal level. Similar to hegemonic masculinity, it is an ideal rather than a lived reality. This means that it is not replicated in toto, but rather that it serves as a model that shapes behavior through both complicity or resistance, and often both simultaneously. As such, it is "stylized and impoverished" and does not represent or correspond with femininities as they are actually lived (Connell 1987, 183).

Emphasized femininity is not the only pattern of femininity (just as hegemonic masculinity is not the only pattern of masculinity), but it does not exist in opposition to other femininities in the way that hegemonic masculinity exists in relation to other masculinities (e.g., by marginalizing effeminate men). Instead, other forms of femininity are defined in opposition, and in resistance, to male hegemony (Connell 1995, 183). Emphasized femininity is both opposite and complementary to hegemonic masculinity, and consists of displays of weakness rather than male strength, reliance as opposed to male support and self-reliance, shyness rather than male confidence, ignorance and deference to male authority rather than male displays of intelligence and knowledge, self-sacrifice rather than aggressive decisiveness and self-promotion, titillation and flattery towards men, and an orientation towards motherhood.[2] This behavior can be seen in the clothes that women wear (the elegant but impractical *áo dài* that is a ubiquitous symbol of Vietnam's beauty, and of Vietnamese femininity, is not countered by male traditional dress), in the way they ride their bicycles or motorcycles (slowly, with good posture and with elbows and knees tucked in), in the way they speak (softly and politely), and in the way they act (submissively, deferring to men's authority and being complicit in the reproduction of a hierarchy that places them below men).

In relationships, compliance to the ideals of emphasized femininity become even more pronounced, so that women I knew to be strong-willed and self-assured on their own would be sweet and submissive with their boyfriends and appear to relinquish control to them. At times, this compliance to the ideal of emphasized femininity may be less complete, as with Yến and the other woman described above, but the expectation is so intense that I have never seen displays of total resistance that are seen in the West. An example of the kind of submissive behavior that is expected of women, and is considered attractive, can be seen in the common practice of letting boyfriends decide what activity to do, or where to go, on a date. This was explained to me by one young woman as being because "it is not romantic for a woman to be too pushy," and by another because "if a woman loves a man, she will follow his decisions."

This quality of women as compliant and soft-spoken is frequently referred to as *hiền* (gentle, meek, and virtuous). The value of this sort of behavior in women is exemplified by the fact that Hiền is also a popular girl's name. Men often spoke of Vietnamese women in this term with obvious national pride, with the subtext being that Western women were perceived as being garish, loud, pushy, and pro- miscuous. I had a long conversation with a group of women who sold clothing in booths at the market near Phúc Lộc Pagoda. The oldest of the group, Mrs. Hà, insisted that it was good that I had married a Vietnamese woman because they are more obedient, because they loved their families and put their families above all else, whereas "Western women love their children less."

> Mrs. Hà: When a Western man marries a Vietnamese woman, most of the time it works, but when a Vietnamese man marries a Western woman, they break up very easily. Do you know the reason? The reason is because Vietnamese women can bear more hardship than foreign women. Vietnamese women are *hiền*. Really gentle. If her husband says something, she must follow—she must agree with him. Even if she knows he is wrong, she still agrees with him.
>
> Me: You too? When your husband is wrong, do you still follow him?
>
> Mrs. Hà: Of course! And it is the same with everyone in this "gang." If they don't, then they are ill-mannered [*hư*]. Doesn't your wife follow you?

Both hegemonic masculinity and emphasized femininity are prominent in media representations. Images of emphasized femininity, in particular, are used in mass media and marketing, instructing women how to be feminine in order to attract the "perfect man." In this way, media images create standardized modes of female presentation for male consumption, usually called "fashion" (Connell

1987, 113), which objectifies women as objects of male desire. These standardized expectations also generate feminine performances specifically intended for male consumption. In Vietnam, there are a large number of magazines dedicated to imposing a unified notion of feminine beauty and behavior. Vietnamese women's magazines accounted for half of the magazines sold at the stands in Hanoi in 1997. Significantly, Vietnamese magazines primarily portray women in "nonproductive roles: wife, homemaker, girlfriend, mother, tourist, entertainment-seeker, and so on" (Drummond 1999, 109). The role that fashion has played in influencing performances of emphasized femininity has only increased in recent years. Pre-Renovation ideology expressed equality between men and women, seeing the domination of women as a feudal remnant. However, since the late 1980s femininity has increasingly been emphasized, with fashion—especially urban middle-class fashion—following Western styles. Consequently, there has been a substantial change from the 1980s, when clothing styles were dominated by "an aesthetic of socialist androgyny that prized simplicity, labor, and frugality" (Leshkowich 2003, 93). Femininity is now portrayed in magazines as at once revealing and girlish, accentuating the simplistic and submissive image of women (Drummond 1999, 112). Not surprisingly, the switch from socialist androgyny has been concurrent with a decrease in the number of women who hold positions within the government (Fahey 1998, 237).

These images of women are both descriptive and prescriptive in that they simultaneously define standards of appropriate feminine behavior, and also create expectations and demands on men and women to enact those standards. Deviation from the norm calls into question one's gender identity, and invites derogatory comments. Women who are too bossy or loud, or who speak their minds are said to be "like men" (Gammeltoft 1999, 178). One female informant told me, "Women can't speak strongly—they have to speak skillfully. My friend always speaks directly because she works a lot with foreigners. She speaks really directly. But Vietnamese women should be gentle and tactful; they shouldn't speak too directly." An oft-heard expression in Hanoi for women who are overly domineering is that they are "lionesses of Hà Đông."[3]

If fashion leads women to enact specific displays as a "carrot," then the inherent threat—the "stick"—comes from the harsh marriage imperative that becomes a consuming concern for women in their twenties. Marriage marks the transition from adolescence to adulthood for both sexes. However, for women there is a great deal more pressure to marry before the age of thirty than for men, because expectations for success as a woman are tied to the production of the "happy family."[4] Finding a husband and getting married in a timely fashion is a major source of anxiety among young women and their families. Spinsterhood is seen as a mark of absence or lack, commonly expressed as "suffering from a lack of a husband" (*bị ế chồng*). For example, one woman I knew had a difficult personality: she was fastidious with a tendency to complain and speak harshly, and was not fond of children. As a consequence of these characteristics, no one would marry her. Her neighbors would frequently comment that of course a woman with such a personality would be *ế chồng* (lacking a husband). "Lack" (*ế*), here, carries connotations of a store without customers, with shelves of unwanted goods. It is used for women who have passed the age of marriageability without finding a husband, and often is used to tease women in their mid-twenties who are not on track to getting married.

The pressure on women to marry before the age of thirty creates an expectation that a woman must conform as closely as possible to an ideal of femininity in order to viably attract a husband. This is reinforced by parents, who warn their daughters to behave in a suitable fashion lest they have to suffer the consequence of remaining unmarried, with no children to support them in their old age or to make offerings to them after their death.[5] For example, there was one woman who was not physically attractive, who worked for a foreign NGO. She earned a lot of money and was very smart, but for these reasons it was difficult for her to find someone. No one who was poorer or less educated, or who earned a smaller salary would want her, because it went against expectations of husbands being dominant. Her mother bought her dresses and pretty clothing and told her, "You need to wear more pretty clothes, like *áo dài,* dresses, and skirts, and stop wearing jeans. You should wear more makeup, speak softly, and act more gently so that you won't be '*ế chồng*.' You need to speak more gently, like a woman. You speak too strong!" Her mother also would say that she needed to go out more often, and not stay at home.

Public opinion also serves as a potent force that produces pressure on both the women and their families. In the words of one young woman who has been married for five years, "Women who are getting older and still haven't found a husband, their families are very apprehensive about public opinion [*dư luận*]." This public opinion is of great concern to families, and can lead to moral judgments of the entire family by neighbors. The same is also true of barrenness, which similarly assigns moral blame for these kinds of problems—not only to the individual, but also to the family. Public opinion, therefore, heightens anxieties around marriage, as well as around childbirth.

The example of Nhung in Chapter 1 is illustrative of how this concern for marriage spurs many young women into religious action. In order to solve the problem of being unable to find a husband because of a ghost being attached to her and preventing suitors from approaching, she went to see a spirit medium to perform a ritual called *cắt tiền duyên* (a ritual for severing the relationship of the last life). During the course of the spirit possession ritual, a paper effigy of her ghost was burned along with a petition to the spirits. Nhung was twenty-eight years old and worried because she was not yet married—an anxiety, as always, exacerbated by parental pressure.

Although young women have other causes for anxiety, such as passing exams and getting a good job, marriage, and children are priorities, with associated anxieties felt more acutely than from other pressures. For women, visiting pagodas when they have troubles is seen as an appropriate response to these anxieties. Young women frequently expressed to me that they like to go to pagodas when they feel stressed because the surroundings calm them and they feel less worried if they think they will receive help from the buddhas. Vietnamese, young and old, male and female, often related to me that the presumed intention of a young woman praying at the altar of a pagoda or temple was wishing for a boyfriend or a husband.

The act of religious participation also can be considered a form of gender performance that is aimed at heightening femininity. Expectations regarding women, is that they are weak and need divine assistance; in seeking that assistance, they are showing that they are feminine. Inherent in performances of femininity are sometimes self-conscious and sometimes subconscious reproductions of sexual desirability. This becomes more evident when young women ask their boyfriends to take them to pagodas to make offerings, which they often do. Young women's engagement with Buddhism and other forms of religious practice (mostly in the form of offerings on the first and fifteenth day of the lunar month) cannot be understood apart from the broader construction of gender in Vietnamese society. The increased engagement in Buddhism by young women who are trying to find a husband partly assuages a psychological need to relieve the stress of social pressure by enlisting the potent support of the supernatural; at the same time, though, religious practice is an aspect of broader performances of emphasized femininity.

The fact that women feel compelled to undertake these practices, despite male and state criticism, indicates that religious practice is not simply a result of belief, but has relevance to women's identities. Women's engagement in religion should therefore not be thought of as resistance to state discourses on religion because those discourses merely reproduce the masculine framing of religious practice. However, as hegemonic masculinity is structured in relation to femininity, the male view of religion is not intended to change women's behavior but rather to reinforce hegemonic structures. This means that the antireligious rhetoric that has emanated from the state has been largely irrelevant for women because it is not directed at women, but at men. Masculinity has been defined partly through men's nonparticipation in religion, and even their performances of skepticism. By contrast, religious practice endures for women because it is essential to the overall construction of femininity. Male ridicule thereby serves more as reinforcement to gender structures than it does as a censure. Far from challenging their beliefs, male expressions of skepticism merely reinforce the close association between religious practice and emphasized femininity.

MARRIED WOMEN, *LỘC,* AND *ƠN*

I have known Hạnh (introduced in Chapter 3) for more than twelve years. She studied at the National Economics University in Hanoi, and is a chief accountant for an international pharmaceutical company. She is intelligent and has been very successful in her career. She married when she was in her late twenties. In 2010, when she was in her mid-thirties with two small children, she took a pilgrimage and described it to me afterwards. It was the end of the lunar year and her company decided to go to the Perfume Pagoda as a group. There were around twenty-five people who rented a bus and prepared all of the offerings for the trip. When the day arrived, it was raining heavily and a few of the people had second thoughts about going. But Hạnh still wanted to go because she believed that if the decision was made and the offerings were prepared, they were obliged to follow through. So, she bought a raincoat and persuaded everyone else to go, too.

When they arrived, the rain stopped and the day ended up being perfect. They went to the first pilgrimage stop, Chình and Bến Đục Temples, where people announce to the buddhas that they have arrived. Luckily, the temple, which is usually shut, was open because a ritual was taking place. She was able to enter and made a request of the temple guardian to supplicate to the spirits on her behalf, asking for her family to be healthy, for her kids to be obedient, for good fortune, and for her husband to be happy and successful. The group then got in the boats and went down the river to Thiên Trù Pagoda, where she offered sweet offerings of five kinds of fruit, sticky rice, cookies, and a petition asking again for health and good luck for her family.

She climbed the mountain rather than taking the recently installed aerial tram, believing that if she went on foot the Buddha would take greater pity on her and support her. When she arrived at Hương Tích Cave, the main shrine in the complex, she made more offerings with fruit and another petition. She bowed at the main altar and asked once again for health and luck for her family, respectful and bright children who study well, and that both her career and her husband's career would be successful. Then she went to the other altars. She rubbed the Gold and Silver Mountains (stalagmites), asking to become rich. She cupped the water at a special place called the Mother's Milk Gourd, gathering the dripping water and washing her face in order to have strength and good health. A few of her friends who had no children asked some monks who happened to be there to perform a ritual on their behalf so that they could have children. When they left, everyone was very happy because they believed that the day had been very lucky. As she was leaving, she bought some live clams and snails, releasing some for good luck and keeping others to take back for her family, along with the *lộc* from her offerings.

Such religious supplications by women on behalf of their husbands and children are commonplace and are linked to self-sacrifice, which is a key characteristic expected of mothers and of women more generally. It is performed by unmarried women through acts of deference to male decisions, and willingness to labor on their behalf. However, it becomes more important in the performances of femininity for married women. A central aspect in the division of labor in Vietnam makes women primarily responsible for maintaining harmony in the family and ensuring that the physical and emotional needs of the family are met. Women's work becomes bound to the family in a way that men's does not, and it is on women's shoulders that the wellness of the family rests. The work of women outside the home is typically seen as expedient, perhaps necessary, but never central to women's identity in the way that careers tend to be central for men.[6]

The term "family happiness" (*hạnh phúc gia đình*), frequently used to describe the ideal product of women's labor, is characterized by a home where there is no friction between husband and wife, where everyone is content and well fed, and where the children receive proper education, are well clothed, and are respectful to their elders. Women are taught from an early age that they should value this ideal and strive for it above all else. Their expectations and the desire for such a family help them endure adversity in marriage, and are largely responsible for this ingrained moral expectation for self-sacrifice. In a concrete way, these expectations translate to women trying to avoid causing disharmony, and making sure family resources are properly used to keep the household running and the family fed (Pham Van Bich 1999, 67).

Gammeltoft (1999) points out that the value of the happy family is emphasized both among women and by "a more general celebration of the 'happy family' in Vietnamese political and popular culture" (pp. 74–75; see also Barry 1996). The concept is prominent in the media and everyday discourse, and *Hạnh Phúc Gia Đình* (family happiness) is even the title of a prominent women's magazine. However, while emphasis on the family is not new (being also crucial in Confucian thought), the way in which it is approached by the state today is particularly systematic: it is embedded in the 1992 Constitution, which describes the family as the "core" or "basic cell" of society. The Vietnam Women's Union is responsible for indoctrinating this view, and goes so far as to arrange competitions that test women's knowledge on how to create a happy family (Gammeltoft 1999, 75).

SELF-SACRIFICE AND MORAL DEBT

Self-sacrifice as an ideal characteristic is seen as being a necessary prerequisite for the creation of the "happy family." Furthermore, self-sacrifice is defined as a characteristic that women naturally possess. Jamieson writes, "A 'good' woman was self-sacrificing, frugal, industrious, chaste, and totally devoted to her husband" (1993, 27). One monk I spoke with attributed these characteristics to mother goddesses, as well, saying that this is why those goddesses are so approachable. He went on to compare men and women in these terms: "Mothers always give in to their children's wishes. Women are always closer to children. Mother's love is like… For example, men can go to work and when they are done their friends ask them to go for a drink, and they go. But women say 'No! I have to go home to prepare dinner for the children.' At that moment they always think of their children, right? Men think: 'OK, my wife, or someone else, is there to take care of them, so good enough.' Right?"

Though the expectations of female self-sacrifice create many disadvantages, its performance can provide a point of leverage for women in the family. Being the creators and sustainers of the family, women embody the core of Vietnamese society. Mothers invoke their self-sacrifice to make power claims within the family. By performing their role well, even if it is a role that is intrinsically subordinate, they make claim to, and are recognized as, being good mothers and wives. This in turn creates an obligation to reciprocate, as seen in this description given to me by a woman of her mother-in-law:

> Old ladies are very scared that their children will forget the debt owed them. Therefore they always remind them and stress this debt. So then when mothers are old, ill, in pain, and cranky, their children still have to take care of them. Mothers don't have money of their own, so the children have to provide them with an allowance and take care of them. My

husband's mother is the same; every mother is the same. His mother always points out to all of the children that in the past she was poor and suffered a lot. His father went to work far away and could not take care of the children so she had to take care of all six of them on her own. When I just married my husband, she right away started to point this out to me, and she continues to do it all the time. A couple of months ago when I gave birth to my second son she came and took care of the baby for me, and she repeated again how she suffered: "In the past, when I gave birth to your husband and his brothers and sisters, his father went to work far away and just came home once a week, so I had to take care of the kids all by myself. With the money he made he just took care of himself and didn't help me to take care of the kids with his salary. I had to work and raise the children by myself. The big piece of land we have—I also worked to buy that piece of land by myself. Now I have divided it for my children. It is from my own labor. When the kids were sick, I bore the burden alone." She always reminds them about the work she did on their behalf. So, I just reply "Yes." She said that it is very important for women after giving birth in Vietnam to avoid certain things; in the first few months you don't have to do anything. For example, if you eat fishy things or touch water too early, later you will suffer. You will get weak and sick because the weather in Vietnam is very harsh. So his mother said that after she gave birth there was nobody there to help her, so she had to do everything: to feed the children, to work, to bring up the children, and take them to school. So now, because she did not avoid those things, she says she has chronic stomach aches and when she touches cold water it is easier to get sick and to have headaches. She claims that the reason for her getting sick so easily and for her arthritis is because when she gave birth she couldn't avoid the things that she was supposed to, so now she suffers.

A great deal of women's energy is spent cultivating moral debts (*ơn*) with their husbands and children through performances of self-sacrifice, such as that described above. *Ơn* is a word that is pervasive in the language of relationships in Vietnam, and signifies a latent obligation or debt. It is mutually recognized, though perhaps unspoken, that the debt will continue to exist until fulfilled.[7] In the Vietnamese symbolic economy, *ơn* represents the currency of exchange.

The value of *ơn* lies in the imbalance that it represents in a relationship; it is through this imbalance that emotional ties are felt and relationships are actualized. For friends and social relations (other than between family members), the imbalance must not be too great. To owe too much is oppressive and fosters resentment, but to owe a little builds sentiment or feelings (*tình cảm*) between individuals, and this is the cement of relationships. O'Harrow describes how there are ongoing efforts between women to gain the upper hand in friendships by giving favors and gifts. However, he also describes how this power is acutely felt and can foster resentment if not executed in a skilful manner, so that the balance of debt is only ever slightly in the favor of one person (O'Harrow 1995, 174).

Gift giving in Vietnam, similar to the way Kipnis describes gift giving in China, is important to the production of relationships (*quan hệ*) in that it involves not only the exchange of material goods, but also an exchange of sentiment, which elicits memories of relationships and obligation (Kipnis 1997, 58). Sentiment is regarded as being the basis of any relationship, and denotes "mutual respect and obligation that attenuates any social asymmetries which exist between parties in the relationship" (Malarney 1993, 187).

Jamieson makes the important point that *ơn* is as crucial for relationships inside the family as it is to relationships outside the family (1993, 16–17). The mother's position in the family is particularly dependant on the power of *ơn*. The father's position, Jamieson argues, is structurally assured by patriarchy and the imperatives for filial behavior. Women, however, are somewhat peripheral to this power structure and therefore depend more on the less structured feelings of *ơn*.[8] Jamieson writes, "A great deal of women's energy is spent cultivating *ơn* from their husbands and children especially. It is these debts which provide security for them, and children are made to feel this debt keenly" (1993, 16–17).

Women create *ơn* by taking overt actions on behalf of their husbands and children, and demonstrating (and often describing) the suffering that they have undergone as a result, essentially performing self-sacrifice. Women's behaviors often accentuate or create this *ơn* through self-effacement that makes clear the sacrifices they have made and the care they have given. Often mothers speak with extreme melodrama and exaggeration of the suffering they have undergone for their children, thereby pointing out the great debt that is owed. This is used, for example, to chastise and instill feelings of shame in a child for misbehavior. The misbehavior is turned into a direct affront to the mother and ties in to all aspects of their intertwined lives. The debt of children (and the debt of husbands, to a lesser extent) is seen as a moral one, behind which lies the threat that an affronted mother (or wife) will make her grievances public, causing embarrassment and loss of face for the family (O'Harrow 1995, 173). One example of a public claim of lack of piety from children came to me from one old woman with whom I spoke in 1997 at Quán Sứ Pagoda:

Woman: My life is so very hard, but following Buddhism enables me to stand it. Buddhism teaches me to accept it and try to endure so that I can succeed and escape.

Me: How many years have you been coming here?

Woman: For about three years.

Me: Why are you selling matches here?

Woman: To live. I have to do something to survive.

Me: But you are old. Why don't you retire?

Woman: My children lack respect and are disobedient. They live in Hà Tây Province.

Me: And they don't provide for you?

Woman: I don't ask them because they are so disrespectful that there is no point in asking for their help, I would rather turn to society for help.

Me: Do you still have a husband?

Woman: He is dead for five years already.

Me: So sad, so much suffering!

Woman: But when I turn to Buddhism it isn't suffering. With Buddhism I am happy.

More common than airing public grievances are private claims of *ơn* by mothers made on their children. Mrs. Tu (introduced in Chapter 1), whose children were already adults, bought a mass-produced red velvet hanging in 2009 with an image of the Bronze (Đồng) Pagoda on the top on Mount Yên Tử (an important pilgrimage site in northern Vietnam) and hung it prominently in the main room of her house. Below the image is the word for filial piety (*hiếu*) and the following verse in Vietnamese:

> In all the world
> No one is as good as Mother.
> For shouldering the weight of the world
> No one will suffer like Father.
> All of the water in the seas
> Cannot match the love of Mother.
> The clouds in the immense sky
> Cannot overshadow Father's merit.
> Striving throughout the day
> Mother raises her children to grow up smart and healthy.

> With his worn out body
> Father continues to protect his children.
> Whoever has a mother
> Please don't make her cry.
> Please don't make the sadness
> Come to Mother's eyes.[9]

The hanging clearly resonates enough for this woman to hang it in her living room, and it does so for enough women for the manufacture of such hangings to be profitable. However, equally important is that though the hanging is seemingly about filial piety, the accent is on both the mother and on the debt owed not by virtue of the mother's position in the family, but by virtue of the suffering undertaken on behalf of the child.

Another example of how mothers use this self-sacrifice to underline the moral debt owed them by their children was played out in front of me when Mrs. Tu scolded her (then) twenty-year-old daughter. Northern Vietnamese rural women frequently mix l's and n's in their speech, and such was the case with her. She said to her daughter:

Mother: You are stupid like a pig (*ngu như nọn*)!
Daughter: (insolently) You said it wrong, Mother. You have to say "stupid like a pig (*lợn*)" to be correct. Next time if you want to say that, say it softly. If you say it softly I can correct you. Saying it loud and wrong will make everyone laugh at you.
Mother: Yes, I am stupid. I couldn't go to study because I sacrificed my whole life for my husband and children so I don't have time for friends and no time to go to study. (Soucy 2000, 194)

It is partly through performances of self-sacrifice such as this, meant to accentuate *ơn,* that women empower themselves within an overall social context that subordinates women. As such, these performances are not resistance strictly speaking, because they are working within the system to strengthen their position. Though the gender structures in Vietnam enforce an inequality, and relegate women to inferior positions, there is room for negotiation. There is, in fact, so much room that women can often end up in a position where they have a great deal of power within the family. However, it is not from an obstinate confrontation with the structure, but by working within the framework of the system that this power usually can be achieved.

ƠN AND LỘC

The view of women's labor as being properly directed towards the production of the happy family and the self-sacrifice that is reiterated by mothers has important ramifications for the religious practice of women. Many young mothers go to pagodas to make offerings and wishes for their family and to collect *lộc* on their families' behalf. The intent of women's religious practices, especially those concerning *lộc,* are often described by both men and women—practicing and non-practicing Buddhists—as being family focused. I have been told countless times by married women that they go to pagodas in order to achieve good luck and health for their children. Women who have families commonly see their religious practice as an extension of their role as family caregivers. Responses to the question of why women go to pagodas more than men also reflected this view: a sixteen-year-old female student told me that women go to pagodas more than men because "women are more concerned about the family than men," and another young woman told me that "they care about the family." A sixty-two-year-old housewife said it is because, "in Vietnam, women are the ones who have the main responsibility for devoting themselves to the family. They always want everything good to come to the family." A fifty-five-year-old female teacher claimed it was because "women like to do charitable work more than men do." A forty-four-year-old female accountant told me, "Women care more and are more concerned than men. They want to bring about good things for the family." Finally, a twenty-five-year-old male student stated that it is because "in the family women are the ones who worry about the family more than men do."

When I asked Thảo, who describes herself as superstitious, what she wishes for when she makes offerings at a pagoda she replied, "I wish for a lot of things. Not for money or those kinds of things, but, starting from the top of the list: for [the continuing happiness and good fortune of] my dead grandmother, for my parents, then my sister, brother, and his child, and finally, for me."

The transferability of merit, along with the notion that one does not have to believe in *lộc* for the practice to be efficacious, means that women can go to the pagoda for the entire family. Thầy Tâm explained when I asked whether everyone needs to go to the pagoda individually: "No. It is like this: Only the mother needs to go. For example, if someone is young and has to go to work and doesn't have time, his or her mother can go and say prayers on their behalf. When we go to pray to the Buddha or to the spirits, we name the child and the husband. Today, no matter what you do or where you live, if you pray to the Buddha, he will help anybody to be healthy, have work, intelligence, luck, and peace."

Due to the transferability of merit, women are able to engage in religious practice for their entire families. The explanation that a businessman gave me regarding the increased wealth of pagodas by the late 2000s demonstrates that the transferability of merit from women to men is an assumption that underlies much religious practice: "Women whose husbands have power, rank, and money that they achieved from bribery—that kind of woman—they go to the pagoda to make merit by doing charity. They are essentially buying merit. For example, the police stand on the side of the road to take money from people so that they can become rich and build big houses. Then their wives have to bring the money to divide the *lộc* so that their luck will continue. They buy luck for their families because their husbands are doing work that isn't good [i.e., that is immoral]."

Lộc is particularly important in these performances because it represents the spiritual labor that has been done by women on behalf of their families. Husbands and children are then enjoined to consume these gustatory symbols of emotion and, in the most immediate way, thereby to incorporate debt into their bodies. As mentioned in the previous chapter, the efficacy of the *lộc* is not believed to depend on whether the consumers themselves have faith in its potency or in the supernatural beings that infused the items with power. *Lộc* thereby serves as a symbol of the transfer of women's production of religious merit to the family and represents their desire to create a happy family, regardless of the receiver's views on religion and the supernatural.

The practice of making offerings and taking home *lộc* is, therefore, part of the same process by which women build both emotion and debt in the family through statements of self-sacrifice. It is meant to strengthen the bond of the mother with her children and the wife with her husband. It is done through a performance that reiterates the role that the woman plays as the family caregiver. At the same time, it underlines notions of *ơn* that are a pervasive part of Vietnamese social life. So, while the supernatural effect of *lộc* may or may not be believed by the recipients, the act of giving builds the emotional bonds of relationships. This was underlined to me by the universal response of men receiving *lộc*: I was always told that *lộc* was appreciated because it showed that their wives or mothers cared about them and their families, whether or not they thought the offerings actually brought good luck.

This role for women begins, especially, after marriage, but does not end when children grow and have families of their own. Women in their nineties still expressed to me that they continued to make wishes on behalf of families and bring *lộc* home for them. They just add grandchildren to the list of people for whom they pray to the buddhas and who receive the *lộc* that they have acquired.

CONCLUSION

The gender patterns that I have highlighted largely inform the ways in which individuals interact with and constitute religious practice and symbolism. Because making offerings and more general religious participation is considered to bring luck to the family, the act of making offerings on the part of women is a demonstrative action that shows that the women are taking care of their family and are therefore "good" women. The importance of *lộc* lies in the specific qualities embodied in these objects: the benefits are imminent, its efficacy is not dependent on faith but its power is transferable, and the objects represent sentiment that has deep social implications involving reciprocity.

Making offerings on altars to the buddhas is an expression of femininity that builds on a complex of actions related to the construction of gender identity. For both young unmarried women and married women, the motivations for participation are somewhat different, driven by their respective chief concerns. For both groups, however, engaging with Buddhism through offerings and appeals to the supernatural is an important part of being a Vietnamese woman.

6   Sutra Recital and Buddhist Identities

Buddhist practice in Vietnam, being nonprescriptive, can take a number of forms. However, the various options for practice are interpreted as leading to different ends and are given very different values, depending on perspectives. There is no systematic or authoritative stipulation regarding which activities are mandatory for a Buddhist, which activities are beneficial but not essential, and which are superfluous or even undesirable from a Buddhist perspective. There is also no authoritative consensus or social pressure regarding what the goals and intended outcomes for particular practices ought to be. Consequently, Vietnamese Buddhists take part to a greater or lesser extent in Buddhist activities, choosing some and avoiding others, based more on personal preference than on any other reason. Even those Buddhists who can be viewed as authoritative view the variations as acceptable. As a result, there are many potential ways to become involved in Buddhism, ways that are broadly informed by dynamic gender structures that draw on understandings of masculinity and femininity that shift in accent with age.

As we have seen, the most common form of engagement with Buddhism is through the practices associated with *lộc*; this is particularly women's practice, and usually is the only form of engagement for young women. Many older women, however, participate in other Buddhist activities with a pronounced religious zeal. The religious practice of women frequently intensifies as they age, and they supplement the usual supplication with additional activities at a time that coincides with the decrease in family responsibilities as their children become adults (Hoàng Bá Thịnh 2002b, 198).

The people who chant sutras are typified by a self-conscious commitment and faith in the efficacy of their practice that is not present in those who engage in only the practices that surround *lộc*. Those who chant sutras are devoted Buddhists and describe themselves specifically as "Buddhist" (*phật tử*). This, of course, does not mean that they are necessarily exclusively Buddhist because all have additional religious practices that they recognize as not Buddhist. Full Buddhist engagement means a greater commitment to a specific activity (such as attending sutra recitals four times a month), to a specific group of people, and usually to a specific pagoda. None of the people I met at these sutra recitals ever expressed skepticism or hedged their devotion by saying that they chant sutras "just in case," as did those who came to pagodas only to make offerings and wishes. The participation of Buddhist devotees who engage in chanting sutras takes up a much larger part of their time and energy and is more central to their identity than it is for those who only make offerings.

Mrs. Bình is a good example of a devoted Buddhist who recites sutras. She was in her late fifties when I met her in 1997. She worked in the office of the *Research Journal of Buddhist Studies,* published at Quán Sứ Pagoda. She habitually wore a brown smocklike shirt that was reminiscent of monastic clothing. Although her family was poor and her home had only two rooms, the smaller of these rooms was given over to a large altar for the buddhas. She chanted sutras twice a day at this altar; on several days a month a few Buddhist women in the neighborhood would join her.

Such devout women form the core of their pagoda communities, and are active in ensuring its maintenance and cleanliness, feeding the monastics, participating in the performance of rituals, and donating money. They also form a fairly cohesive, but informal, pagoda association. Many are friends that also spend time together outside of the pagoda. They form a bond and have a sense of belonging and identity that is grounded in their Buddhist participation. While some men take part in these activities, they usually distinguish their practice from that of women and, in effect, form a group distinct from the women. (I will discuss these men in Chapters 8 and 9.) This chapter will look at the motivations for increasing participation in the activities of this group of women, and the importance of their practice and their inclusion in the group for their identity.

INTENSIFICATION OF RELIGIOUS PRACTICE: AGE AND RELIGIOSITY

The greater time commitment that is required to be a more active Buddhist means that this level of engagement is not open to all people.[1] Involvement in the Buddhist group that gathers to recite sutras on appointed days means participation may be requested for mortuary rituals as well, rituals that are not timed conveniently for those with young families or work obligations. Young women in Hanoi have busy lives, either studying or working in addition to taking care of the household if they are married. Few today work only in the home unless they have small children. Even those who work outside the home are nonetheless expected to do the lion's share of cooking and cleaning in most families. This means that young women have little free time to spend at the pagoda. Making offerings twice a month is all most are able to commit to, even if they are fervent Buddhists.

Special occasions such as Lễ Giỗ Tổ, which celebrates the deaths of a pagoda's monastic "ancestors" and is the largest celebration in the ritual calendar, might draw a greater range of ages, but most participants are older women, who also organize the celebration and prepare the feast. Although the increased free time has the effect of allowing these women to be more involved in Buddhist activities, there are other factors that contribute to the appeal of Buddhism for older Vietnamese women, including approaching death, social meaning, community, and expectations.[2]

APPROACHING DEATH

Anxiety over what will happen after death is universal. Although in Vietnam conceptions of what happens after death are usually unsystematized and unarticulated, the rituals are very clearly spelled out. So, for example, most hold an idea of reincarnation, but are hard-pressed to say how reincarnation fits with ideas of ancestor worship. People are usually unable to discuss in much depth where ancestors reside, and what life after death is like. They know that offerings are essential, that the needs of the dead are not dissimilar to those of the living, and that funerals must have a particular form for the spirit of the dead to be at peace. Better articulated are the repercussions of not conducting rites properly: wandering spirits and a negative impact on the living. I attended a secondary burial in 2004, in which the decomposed remains of my wife's grandfather were exhumed, the bones cleaned and arranged in a new smaller casket before being taken for reburial in his home village. I spoke at length with family members while the bones were being cleaned by a pair of hired workers. They were able to tell me that this was their tradition, and that they envied southern Vietnamese who did not have this tradition (which most found to be a dirty and unpleasant task), but they were unable to elaborate on why it had to be done, other than stressing that it was their responsibility.

Vietnamese people do not generally think deeply about the nature of the soul. Nonetheless, there is a commonly held but loose set of beliefs that the dead remain for a while around the place that they died and, if they died well (in old age, of natural causes, with children and grandchildren, and in the home) and the correct rituals are performed, they are sent to an afterlife that is much like this one. The afterlife, in this view, has much the same requirements that this world has. The soul needs to be fed, to have money and other essentials, such as transportation, cell phones, and clothes. To provide these things for loved ones, living family members burn votive items for those who have died. Ancestors need to be well treated by their descendants: given a good grave and a tablet on the ancestor altar, and given regular offerings in the form of incense, alcohol, cigarettes, betel nuts, and feasts on special days (such as the death anniversary and on New Year's Day). If these conditions are met, then the soul will prosper; if not, the soul will suffer and become a hungry ghost.

Another explanation of what happens after death is provided by Buddhism, which describes rebirth into a new life after a sojourn through hell to pay for past sins. Again, this stint in hell can be eased through the correct rituals. Those who believe in the vow of A Di Đà Phật may be reborn in the Pure Land by reciting his name and his sutras in faith. Although beliefs in ancestors and ancestor offerings outlined in the paragraph above contradict the Buddhist views of what happens after death, all of these beliefs are usually held simultaneously in Vietnam, and the contradictions left unaddressed. Instead, explanations of what happens after death are usually contextually formulated so that people may speak of reincarnation in one instance and of the need to feed ancestors in another.

Anxiety and preoccupation over what will happen after death plays an important part in the lives of Vietnamese as they age, becoming a central concern as a person reaches old age. I saw this concern with the approach of death in a small village in Hà Tây province, in 1998. The old lady in the family I was visiting saw that I had a camera and asked me to take a picture of her. She then went and put on her best clothes in preparation and, with her family looking on, sat to have her portrait taken. Only later was I informed that the portrait I had just taken at the insistence of the old woman was to be placed on their ancestor altar after her death. It is also common that people prepare other aspects of their ancestor cult in this way, for example by purchasing a burial site before death. One woman described the process that her mother and mother-in-law were going through in anticipation of their deaths:

> First, depending on each place, they go to pray more often so that the
> Buddha will let them die easier and go to the Buddha's paradise. They
> prepare to buy a plot for themselves and then they prepare their will just
> in case they die suddenly. And they also prepare their picture with their
> nicest clothes. But I see now most of the women are not so worried about
> their clothes, but before that they were really concerned about clothes. For
> example, my mother took a picture of my grandmother wearing new bright
> red clothes. Normally she doesn't wear that kind of clothes, just for special
> occasions, like her longevity ceremony when she turned ninety years old.

The people who serve the spirits have to wear special clothes, not like normal people [the grandmother used to be a spirit medium]. Old women also chant sutras at the pagoda to ensure that they will have people to chant sutras for them when they die. They are really scared that no one will chant sutras for them. My mom is very scared too, but I told her when she dies I will make sure to ask a monk I know and all of the Buddhist women around here to go and chant sutras for her. I promised I would prepare very carefully and ask a monk—because, you know, she just likes the monk to do it for her, not the nun. She says she doesn't like nuns, she says they are not good. So when I said that I would get the monk to do it, she was very happy with that. My husband's mother often goes to the pagoda because she thinks that if she goes often, her death will be fast and easy and then she will go to paradise instead of to hell. When my father was young my paternal grandfather (who knew about geomancy) took him around the village and pointed and told my father, "When I die you should bury me in this place where I can see that direction. The grave has to be placed in this way." Like that. So each person has a different way to prepare.

People turn to Buddhism as one way to deal with the approach of death, but also as a way to make arrangements to ensure that everything possible will be done for them after their death. Many women expressed to me the opinion that having more people chanting at a funeral increases the benefit to the spirit in the afterlife and for their rebirth. One woman in her sixties voiced an observation, repeated by others, that if the person was not an active participant in a pagoda association, then only a few Buddhists would show up to chant sutras on his or her behalf, even if the family invited the society members to come. It is common that older people in the pagoda association will ask fellow members to be sure that they will have people chanting for them. Mrs. Tu told me, "An old woman recently told my group, 'When I die I want you sisters in the pagoda association to come to chant for me.' Everyone agreed and said that they would come when she died and they put her in her coffin. Afterwards, she felt much happier knowing that people would help in this way." Thus, participation in the pagoda association is one way to ensure an optimal afterlife.

SOCIAL MEANING

In the Vietnamese context, the centrality of the ancestor cult means that religious and existential concerns regarding the meaning of one's life are not important: everyone is concretely part of a web of social connections that span the line between life and death. Questions on the meaning of one's existence are concretely answered by ingrained understandings that place emphasis on the family and on the individual as a link between the past and the future. People understand that they have a responsibility towards ancestors, and part of that responsibility is to produce offspring who can continue the family and maintain the ancestor cult.

The loss that may be experienced because of a diminishment of social roles may be more of an issue for Vietnamese, as is the problem of increased leisure time. In Vietnam, increased religiosity is a standard and sanctioned way for women to deal not only with their free time, but also with the emotional anxiety surrounding that extra time. As we saw in the last chapter, much of women's identity is tied up with their children and the enterprise of creating the "happy family." There is a feeling of loss and a diminished social worth that is attendant with changes when children become adults. Becoming more involved in Buddhist activities provides a common way to feel more important and part of something bigger. So, for example, two elderly women live at a pagoda I know on the edge of Hanoi to do chores and cook for the resident monk. One of them was widowed at the age of thirty-five, during the war. Her children have all left home and have their own children. With nothing of value left in her daily life, and feeling alone, she has found meaning and purpose by taking care of the pagoda full time.

Increased leisure time is one of the most prominent reasons that people offered as to why active Buddhists are overwhelmingly older women. The increase in religiosity correlates to the time when children become more independent. In Hanoi today, and even more so in rural areas, there are few activities that are open to older people. There is the government-sponsored Elder People's Association, and there is the possibility of Tai Chi exercises in the morning. Some elderly men play chess in the park or take up a hobby such as raising birds. One co-ed group I knew gathered once a week to sing folk songs from northern Vietnam (*quan họ*). However, in general, there are few activities open to older people, and this is amplified even further in rural areas. Involvement in Buddhism activities provides not only a new purpose, but also activities to occupy time and hopefully improve chances for an easier passage through hell and a better rebirth.

More intense Buddhist practice on the part of women is also a way to continue the role of care giving for the family, at least at a supernatural level, and therefore symbolically maintaining that central role in female identity. Mrs. Tu continues to see Buddhist practice as being centered on the family: "There are two reasons why older people believe more in the Buddha, worship the Buddha, and go to the pagoda more often. The first is to get blessings of happiness for their children and grandchildren and to make everything good for them. Young people like my daughter don't have time to go to do it, and young people also don't believe as strongly in the Buddha. Older people understand more about Buddhism and they also want to worship the Buddha to make wishes of wealth, happiness, and talent for their families, their children, and their grandchildren."

COMMUNITY

Old age can be an isolating experience for many. In Vietnam, this isolation may be somewhat mitigated by the need to take care of grandchildren while parents are at work. Although this sort of labor does provide human contact, some older people confided in me that they found their young grandchildren tiring. The pagoda group, some told me, provided a chance to escape their homes and to spend time with like-minded people. One woman in her late sixties commonly went to Phúc Lộc Pagoda to volunteer. She went especially on days when people came to get *lộc* (the first and fifteenth of the lunar month and on special days like Lễ Giỗ Tổ [the feast for pagoda ancestors]). She would sit on the platform by the reception area and assemble bags of *lộc* for people, spending her time chatting with those who came in. She told me that this was her way to serve the buddhas and that she had nothing to do at home.

The people who take part in group sutra recitals often interact as peers outside the context of the pagoda as well. As one woman admitted, "Of course, I go to Quán Sứ Pagoda because I have many friends who also go there." Others, such as Mrs. Tu, do not spend much social time with their Buddhist friends except when they go with them to religious activities. However, Mrs. Tu says she does not have friends other than those from her Buddhist group, so all of her social contact comes through Buddhism, though she says that this is not her principal reason for participating: "The first reason old women go to the pagoda is to follow the Buddha to learn from the Buddha Dharma. The second is that at home they don't have to take care of the children or grandchildren, so they go to the pagoda to relax and be comfortable. This is not the main thing for me. The main thing for me is to learn the Buddha Dharma. Of course, getting together with people is fun, but the main thing is whether you want to follow the Buddha." Another younger woman, however, was clearer that motivations often revolved around the social aspects:

> I think the biggest reason old women go to the pagoda is that it is fun to go and be with friends, who are the same age and think the same kind of way. Second, I think that they will be more healthy, and when they die they will be more content. They also go for social interaction. Old women feel that

it will make them healthier, have a chance to chat with others and find out what is going on with everyone, and to have relationships—to have more friends. I think this is why old women go to pagodas. Like a social club. And old women always say that they go to pagodas to give morality and merit to their children and grandchildren.

Most often women can be seen arriving in small groups rather than alone. Thus, there is a sense in which the pagoda and the pagoda association provides community and fulfills a human need for belonging.

EXPECTATIONS

While the points outlined above are important draws for women to become increasingly involved in Buddhism as they age, there is another important factor. Young women do not participate because the group that chants sutras is defined by the age of those who take part. More intense Buddhist activities are appropriate for old women, and therefore draw them. Simultaneously, and for the very reason that it draws old women, chanting sutras is not an activity that will draw younger women, even if they are strongly devoted to the Buddha. This is how Thảo, who described herself as being very religious, explains why she does not go to chant sutras at a pagoda:

Me: Do you take part in any activities other than making offerings?
Thảo: No. Actually, I don't have time, and most of the participants are very old women. I find it very difficult to get the chance to participate because I am still young. Mostly they do it when they are retired or have a job in which they are very free.
Me: Why do only old women, and not young women, participate? Is it only because of lack of time?
Thảo: Maybe partly because they don't have time, but to join them you have to... [hesitates]. They are really difficult to get close to. They have a different way of thinking, from a different time, with different concepts. Their level is different. They are very difficult to talk with.
Me: So, even though you are very religious, you don't participate?
Thảo: No. But I have an older cousin, and she is not married. She is over fifty years old and she is a very devout woman. She knows very clearly about the procedures, chanting sutras, and other things. Sometimes I go with her to the pagoda and talk with the monas-

tics and other people as well, but only when she is available and takes me along. If I am alone I am very scared.

There are a range of motivations for older people, especially women, to increase their participation in Buddhism, and draw a large number of women whose children have grown. Once committed, these women typically become involved in a way that absorbs a large amount of their energy, free time, and financial resources.

ACTIVITIES OF THE COMMITTED BUDDHISTS

The activities of these older Buddhist women differ significantly from those individuals who arrive to make personal offerings on the first and fifteenth of the lunar month. The differences are particularly evident at Quán Sứ Pagoda, where a large group will gather to chant sutras together in the center of the large main hall, while individuals will continue to come in, place their personal offerings on the altar, and make their supplications.

As mentioned earlier, there is a substantial change in practice for older women who become Buddhist adherents. They still make offerings on the first and fifteenth of the lunar month on the altars of the buddhas and at other non-Buddhist sites. However, they add to this a number of other activities. These activities typically demand a much greater time commitment and emotional investment.

The main sutra recital is the penitence ritual, during which laywomen and laymen chant sections from a liturgy titled the *Sutras for Daily Use* (*Chư-Kinh Nhật-Tụng*, 1964), which includes the *Sám Nguyện Sutra* (*Kinh Sám Nguyện*) and sections of the Amitābha Sūtra (*Kinh A Di Đà*).[3] It also includes the recitation of some *dhāraṇīs* (verbal formulaic mantras), the names of 108 buddhas, and the repetitive chanting of "*na mô* A Di Đà Phật" (homage to Amitābha Buddha) one hundred times. The sutras themselves are translated into Sino-Vietnamese rather than the vernacular, so they are difficult to understand for the vast majority of participants. The *dhāraṇīs* are transliterations of Sanskrit and are considered important, but to the participants are just sounds without intelligible meaning.

My informants draw a distinction between chanting sutras (*tụng kinh*), on the one hand, and ritual (*lễ cúng*) on the other.[4] Chanting sutras does not involve a ritual specialist (i.e., it is led by the laity) and can be done in a group or alone at home. Unlike ritual, it does not involve experience or training to any great extent to join a group. It takes no more than one or two sittings to be able to chant the sutras adequately, following along from the book, and there are CDs available for those who want to chant with someone when they are alone. Sutras are written in the modified Latin alphabet used for writing in vernacular Vietnamese, but, as I said, they are written in Sino-Vietnamese, which is incomprehensible to most.

"Ritual," as the term is used by my informants, is performed only by specialists, inevitably men or monastics. It requires training and practice, both to read the texts (which are often written in Chinese characters), to chant the more complex rhythmic and tonal patterns, and to play the percussion accompaniment. Before most sutra recitals, the all-male ritual group at Phúc Lộc Pagoda usually performed a ritual in which a sutra from the liturgy *Thỉnh Phật Khoa* is chanted.[5] This chanting is far more elaborate than the regular sutra recital, and requires practice and study. While there are occasionally women who sit behind the men who do this chanting and count rosary beads during its performance, the majority of women who take part in the penitence ritual do not show up until after the conclusion of this ritual. This all-male ritual group also performs the special rituals that are held throughout the year.

NGHÊ GIẢNG: DHARMA TALKS

Many of the more devout not only meet at their local pagoda to chant sutras regularly, but also take part in other Buddhist events. Every Sunday morning at Quán Sứ Pagoda "Dharma talks" are held that draw large groups of devotees from all over the Hanoi area.[6] Mrs. Bình, who worked at Quán Sứ Pagoda, would ride her Honda Cub motorcycle from the far side of Gia Lâm, past Đuống Bridge (around thirty minutes from the city), in order to sit in on these talks. The crowds would fill the large lecture hall, and a sea of brown-robed old women would pack themselves into the courtyard and alleys of the pagoda in order to be present. A few old men could be seen seated inside the hall at tables, but the vast majority consisted of women sitting on mats on the ground, many of whom could be seen telling their prayer beads while the talk was being given. The term *"nghê giảng"*—"listen to a lesson"—would suggest that these were sermons. In fact, they mostly consisted of a senior monk reciting from the Mahāvagga Sūtra, which mainly gives rules of conduct. However, because it was written in Sino-Vietnamese, its lessons were largely unintelligible to most present. On occasion, the monk also would give a small sermon. The contents of these lectures usually revolved around the importance of moral behavior. At times they reflected state positions and warned of the increase in social evils and materialistic greed coming from the West.

It was clear that some women were not as interested in listening to the talk as they were at being present. A number of older women expressed to me that they

Dharma talk at Quán Sứ
Pagoda

believed that it was meritorious to attend these talks but confessed that they did
not learn anything. One older woman I sat beside at one of these talks told me
that she believed it was important to be present because it calmed your spirit and
brought good luck. The tie between the delivery of these "lessons," the importance of the figure delivering them, and the accent on merit making was demonstrated by the fact that events were cancelled whenever a senior monk was not
available to deliver them.

FUNERALS
One of the key functions of the pagoda association is to chant sutras at funerals
and other mortuary rituals for those who were associated with the pagoda. The

importance of having people chant sutras at a funeral was stressed by many with whom I spoke, echoing the opinion of this old woman: "Chanting sutras helps them leave their body to go to the Buddha's place and to be at peace." The groups of sutra chanters will also accompany the pagoda's monastics when they have been requested to perform rituals at funerals or when families that are not associated with the pagoda ask the women of the association to chant for them (though only a few of these women will show up in these cases). People sometimes arrange for lay Buddhists to chant even if the deceased was not Buddhist because it is still thought to be beneficial. There are key phases when the group's services are required. The group will frequently gather at a deathbed to lighten the karmic load of a dying person. The group also gathers to chant sutras by the coffin while it is being viewed. Groups usually can be seen leading funeral processions down the streets of Hanoi, holding banners in Chinese characters reading, "Honor to Amitābha Buddha." They again chant sutras while the coffin is being lowered into the grave and while the first shovels of dirt are thrown in.[7] Finally, they chant sutras every seven days until a concluding ritual on the forty-ninth day (though some choose to have this ritual on the thirty-fifth day). The Buddhist ceremonies performed for the dead are collectively known as *cầu siêu* or *siêu hồn,* and the chanting of sutras by women from the pagoda association at these ceremonies is seen as one of their most important activities.

As discussed above, preparation for death becomes increasingly important as people become old in Vietnam, as is true everywhere. Taking part in the pagoda association allows the chance to be more intimately and frequently involved in the process by becoming active at the funerals of other Buddhists. This participation allows time and opportunity to confront death and to reconcile oneself to the approach of one's own. Being part of the pagoda association and chanting at others' funerals also give merit, which will aid in one's own process of death and reincarnation. Finally, by being an active member, participants can be sure that fellow members will assist at their own funeral, when the time comes. This last point is an important consideration because I have been repeatedly told that few will show up to chant for someone who was not a member of the pagoda community, and it is thought that the more people who chant, the greater an impact it will have on the spirit's experience after death.

PILGRIMAGES
The pagoda association also organizes pilgrimages to famous Buddhist and other religious sites. These pilgrimages are usually undertaken by core members of the pagoda community, though frequently friends who are not part of the inner circle

are invited, to defray costs. They usually take place in the first month of the lunar year, in the spring, when the weather is cool and conducive to travel, and when there was traditionally a lull in agricultural production. This time is especially understood to be supernaturally potent. It is a time when festivals take place, centered on the communal houses in northern Vietnam. Buses packed with women, most of them more than fifty years old, can be seen on all of the highways around Hanoi in great numbers, recognizable by the flags tied to their side-view mirrors. Spirit mediums are also particularly active at this time, business people are borrowing supernatural loans from the Lady of the Storehouse, and large crowds head to the Perfume Pagoda to wish for the conception of sons and fortunes of families. The more adventurous might climb Mount Yên Tử, famed as a northern center of Vietnamese Zen Buddhism.

Such pilgrimages have become more popular in recent decades. Until the 1990s, sites that are now favored destinations lay empty. For urban youths, it is now a simple proposition for a group of friends to ride their motorcycles for a day trip and picnic to a scenic site outside Hanoi, whereas in the past very few had access to a vehicle. Today, many companies organize trips for their employees, and of course religious groups routinely go on pilgrimages together.

On one occasion, shortly after New Year's Day 1997, I went along with a busload of older women to visit religious sites. While trips in the beginning of the year are invariably a mix of tourism and devotion, this trip was overtly religious. Rather than saying that they were going on a trip (đi du lịch), a term often used to describe trips to religious sites by younger people, they said that their purpose was explicitly religious (đi lễ—go to worship). Nonetheless, they spoke as much of the enjoyment of the trip (consisting of a succession of visits to various temples and pagodas in the vicinity of Hanoi) as they did of the religious benefit. It was one of the few times every year when these women had the chance to get out of their village in Gia Lâm and tour the area's scenic sites.

The first, and farthest, destination of the day was to the Temple of the Lady of the Storehouse. Offerings consisted of processed pork (giò), boiled chicken, and a cake made from sticky rice and fatty pork meat (bánh chưng). Some women made offerings of money, which were later distributed to members of the group. After collecting the lộc, we proceeded to the next destination, a temple dedicated to Lý Thánh Tông, where the sweet and salty offerings were eaten for lunch, before heading on to seven pagodas in and around Hanoi.[8] The combination of Buddhist and non-Buddhist destinations in the day's itinerary is indicative of the way that both sides (i.e., Buddha side and spirit side) are usually integrated in the practices of northern Vietnam.

As an example of a more ambitious pilgrimage, I went on a multiday trip with Thầy Tâm (a nun, discussed in Chapter 2), Thầy Linh (a monk, discussed in Chapter 1), and a group of laywomen who were the followers of Thầy Linh. The trip included a dawn visit to Côn Sơn Pagoda and a stop by Kiếp Bạc Temple on the way to our main destination, Yên Tử Pagoda.[9] We arrived at the pagoda at around eight o'clock in the morning. It is a famous pilgrimage site in northern Vietnam, said to be the center of Vietnamese Zen and the location where King Trần Nhân Tông founded the only Vietnamese Zen school. We then embarked on a strenuous eight-hour hike up Yên Tử Mountain to reach the Bronze Pagoda (Chùa Đồng), a small shrine at the top. We continued to the coast to spend the night. In the morning, we visited three more religious sites (a Buddhist pagoda, a temple, and a shrine dedicated to the pantheon central to the mother goddesses), made offerings and reclaimed the lộc. We then hired a boat that took us on a leisurely sightseeing cruise around the scenic Halong Bay for an afternoon, eating the lộc from the offerings made earlier and looking at the spectacular landscape of jagged pinnacles erupting out of the bay's green waters, while chatting and joking.

Such trips, organized by pagoda associations, serve as important moments in the groups' calendar. Not only do they provide opportunities for these older women to go on a trip with peers and experience something beyond the scenes of their everyday lives, but they also are important for the health and cohesiveness of the groups. They strengthen communities and increase the spirit of shared purpose.

INDIVIDUAL PRACTICE

The most committed Buddhists also undertake a variety of practices at home as individuals. Already mentioned are the sutras that some chant at home. The most common individual practice is abstaining from eating meat and other forbidden substances (alcohol, cigarettes, eggs, milk, and vegetables with strong aromas such as onions, garlic, and shallots [Hữu Ngọc 1997, 92]). The degree to which one chooses to be vegetarian depends entirely on personal proclivity. Some options include total vegetarianism (usually only undertaken by monastics); abstinence one time, two times, four times, six times, or ten times a month; and abstinence once a quarter (Hữu Ngọc 1997, 93).[10] The most common, by far, is eating vegetarian twice monthly. Buddhist adherents also make donations as part of merit-making practices.

Another activity that is done individually is making donations. All pagodas have donation boxes, though many believe that money given directly to resident monastics is a more meritorious action and generates more luck for the supplicant. Even better is making substantial donations to sponsor a major feast or a construction project, though this is done less frequently and is not something to which most people aspire.

BUDDHIST IDENTITIES

Being a committed Buddhist can best be described as a group activity. Indeed, many of the functions that religion plays for the elderly are predicated on community practice. Pilgrimages, chanting sutras, volunteerism, and service at funerals all bring the group together and foster a sense of inclusion in something that transcends the individual beyond the family. Being an active Buddhist ties older people, who might otherwise spend much time alone at home, into a network of people who share common beliefs and work as a group towards common goals.

Generally speaking, the pagoda association is loosely defined, and membership is not strict. In many pagodas there are no formal requirements for joining, nor is there an initiation ceremony. Some may take the Three Refuges (in the Buddha, the Dharma, and the *sangha*) and Five Precepts (to avoid killing, stealing, sexual misconduct, lying, and intoxication), but many do not, and initiation rituals or requisite actions are not discussed in a way that signifies that any action is centrally important or defining of being a Buddhist. Joining the group in a formal way is also not necessary for participation in sutra recitals. Some pagodas, however, hang pictures of the members on the wall in the courtyard. This did not happen at Phúc Lộc Pagoda or Quán Sứ Pagoda (in the latter case because the large size of the group would have made it impossible). However, on the wall of the lecture hall at Quán Sứ Pagoda there are plaques with the names of deceased members, and some families have chosen to pay for their deceased member's tablet to be installed at Phúc Lộc Pagoda.

The group bond that is achieved can be usefully understood through the notion of *communitas*. It stands in opposition to society as structured, differentiated, and hierarchical. *Communitas* is an unstructured, "relatively undifferentiated comitatus, community, or even communion of equal individuals" (Turner 1995 [1969], 96). The pagoda space represents, especially when juxtaposed with the communal house, a relatively unstructured space in which community is stressed over hierarchy, "anti-structure" over structure.[11] *Communitas* is achieved to some degree within the group that participates in sutra recital through the uniforms and the sense of shared purpose. It makes members feel different from others, and set apart as a group. It is this sense of community that is part of what compels some people to become involved in pagoda life at this level. *Communitas* is especially present during pilgrimages or when the community pulls together to organize a feast or ritual. However, *communitas* is only one dynamic, and excessive stress should not be placed on this group dynamic to the exclusion of individual motivations and aspirations.

Inclusion in these groups has emotional importance for those who choose to be involved. Their participation and commitment to Buddhism comes to be an important part of their identity and of the way that they present themselves to the outside world. The people who take part in these group rituals come to define themselves to a far greater extent as Buddhists than do people who only make offerings. These latter individuals usually go to the pagoda alone or in pairs and do not define their activities as a group activity. The people who chant sutras, however, show a high level of involvement; some may even take on a Buddhist name that they use when in Buddhist circles.

Inclusion in these groups is important as an aspect of these older women's overall identity, and, therefore, markers are used to define themselves as Buddhists. These markers play a dual role of showing inclusion in the group of devout, but also serve to draw a distinction with those who are not part of the group. These markers are not qualifications bestowed by the Buddhist establishment or the group so much as they are investments by those who seek inclusion, and can be seen as statements of affiliation. Similar to devoted fans of a football club, the identity of the committed Buddhists shows itself in a myriad of small ways: choosing certain styles of dress, wearing bracelets of prayer beads or a necklace with an image of Quan Âm, or assuming a vegetarian diet to varying degrees. Commitment also influences living space, so that many of the people who take part in sutra recitals decorate their houses with Buddhist calendars and Quan Âm clocks with neon halos, display *lộc* from famous pilgrimage sites, and erect altars in a room of their house.

Clothing is the most obvious marker of inclusion/exclusion used by many of the Buddhist laity, especially women. The people who have the closest relationship with the pagoda will frequently dress in brown shirts at home that echo Buddhist monastic robes. The women who ran the bookstore at Quán Sứ Pagoda, for example, always dressed in this way, as did Mrs. Bình, who worked at the Institute of Buddhist Studies. At Phúc Lộc Pagoda, the mother of the resident nun performed daily chores around the pagoda, and dressed similarly. Sometimes a brown woolen hat would heighten the monastic appearance of such people in winter months. Often, women who dressed like this would also cut their hair short, though they did not shave it completely. Some, Mrs. Bình and Mrs. Tu, for instance, would carry a monastic handbag rather than a purse.

More importantly, there was a kind of uniform worn by recital participants that consisted of a brown robe worn over street clothes. These robes are loose, have slits down the sides, long sleeves, and are made of light fabric so that they can be slipped over the top of street clothes without being too uncomfortable on hot days. The robe is often supplemented by a Buddhist rosary hung around the neck, with the red tassel hanging at the back. The robe is worn during rituals, sutra recitals, Buddhist lectures, funerals or memorial services, pilgrimages, and pagoda activities generally. These robes, or uniforms, were not enforced in any way, but all who became involved in these groups wore them.

On pilgrimage tours, the buses would be packed with women who were both regular practitioners as well as women who only went to pagodas on occasion, and the two types of participants could be distinguished by the robes. At large Dharma talks, the courtyard of Quán Sứ Pagoda would be a sea of brown-robed laywomen. However, the robes were not worn by all participants, but only by the regular participants who actively recited sutras and took part in other pagoda events.

The relevance of robes as identity markers can be seen in the case of a recently established Zen center in Hanoi. This center is part of an organization led by a famous monk named Thích Thanh Từ. The lay followers dress in a manner that is distinct from the regular devotional Buddhists, wearing gray robes rather than the usual brown, in the manner of Buddhists from southern Vietnam. The gray robes were adopted because the organization is based in Đà Lạt, in the south, and the leader is southern. The robes stand out as distinct from the vast majority of Buddhist practitioners in the north. They serve the purpose of making a visual distinction between the Zen practice of this group, which is viewed by them as a higher practice than the devotional practices that are the norm in Vietnam.

Objects of clothing as markers of inclusion/exclusion and distinction can also be sources of contention. Mrs. Tu was a regular participant at Thích Thanh Từ's center as well as Quán Sứ Pagoda, but also was actively involved as a devotee of a certain Theravada Buddhist monk based in Ho Chi Minh City. When Mrs. Tu was visiting this monk in the south, she wore a thin mantle around her neck, which marked her as his disciple. When I asked another follower of Thích Thanh Từ about the significance of this mantle (without identifying Mrs. Tu), she became alarmed that a follower of Thích Thanh Từ was involved with a different group, and exclaimed that she would have to tell her friends about this breach in the dress code. For this woman, membership in the group, as signified through clothing, was exclusive.

In 2010, at a feast for pagoda ancestors at Vẽ Pagoda, I saw a good example of how Buddhist clothing serves as markers of inclusion within a group. In this instance, a group of women arrived together as a cohesive group on a bus that had been organized by their pagoda association. They emerged from the bus wearing the usual brown robes and prayer beads and carrying monastic-style brown bags. On the side of each of their bags was an embroidered design with the Chinese character for Buddha over a lotus flower, and below that the words (here translated into English),

Tinh Tiến Sutra Team
Devotees of Nôi Đồng Pagoda
Western Thiền Temple—2009[12]

A few of these women had gone a step further by also embroidering their Buddhist names onto their bags.

On my first attempt to participate in the penitence ritual at Phúc Lộc Pagoda in 1997, I tried to sit at the back of the sutra hall in order to watch what was happening. At this particular pagoda in front of the altar was a raised platform. The men would sit on this platform, which was quite small, perhaps measuring four meters by four meters in surface area. I was urged to go up to the platform by a number of men and women, but one woman spoke up saying that I should not be allowed because I was not wearing the brown robe that is worn by all devotees. She was the only one who protested, and the eventual consensus was that I should sit up with the men despite my improper dress. The men themselves were happy to have me, and in the end it was their voice that stopped the protests of this woman. However, the incident made it clear that the marker of a brown robe had significance, at least for some.

Just as they stress internal equality, uniforms also serve to delineate those who are part of the community from those who are not. It is perhaps a recognition of this aspect of exclusion to which Thảo was pointing when she said she did not participate in sutra recitals because the people there were difficult to get close to, were difficult to talk to, and had different ways of thinking (see Chapter 5). These groups, being primarily made up of old women, do not actively recruit members, but instead seem to form a fairly tight cohesion that can be difficult to penetrate.

Books and magazines are important for their symbolic value and serve as markers of inclusion as well. Chau has suggested that in the Chinese context the value of the text surpasses the content. Due to the history of writing and its association with formal power of the state, text assumes a "fetishistic" fascination that produces "awe, submission, recognition" and is used to display both political and cultural legitimacy by their association with state power and literati high culture (Chau 2006, 97). In Vietnam, text plays a similar role. In pagodas, temples, and shrines, inscriptions in Chinese and Vietnamese are ubiquitous. Books and magazines similarly hold value as material objects, value that transcends the content. Thus, books serve as markers of inclusion in their own right, as pieces of material culture for display. They are very often collected and kept at home, but not necessarily read. Mrs. Tu had a prodigious collection of back issues of the two main Buddhist magazines in Vietnam: *The Research Journal of Buddhist Studies* and *Enlightenment Weekly Magazine*. However, these magazines mostly sat in piles in her room untouched and, more often than not, were left in their plastic wrappers.

The bookshop at Quán Sứ Pagoda always has a small crowd of people buying the latest issues of Buddhist magazines, books explaining Buddhist philosophy, sutras, and various Buddhist paraphernalia (small statues, Buddhist robes, rosaries, incense, tapes of Buddhist sermons, and so on). These material objects become symbolic badges of association for the inner circle of devotees. The potency of these symbols was illustrated to me when I asked a woman at Quán Sứ Pagoda what sutra had just been chanted. She gave me the name of the sutra and asked a friend who was with her to show me a copy of the sutra. The woman refused, saying that I was not a Buddhist and therefore was not allowed to see. Although this was the only time that this happened, it indicated that, at least for this woman, feelings of inclusion also entailed boundaries of exclusion.

Other markers of inclusion are less tangible. Especially in the pagoda or on pilgrimages, the devout change their usual speech patterns and make a conscious effort to avoid confrontation. They speak of Buddhism, of past pilgrimages, of the efficacy of particular shrines and spirits for granting wishes. The way that they speak and the subjects they talk about are a part of their Buddhist performance. In short, people who become involved in sutra recital rituals infuse their lives with symbols of their devotion and display it for others. Their involvement in the Buddhist community often becomes a defining feature of their lives so that their status as Buddhists is increasingly important to their overall identity.

CONCLUSION

Aging is a difficult process in Vietnam, as elsewhere, and is frequently characterized by a diminishing role in society, and drastic changes in key elements of the identities people have constructed over a lifetime. For men, retirement brings an end to a career and productive capacity; for women, old age brings an end to their fertility and their role as mothers. For both, sexuality is no longer central, though this change is more pronounced for women.[13] When children grow up and leave the home, or at least no longer require the same level of effort, there is a diminishment of responsibility and a challenge to women's feminine identity as mothers. Older women frequently turn to the supernatural (buddhas, bodhisattvas, and other gods) to address the concerns brought on by old age. Going to pagodas allows women to continue to care for their families and thereby maintain their feminine identities. This explains why so many women described to me that they went to pagodas and recited sutras in order to help their families by bringing them good luck.

At the same time, participation in Buddhism provides for a way to deal with death. It reinforces ideas that there are positive ways to influence the outcome. Participating in Buddhist rituals can improve one's karma to influence punishments in hell and future rebirth. The vow of Amitābha Buddha also offers the possibility of salvation through rebirth in the Pure Land. In a more mundane way, involvement in a pagoda association helps to ensure that greater numbers of lay Buddhists will be present at one's own funeral to chant sutras and thereby improve a person's fate in the afterlife.

However, one of the most pronounced reasons for becoming more involved in Buddhist activities later in life is that it provides a community. Being Buddhist occupies a significant part of the identities of these older women, and their inclusion in these groups is marked by dress, home décor, and mannerisms that are especially assumed in the pagoda context. Being Buddhist can come to be a central aspect and an all-consuming activity for older women.

Involvement in the Buddhist community becomes a central part of the identity projects of older women. Their participation can start to take up a great deal of time, and often an increasing amount of money, as these women come to believe that their worth as a Buddhist is tied to the size of the donations they make. This expenditure can create resentment in the family, because children and husbands often do not share their enthusiasm for Buddhism and see only the absence of the mother/wife and the money wasted. Nonetheless, the women who are involved see their practice as benefitting themselves, but also their families, and so they persevere in the face of family objections. In addition, there is a competitive element in the display of this commitment that is the subject of the next chapter.

7 Conspicuous Devotion and Devotional Distinctions

I went on a one-day pilgrimage touring temples with a busload of women from a village on the outskirts of Hanoi in January 1998, shortly after Tết Nguyên Đán (the Vietnamese Lunar New Year holiday). It was similar to the pilgrimage described in Chapter 6, though it was with a group from a different pagoda. The trip was organized by three women: two were retired teachers, and one was the leader of the local pagoda association. The leaders had obtained help from a number of women who had volunteered to phone other Buddhist women to ask them to come on the trip so that each woman would pay less for the bus rental.

My companion and I arrived on foot at a spot beside the highway early in the morning and joined a large group waiting for the bus to arrive. Apart from me, the group consisted entirely of women. When the bus finally arrived, everyone surged forward towards the door to get a seat. It was obvious that the bus size was woefully inadequate for the number of people who had shown up for the trip and we were uncomfortably crammed on the bus after picking up a second group along the way. The situation caused a great deal of grumbling and some suggestions that they try to get a second bus. One woman in particular complained bitterly about not having a seat, until an old woman with blackened teeth and a black velvet traditional head wrap silenced her with a litany of "A Di Đà Phật"— the name of Amitābha Buddha, often repeated in statements of pious greeting or after a Buddhist sermon. Others nearby declared that, because they were going to pagodas, they should fill their hearts with good feelings. The protestor eventually gave up after several others joined in, telling her it was important to have a pure heart when visiting religious sites.

On the bus a couple of women sang Buddhist chants. It was the only time I have ever seen this sort of chanting, and it reminded me of the singing that takes place on school trip bus rides. At every pause in the chant people intoned "A Di Đà Phật." This exaggerated piousness continued to be displayed throughout the trip. At every pagoda we visited, women would display their devotion. Around me some women prayed in loud "whispers" and exaggerated waving of clasped hands. They punctuated their prayers with a sucking noise through pursed lips and clasped teeth, seemingly intended to indicate the depth of concentrated devotion that they were putting into their supplications.

It occurred to me at this point during my research that there was a specific kind of affected behavior that occurs in the context of the pagoda that involved performances of piety and moral rectitude out of character from the way that I saw the same women act in their everyday lives. Some, whose identity projects were closely associated with their Buddhist practice, spent a considerable amount of time in pagoda-related activities. For example, a young woman once related to me how her mother often spent her days on the phone, calling her network of Buddhist acquaintances to help organize trips such as these. The young woman claimed, "The main reason they do it, and act in this way, is that it makes them feel important." This comment regarding the volunteer work of Buddhist women was often made by younger people and by men. However, even devout Buddhists would sometimes comment to me about how certain of their co-Buddhists were not sincere, or that the exaggerated displays of piety of so-and-so were contrary to the teachings of the Buddha. The term they used to describe this kind of behavior was *khoe,* meaning to boast, brag, or show off. These forms of behavior (including showing off, criticism, and gossip) were commonplace, and made me start to ask how competition plays out in the religious field.

COMPETITION IN RELIGIOUS SPACES

It has sometimes been presumed that the pagoda is free of hierarchy and competition, especially when compared to the male space of the communal house. Most notably, Neil Jamieson saw the communal house and pagoda as representative of a bipolar *yin–yang* character that runs throughout Vietnamese culture and society (1993, 12–16).[1] Despite this generalized assumption of a lack of hierarchy that a comparison with the communal house brings about, within the pagoda asymmetrical power relationships do exist, by age but, more importantly, by sex. Hierarchical stratification by sex and age is such an intrinsic part of Vietnamese society that it would be hard to imagine it being entirely left at the gates of the pagoda. For example, Luong (1990) describes how the use of pronouns and honorifics, as well as naming practices, contribute to placing men over women in the Vietnamese social hierarchy. For now, I will leave the question of men aside and look specifically at women and status competition in the pagoda.

Within the Buddhist structure, there is a four-part division between monks and nuns, and male and female laity, with the male/female lay division matching the division between monk and nun.[2] In the monastic structure, nuns are subservient to monks. They are required to undertake a greater number of precepts, including the requirement that nuns always bow to monks, regardless of relative seniority. Leadership of the Buddhist institutional structure is entirely in the hands of monks. Pagodas are inhabited by either monks or nuns, but never both simultaneously, and pagodas where nuns are resident are less prestigious and appear to receive less financial support.

Unlike the division between the *sangha* and the laity, and between monks and nuns, the division between laymen and laywomen is not institutionalized. Rather, it exists at an informal but understood level, reflecting the lower position of women in Vietnamese culture rather than reflecting official pagoda organization. The lack of institutionalized hierarchical stratification in the lay community means that seating arrangements and portions of food signify very little when compared to the strict formality and importance placed on these status symbols in the communal house. The absence of formal status markers at the pagoda can be explained by its lack of official political power. A Buddhist monk may have respect within the pagoda, but he does not usually have any sway in local decision making.

Despite initial appearances, however, there is also competition for status within the ranks of female lay practitioners that simmers below the surface that has gone entirely unnoticed by scholars. Rather than being the imagined egalitarian space, the pagoda is often rife with competition between women who make Buddhist practice central to their identity projects. One way that this competition is seen is in the expectations that surround seating.

While seating in the pagoda is not structurally related to status, as it is in the communal house, there are nonetheless expectations that relate status to seating location. Both Malarney (1999, 190) and Luong (1993, 272) remark that the senior women in the pagoda sit closer to the altar than younger women in the village pagoda in the northern Vietnamese villages where Malarney and Luong conducted fieldwork. My experience in Hanoi is that this seating order is by convention rather than by rule. Nonetheless, the association of seating with seniority (most usually in terms of sex and age) is deeply engrained in Vietnamese society and is transferred into the pagoda space despite the lack of a strict rule, so that people assume the position appropriate to them unselfconsciously. At Phúc Lộc Pagoda, where the room was usually not full, there was not a great deal of competition. The men would sit in the front and the senior women would find a way to the front, as close as they could to the main altar. At Quán Sứ Pagoda, however, the desirability to be closer to the main altar would result in many devout women, regardless of age, showing up well before the start of the service in order to claim a spot near the front, though the very front was still reserved for the men.

Competition is usually more evident in less blatant ways—palpable, but not overt. Instead, it is expressed in small actions, mannerisms, and discrete markings. It is mostly not through grandiose gestures but through the minutia of everyday performances that are hardly perceptible but that cumulatively show a pattern. One woman described the difference between those who are showing off from those who are genuinely devout in this way:

> Being devout and showing off are different. If you are really doing it for the Buddha, you don't need everyone to know; you just need the Buddha to know. You don't need to tell people about it. And I think that the Buddha doesn't need expensive things. He just needs your heart, and that is enough. Like one woman I know, she always wants to tell me about all of her pious actions: "I just bought this fruit for offerings. It is very expensive!" She says that to me and to a few other people. If you are really devout you don't tell people like this. One day we went to release living beings on the first of the month. And when we went to do this, she said, "Today I bought a bunch of fish," or "I have some living snails to release." She always brags like this! I also like to make offerings, but I never tell people about it like her. Because I think it isn't necessary. If it is a true action, you help others or offer to the Buddha, you don't need to tell everybody. But many people really like to brag about it. That is the difference between true devotion and showing off.

The competitive aspect of religious practice is usually overlooked in academic studies of religion, probably because it is a difficult subject to broach without coming across as judgmental and dismissive of the sincerity of practitioners. Nonetheless, the tendency for religious practice to be ego building and binding rather than liberating is present and has long been noted even by Buddhist leaders. Buddhist exhortations "not to mistake the raft for the shore" point to an emic understanding of the pitfalls of human nature, which lead even the faithful to become attached to Buddhism, the Buddha, and Buddhist identity rather than staying fixed on the goal of liberation. Chögyam Trungpa Rinpoche, the founder of Shambhala International (formerly Vajradhatu) wrote explicitly about this pitfall for Buddhist practitioners, giving it the term "spiritual materialism": "Ego is able to convert everything to its own use, even spirituality" (Trungpa 1973, 7).

Bourdieu, in an essay titled "The Laughter of Bishops" (1998) argues that within the field of religion it is very difficult, if not impossible, to admit to religion's economic aspects, leading to its economic nature being spoken of only euphemistically. A mutually exclusive double truth is therefore employed, one religious and the other economic, but neither sustainable in the presence of the other. Hence, the "structural double game" necessitates the use of "two words superimposed on each other as if in a musical chord: apostolate/marketing, faithful/clientele, sacred service/paid labour, and so forth" (Bourdieu 1998, 114).[3] It is perhaps this reluctance to admit to this double truth that has led to a relative neglect of the competitive nature of the religious field. Despite the difficulty of the task of describing competitive behavior in the pagoda, particularly when I am sympathetic and indebted to informants, it is nonetheless the role of the anthropologist to lay bare this dual aspect, and it is for this reason that I embark on this discussion, though I find it uncomfortable to do so. Informants, it should be noted, found the subject distasteful because it presented an unflattering portrait of Buddhism and their own involvement. While some admitted to recognizing this sort of behavior in others, none discussed it as forthrightly as did Chögyam Trungpa.

CONSPICUOUS DEVOTION

Women who have become committed to their Buddhist practice, in the sense that they invest a substantial amount of time and frequently a significant portion of available financial resources, identify a large portion of their identities with their practice. Such an identity investment demands not only the perception of the self in a certain way, but also a desire for that identity to be substantiated through the recognition of it by others. Thus, it is not enough to be quietly Buddhist—there is also a deep need to be seen, and acknowledged, as devout.

The economist Thorstein Veblen introduced the term "conspicuous consumption" in 1899, chiefly using the notion of conspicuousness to denote a class-based form of differentiation. The term describes extravagant spending on luxury items as a display of wealth, aimed at attaining or maintaining social status. Veblen believed that such spending was not frivolous and, therefore, insisted that conspicuous consumption should not be viewed as wasted resources (2007 [1899], chap. 4). Rather, he saw conspicuous consumption as the price of social recognition and status.

Veblen's term explains adequately the potlatch type of competitive donations and offerings in Vietnam that form a significant part of some people's practice in their search for prestige or status, as described by Đỗ Thiện (2007). But this consumption is only part of a broader pattern of religious behavior that is prominent in pagodas throughout Hanoi (and I suspect elsewhere, as well). Twisting Veblen's term slightly, the displays of differentiation that are a part of Buddhist practice in Vietnam could usefully be described as "conspicuous devotion," being overt displays of piety and devotion that are substantive and purposeful rather than frivolous or secondary to the practice, having as their prime purpose the attainment of status or recognition within the religious field. However, while the focus here is on this aspect, it should not be seen as a nullification of other motivations. That is, a woman may be concerned with her status in the pagoda, and may engage in overt displays of piety, but this does not make her engagement any less important to her view of herself in the world, nor does it undermine the fact that she likely sees herself as engaging in moral practice and in significant interactions with the supernatural that will materially help with her life in this world and the next. Furthermore, it does not diminish the fact that she may also be motivated by a strong, selfless desire to have a positive impact on her family's health and wealth. Therefore, religious practice cannot, in the final analysis, be reduced to a search for status or power, but rather includes multiple and contextually shifting motivations.

In seeking attention for one's commitment to Buddhism, there is often an element of competitiveness constitutive of the way they present themselves through their activities and in the accumulation and presentation of the paraphernalia emblematic of their Buddhist identities. They, in essence, perform their devotion for an audience, comprising their Buddhist peers, by overt displays of devotion, as described at the beginning of the chapter.

Such performances of distinction are not typical of everyday behavior, but are instead performed in particular circumstances. Conspicuous performances of piety seem natural within the pagoda space, particularly for those engaged in the field. Those on the outside often see these performances as false, hypocritical, or two-faced. This discrepancy in the way that performances of devotion are received (either accepted or rejected) indicates the extent to which there is an internal acceptance of the rules of the game within the field. Participants internalize the rules and enact them as natural, while outside observers perceive the rules of the field as transparently artificial.[4]

It was often not the actions themselves that led me to see a person's devotion as intentionally conspicuous, but rather the way in which the actions were carried out. There was a qualitative aspect that signaled the conspicuous performance of some of the devout. Praying in front of an altar, for example, is an ordinary activity that all Buddhists do, but it can be done discretely or in a way that draws attention to the person's piety.

The fact that they were performances, however, does not necessarily imply full and conscious intentionality. Some may be distinctly calculating, but few, I suspect, enter into this form of devotional display fully cognitive or self-aware of their motivations or the implications of their actions. Instead, it is part of their *habitus*, which shape the way intense devotion is manifested and forms a desire for status within the field. It is a feel for the game rather than a deliberate strategy that leads to these demonstrations. Thus, while Buddhist women may perceive the desire to be recognized as good Buddhists, few would recognize in their own activities performances of conspicuous devotion that are part of a broader pattern that is directly aimed at the attainment of prestige and power within the pagoda.

ACTS OF CONSPICUOUS DEVOTION

I first met Mrs. Xuân at Phúc Lộc Pagoda in 2010. She was leading the older women in chanting on the eighth day of the third lunar month, reciting the penitence ritual. After the ritual, she invited me to visit her at her apartment sometime. She lived one hour by bus from the pagoda, which demonstrated her dedication. At the age of seventy-nine, she was energetic and active. She only went to Phúc Lộc Pagoda twice a month because of the distance, but she also recited sutras at home and went to several other pagodas a little closer to home. Her children had all moved overseas, and though she was proud that they were doing well, she confessed to being lonely, living by herself in her apartment without any close relatives nearby.

I met her again a few days later, again at Phúc Lộc Pagoda. This time she was not leading anything, but sat among a group of Buddhist women who had come to help at a memorial service held on the thirty-fifth day after someone's death. The main ritual was performed by Thầy Linh and by two of the old men from the ritual group. Afterwards, the Buddhist women sat and recited the Amitābha Sūtra, at the invitation of the family. Mrs. Xuân again stood out from the crowd of devotees, wearing a gray robe similar to Buddhists in southern Vietnam, rather than the usual brown robe of lay Buddhists that is customary in the north. On this occasion, she repeated her invitation, this time asking specifically whether I was available on the coming Monday. I gladly accepted her invitation.

I arrived a little after ten in the morning. Her apartment was on the first floor of a small apartment building, so she kept her door open and spoke to people as they passed by—mostly students on their way to class. In preparation for my arrival, she had put out a tray with packets of instant coffee and various kinds of cookies in colorful foil wrappings fanned out around the outside of the tray. In the center was a sweet bun, which, she told me several times, was very delicious. She lived in a small one-room apartment. The focus of the room was a proportionally large altar piled high with offerings of flowers and cookies. There were no statues on the altar, but an icon of Quan Âm hung on the wall above it. To one side of the altar was her bookstand and prayer book that she said she used for chanting sutras every day.

On the opposite wall hung two large picture frames, each with photographs of her family and of her meetings with various Buddhist monks. One of the monks that she pointed out to me lived in the south. In another photo she stood beside Thích Thanh Tứ, the head of Quán Sứ Pagoda. She also pointed out a few photos in which she was dressed up in costume for a communal house ritual. She spoke at length of her religious practice, how she ate vegetarian only two days a month because of her age, though she used to eat vegetarian ten days a month. She told me how she was the leader of the pagoda association at Phúc Lộc Pagoda, but she said that she could only get there once a month since she had moved so far away. She told me that the standard of lay practice had declined in her absence because, she said, Thầy Tâm was "too lazy" to take up the slack. Since she moved, she had become more involved at Thầy Linh's pagoda, which was closer. She made it clear that her practice included involvement at a number of pagodas. Finally, she described how she was also "serving the spirits" (*hầu thánh*)—a euphemism for taking part in spirit possession rituals.

All of the neighbors that walked by her front door were invited to come in because she had a special guest from Canada, who could speak Vietnamese and was also a Buddhist. Most of them politely declined, making excuses and smiling awkwardly at me. After a while she put on a video of a monk from the south giving a Dharma talk, saying that Buddhists in the south were much better than the ones in the north. She never directly explained whether that was the reason she chose to wear a gray robe of the south rather than a brown northern one, only saying, "It is up to the individual what color they wear."

After four or five people declined her invitations to speak with me, a young woman was persuaded to sit down and speak with us. Mrs. Xuân told her about how I chanted sutras and that I was Buddhist. Then she convinced the young woman to come with us to go to a nearby pagoda to eat a vegetarian lunch. Outside the front gate of her building she told the neighbors more about me. We stopped along the way to pick up a friend of hers and then proceeded to the pagoda.

Mrs. Xuân was typical of many Buddhist women I met who had made Buddhist practice a central focus of their lives. In the case of Mrs. Xuân, her practice was particularly intense because she had no family obligations. Nonetheless, the way that she displayed her Buddhism was typical. I have often gone into the homes of Buddhist women and noted the Buddhist decorations that adorned the wall and the pictures that they displayed of themselves in the company of famous monks.

Her clothing and accessories also displayed a strong desire to be singled out as a Buddhist. She carried a monastic-style handbag and a prominent Buddhist necklace. She distinguished herself from other Buddhist women by choosing to wear a robe that was markedly different from the robes the other women wore, and seemed to imply that she belonged to a group that was more earnest in its Buddhist practice than were the average northerners.

There are many ways that conspicuous devotion is manifest, with donation perhaps the most obvious form. Public generosity is an important part of Vietnamese social life and has traditionally been a way in which people rise in status in the community. It is therefore not surprising that making donations to pagodas is an act that is displayed openly. When donations are made at the donation offices

Tablet recording names and donations at a pagoda in Hanoi

of major religious sites, the donors are issued with a certificate to bear witness to their actions, which are then often displayed in homes. Inscriptions or posters are commonly placed on the walls of pagodas that list the names of generous benefactors. Frequently, the names of donors and the size of donations are broadcast over a loudspeaker during the busy season at major sites. So, for example, in 1998 I went to Bà Đá Pagoda to listen to Dharma talks that were being given for devout Buddhists, and at the end of each session a list of donations and donors was read over a loudspeaker.

There appears to be a strong desire by many women to be recognized in this way and for their generosity to be displayed. Families of these devout women often articulate their frustration at the amount of money being spent on pagodas and being sent to famous monks to fund their projects. Frequently viewed as wasted money, there are sometimes attempts to curtail this generosity, which sometimes leads to open conflict in the home. Such is the case with Mrs. Tu and her family. She is dedicated to her Buddhist practice, but her family views her donations and involvement as excessive. Her husband told me, "Most of the donations that women give to pagodas are out of a lack of understanding in that they think it will directly affect their lives by bringing them good luck. This way of thinking is wrong because bigger donations will not improve a bad life." He went on to say that many women give big donations so that the monk of the pagoda will pay more attention to them, but he sees these donations as a bad thing. Even her daughter, who is quite religious, does not agree with the amount of money that she spends on Buddhism, and questions her motivations:

All of my father's pension goes to my mother and she spends it all on donations to pagodas so that the monks will like her. We sold some ancestral land and got a few million *đồng* from it, and it is probably all gone now.[5] It has probably gone for making merit already. I have to buy the food for the family or my father wouldn't be able to eat! She doesn't put it into the donation boxes either, but gives it directly to the monks, so that they will like her more. Then if my mother has some business the monk will come to meet her and everyone will say, "Ah, she knows a lot of monks. A lot of monks like her." So then she will have more prestige with other people. One time she invited over thirty monks to eat vegetarian and she was so proud when her neighbors could see all of the monks at our house. She went around telling all of her friends. One monk gave her a relic, and she is always telling people about it. She doesn't let people near it for fear that they are not good and will spiritually pollute it. My father has spoken to her many times about her spending, but she doesn't listen. He is afraid to cut her off because she will go crazy. She also always calls this monk in the south. My father didn't like her to be calling the monks all the time, so she bought a cell phone so that he wouldn't know how much she calls.

Pagodas capitalize on these urges to gain status in the pagoda by creating opportunities for generous followers and benefactors to be recognized and publicly acknowledged for their generosity. Some prominent monks give gifts, such as inscribed books and portraits, to generous donors, who then prominently display the items and show their friends. These items, along with donation cards, ribbons that attest to involvement in volunteer committees, inscriptions on walls, and broadcasts of donors' names all take advantage of the competitive drive for status-giving recognition.

Some women donate time by volunteering to help with pagoda upkeep and special activities and become central to the pagoda in this way. All pagodas have groups of women who volunteer to act in various capacities, in order to ensure the smooth running of the pagoda, as described in Chapter 6. Large pagodas such as Quán Sứ Pagoda also have groups of women who are associated with the pagoda. When the pagoda holds special events or the monks want to send out information, they call on these women to phone their friends and fellow devotees so that there is a broad network of dissemination of notices regarding upcoming events.

MARKERS OF DEVOTION AND DISTINCTION

Goffman (1959) draws attention to the parallels between theatre and the way that people construct their social persona and present it to the world. Similar to theatrical performances, social performances make use of props and gestures that are accepted as signifiers by the audience. These are termed "fronts" by Goffman (1959), and defined as "the expressive equipment of a standard kind intentionally or unwittingly employed by the individual during his performance" (p. 13). Performers of devotion, too, use fronts that serve as markers of distinction that establish status within the field. Like actors in a play, physical props and costumes are combined with gestures and dialogue to make the performances "believable" to the audience, in that they are accepted as expressing particular meanings. In the Buddhist field, these performances serve to mark the performer as part of the community, but they also are used to create distinction and build symbolic capital within the community.

In Chapter 6, I noted how brown robes were markers of inclusion, showing who was a member of the group of devout Buddhists and instilling a sense of belonging and identity to participants. At the same time, objects such as clothing can be used as signifiers of distinction, marking the "other" as being those who do not use or even possess these objects. As Arthur notes, "Dress functions as an effective means of non-verbal communication during social interaction; it influences the establishment and projection of identity" (1999, 3). In this way, identity becomes associated with membership in the group and is a positive signifier that heightens this association of the self with the group.

Furthermore, there often arise microdistinctions that serve to mark, create, and sustain status distinction within the group ranks. Members try to distinguish themselves as being exceptional members of the group by more rigid adherence to moral restrictions (for example, eating vegetarian on more days of each month), by donation and volunteerism, and through the acquisition and display of objects such as clothing. One old woman at Quán Sứ Pagoda made a point of telling me that most people wore the prayer beads incorrectly. She insisted that the tassel should not hang down the back, but over the right shoulder. The prescription she gave me was not accompanied by an explanation, and did not appear to be shared by most others. Apparently, instead of being directed towards ensuring my conformity to a widely understood and tightly regulated dress discipline, she was indicating specialized knowledge to me that sought to distinguish her from the many other Buddhist laywomen who, in her words "did not understand the correct way to wear it." When I brought it up with others, they disagreed and accused whoever told me of trying to show off.

As in the case of Mrs. Xuân, robes could be used as statements of distinction. Many women tried to wear the most expensive robe they could buy, so that the robes were not only a badge of inclusion in the Buddhist group, but also objects of competitive distinction within the group. As one woman described,

> They wear robes from Taiwan and India, because only those ones are considered beautiful. Bags are also like that. If they are from Vietnam, for example, or China, they aren't as nice as the ones from Taiwan. Bells and wooden fish are the same. The production of these items in Vietnam or here in Hanoi is not good. They have to be from Taiwan or India. People particularly like the ones from Taiwan. The monks like to use things from Taiwan, so the old women copy them. The items from Taiwan are a lot more expensive than the ones from Vietnam. Robes, bells and wooden fish, sandals, are all better from Taiwan. There is a store across from Quán Sứ Pagoda that sells items from Taiwan. It is very expensive, but it is always crowded with customers. People can see the difference. The quality of the

fabric for the robes is much better. Everyone will know, so the person really enjoys it and feels very refined.

Women who are especially devout start to show this devotion outside of the pagoda as well, not only as a matter of identity, but also as a way to display their commitment. A number of women I knew made a point of wearing monastic-like brown loose shirts when they were in a Buddhist context (such as going to the pagoda or meeting friends who were Buddhist). Others wore prayer beads around their neck or wrist as Buddhist accessories. Others used Buddhist bags instead of purses.

Other objects are also important for making statements of inclusion, but take on particular importance for competitive behavior within the group. *Lộc* often seem to be involved in performances of piety and devotion and are built into the process of pilgrimage. For example, at major religious sites *lộc* in the form of plastic necklaces (usually with an image of Guanyin and the name of the site) are often bought and worn and can sometimes be seen hung in prominent places in homes afterwards. On the pilgrimage I mentioned in Chapter 6, one of the stops was at Quang Hoa Pagoda, near Lenin Park, south of Hoàn Kiếm Lake in Hanoi. After people had finished praying in front of the altar, some were handed pieces of cardboard on which were printed ten objects of meditation. When others became aware that Buddhist items from the pagoda were being given out, there was a rush by the others to get one. A number of them shouted, "Give me one! I don't have one yet!" Those who did not receive one grumbled about their deprivation. The person who was accompanying me remarked that they would probably never read them anyway. It seemed that it was not the information that was printed on the cardboard that was viewed as valuable, but that the object itself had significance. Hence, the women around me described it as *lộc*. As *lộc*, it was a gift from the buddhas, and would bring benefit. At the same time, *lộc* in this instance was a marker that they had been on this trip, that is, a souvenir, and therefore became an object of competition.

On another group pilgrimage, after we had visited the Temple of the Lady of the Storehouse, a woman insisted on giving me money (*lộc*) in order to bring me good luck. She did it with great show, handing it to me with an explanation given in a loud voice at the front of the bus when all eyes were on her. Her act appeared to be intended to bring attention to her generosity.

Other objects that create distinction are altars, which the very devout will sometimes undertake to build in their homes. While it is fairly standard to have a small Buddhist statue or image in the home, some altars are much bigger, often featuring multiple statues of different Buddhist figures. If a person has a home altar, he or she is usually eager to show it to anyone perceived as sympathetic to Buddhism; sometimes they brag about the cost or quality of the statues. This happened on a few occasions when I was invited to the homes of old women whose involvement in Buddhism was central to their identity. Within a few minutes of entering their house they had taken me to their altar room in order to show me both the beauty of their altar and the depth of their devotion, usually seeking praise by asking me whether or not I thought it beautiful. One woman described an office mate who always boasted in this way:

> Everyone wants to show off their altars. An older colleague of mine also worships the Buddha and she always talks about how well she does it with all of the most expensive things. For example her statues have to come from a certain place, and be made from certain materials, for example made from stone or jade or amethyst from Thailand—which is so precious—not made of ceramic like the ones from Vietnam. I buy them out of normal ceramic, but she buys ones made from jade or amethyst. She says, "I worship very carefully, with the very best sandalwood incense." Every morning she chants sutras, the Sutras for Daily Use, and every night she does rituals and gives special offerings. Her wooden fish is made from jackfruit wood. The meaning is that everything is very precious and special and refined. Expensive things...For example, to buy ordinary pomelos [for offerings] are about 10,000 *đồng* [around US$0.50], but she always buys special ones that are expensive in Vietnam 50,000 to 70,000 *đồng* [US$2.50 to US$3.50], depending on the season. Five to seven times more expensive than the regular ones! Or she buys "Buddha's hand fruit," which is also an expensive fruit—a few hundred thousand *đồng* for a big one, and the fruit can last long. Flowers are the same, lilies and orchids, these expensive kinds of flowers which are very fragrant. She always tells me about this. All these religious people like to talk about it—to brag.

On occasion these altars occupy entire rooms. People who have constructed larger altars often use them as drawing points to form smaller groups who meet to chant sutras more frequently than recitals are held at the pagoda. Thus, building a larger altar room could be used as the basis for claiming leadership of a subgroup of the pagoda community. As with clothes, objects (whether *lộc*, altars, prayer beads, or Buddhist bags) are intended to indicate depth of commitment to Buddhism and to mark a person as devout.

THE PROFIT OF CONSPICUOUS DEVOTION

If conspicuous devotion cannot be correctly viewed as wasting resources, what are the reasons for undertaking these performances? While status within the communal house could bring real political power within the village context, the advantage gained through status within the pagoda is not as apparent. However, as with Veblen's "conspicuous consumption," it is not productive to see conspicuous devotion as frivolous behavior. Women do not attempt to distinguish themselves as devout (or even more devout relative to others) for no reason. There is merit in pointing to the *habitus* of hierarchy in Vietnamese society as having an influence on competitive behavior in the pagoda. That is, Vietnamese in general have an embodied disposition towards the establishment of hierarchies that carries over into the supposedly egalitarian space of the Buddhist pagoda. This disposition is displayed, taught, and reinforced through language and other embodied dispositions.

This *habitus* is inevitably one factor, but there is more to conspicuous devotion. Within the Buddhist field, performances of conspicuous devotion also have the potential for generating symbolic capital. This Bourdieuian notion dovetails with the Vietnamese concept of "face" (*mặt*), most simply translated as public recognition of status. The concept of *mặt* in Vietnam is not significantly different from the Chinese concept of *mianzi*. Mayfair Yang describes *mianzi* as a "combination of a sense of moral imperatives, social honor, and self respect" (1994, 141). Kipnis additionally notes that if someone has "face" it confers respect on the individual, but equally importantly it gives respect to the family, and aids in constructing intrafamily relationships and hierarchies (1997, 43). Thus, *mianzi* not only involves the individual and his or her interactions with others, but also ties those interactions to the reputation of the corporate identity of the family.

Jamieson, who calls the concern for face in Vietnam a "deep-seated" desire to "gain prestige and to have it publicly acknowledged," also brings out the corporate nature of face, and the way that it acts on the family and community as a whole. He stresses that public scrutiny and concern of the opinion for others in the community were driving factors that impelled a basic system of wealth redistribution at the village level (Jamieson 1993, 32–33). The closed nature of the village does not apply completely to the situation in urban Hanoi, but the general principle still holds: families care about public opinion and are privately willing to sacrifice a great deal in order to put forward a public display of prosperity and generosity and avoid anything that would detract from their reputation. In fact, people usually mention face only in the context of losing it (*mất mặt*), whereas people speak more positively of status (*địa vị*) or prestige (*sĩ diện*).

All of these concepts are closely related to the prominent concern for public opinion (*dư luận*), which amounts to expectations placed on individuals by society. The importance of public opinion was explained to me this way: "For example, if I was the director of a company, public opinion would dictate that I would have to drive a nice vehicle, wear brand named clothes. I couldn't use common things. If a company director went around on an ordinary motorcycle or wore Chinese clothes and common things like that, public opinion would say that this is no director but someone without purpose." For instance, a young woman who has not married and is approaching the age of thirty is particularly concerned because of the public perception her unmarried status will give. Or, if a woman is married but has no children, she can fall victim to gossip by neighbors who attribute barrenness not only to medical conditions, but also to the moral state of the family. Lack of children thereby becomes of great concern due to public opinion.

Face and public opinion are major concerns for everyone who I know in Hanoi, who go to great lengths to avoid public approbation and improve the reputation of themselves and their families. The pressure of the public gaze, or the perception of it, has two effects. The first is that it acts as a censure against inappropriate behavior such as premarital sex, public displays of hostility, or stinginess. Second, public opinion also promotes positively valued behavior, such as sponsoring lavish public events, performing acts of generosity, and maintaining strict politeness.

The system implies that there is a critical audience, and indeed there is. Within a community (whether it is a group of students, a village, a neighborhood, the extended family, or a community centered on a pagoda), people are extremely attentive to the actions of others and quick both to judge and to gossip about perceived indiscretions. For example, people can be very critical of events such as weddings and pay particular attention to the finer details, such as the quality and quantity of dishes served at the banquet.[6]

In many ways women appear more concerned with respectability and appearances than men do. They spend a great deal of time and enormous amounts of energy working out how to present themselves and their families in public situations. This can be seen, for example, in wedding gifts of money (the standard wedding gift in Vietnam). The correct amount to give in each situation is carefully calculated, because the amount is an indication of a number of factors, including generosity and closeness of relations. On the one hand, too little money may indicate either that you do not believe the relationship is a close one or that you are stingy; on the other hand, too much money can also be inappropriate, and can be taken as showing off. Also, the ensuing debt (to be repaid at a later time) may cause resentment rather than goodwill (O'Harrow 1995, 174). Thus, wedding gifts serve as markers and are therefore extremely important to the reputation of the family. I have witnessed deliberations regarding the amount to give as a wedding gift on a number of occasions, and each time I was struck by the fact that women were much more involved in the calculations than were men.

At one wedding that I attended, I learned that the mother of the bride had been insistent that the wedding be large. The father, more pragmatically, had said that it was not affordable and wanted it instead to be within their means. In the end, the mother prevailed and the wedding was more lavish than the family could afford. In another instance, this time a funeral, the old women of the family were the ones that insisted that the grown children of their dead mother carry the coffin in the traditional manner. They claimed that to not do it in the traditional manner would be a loss of face. Despite their reluctance to do so, the male children eventually agreed.

Women are particularly sensitive to the intricacies of public opinion, primarily because of the close connection between women's identity and the family. When the family is well respected, the benefits of that respect are shared by women—who are more usually in contact with everyday gossip and feel public approbation more immediately. Men, in some sense, can rise above the problems of the family and can stand alone as honorable people who are well regarded, despite inappropriate behavior of their wives (for example, being too gossipy or stingy). Women are more tied to their families, however, and to their husbands' prestige as they are seen as the bearers of responsibility for creating a "happy family." They also are more prone to bragging about their sons' successes or their grandchildren's intelligence or beauty. Thus, while men are usually publicly active, their strivings are more often geared towards personal prestige, whereas there is a level at which women are constantly maneuvering in this public realm, trying to improve the standing of the family in the community. This sensitivity produces a *habitus* of sensitivity to matters relating to public opinion that crosses over into the Buddhist field.

For women whose Buddhist practice is their principal and consuming public activity, performances of devotion are done out of a desire for peer recognition within the pagoda field. Through these performances of conspicuous devotion they aspire to be viewed as moral beings who have status based on their level of religious commitment. For those who volunteer, become leaders in the pagoda association, organize pilgrimages, take a leading role in organizing festivals and feasts, or make large donations that are publicly displayed or boasted about, there is often a strong desire to be seen as a good Buddhist and to be recognized as important by their peers.

Thus, Veblen's view that conspicuous consumption should not be viewed as a waste of resources holds true—perceivable profit can indeed be obtained from such practices. Likewise, when viewing conspicuous performances of devotion, one could presume that the effort is not wasted and that there is an anticipation of profit. The profit comes in the form of social recognition and prestige within the pagoda community. Recognition within the field does not necessarily give authority in the same way that men can have authority, but it nonetheless gives status among peers (i.e., other women). The immediate profit, in a social sense, is actually quite limited, giving only acceptance among the group and status relative to other women in the group, rather than command over the entire field. The profit is, furthermore, convertible into other fields to only a minor degree. Being regarded as a pious and moral person will improve overall reputation in the wider community, but it will not bring political power. It may bring recognition and *ơn* (moral debts) in children, and to a lesser extent husbands, but prestige in the pagoda community does not significantly affect women's position in the family, for the overall gender structure serves to limit avenues of power for women in Vietnamese society.

To outsiders, the performances that are intended to give status within the Buddhist field are usually given no value, or perhaps even given negative value, because they are commonly viewed as self-serving displays, or showing off, going against the supposed intent of religious practice. Men, even those few who are active Buddhists, view these performances cynically, using them as evidence that women are ignorant of the teachings of Buddhism. Furthermore, even within the field, prestige is contingent on the persuasiveness of the performance. While some women in the Buddhist groups were more active and some were regarded as good Buddhists, others were condemned if it was perceived that their performances went too far. So, for example, one middle-aged woman described the following:

> The woman that lives across from us—her name is Mrs. Nhân and she is a friend of my mother—she often brags to my mother and tells her about what she is doing, but many times my mother said to me, "My god, I can't believe anything she says!" So many times Mrs. Nhân said, "In a few days I will be going to Bái Đính [an important pagoda in Ninh Bình Province]," for example, and "I am the group leader and I have a close relationship with the monk there and he is very fond of me. When we organized a ritual in

that pagoda the monk organized a ritual unveiling of a new statue and he gave me a lot of things [i.e., ritual items as *lộc*]," and she went on and on. But my mother just laughed—she didn't believe her. The woman said that the monk who organized the ritual gave her the old coins [that are flipped in pairs to determine responses from the gods and buddhas], the red fabric that covered the statue, and she also got a lot of the *lộc*. Her meaning was that she is very special, that is why she was given the special items that had the power of the buddhas. So then my mom asked where these objects were and the woman said, "I have put it away already." Because of this, my mom said she doesn't believe. Mrs. Nhân wants to show that the monk really likes her because she is so special. And Mrs. Nhân also comes to tell my mom, "I know this important man, I met that important man" and so on and so forth, and I also don't believe. In general, these old women really like to talk about themselves in this way with each other. Each of them wants to have prestige: "I am the best. I am the 'number one'!"

Another time she described an interaction between her mother and her mother's friend:

She bragged to my mother and I overheard, "That monk just came back from India and gave me a dried bodhi leaf. He brought it back from India, from the land of the Buddha. It is so precious." My mother replied, "Where? Let me see." And she said she would show her, but she never did. She was just boasting. This woman is always acting like this. After that, there was a monk who gave her some *lộc* money or some other small small ritual items and she really liked it. She right away went to tell everyone about it.

Sometimes their activities can get them into positions where they can have some real power. Such is the case with Mrs. Bình. One woman described her power in this way: "They know that Mrs. Bình is a show off, but because Mrs. Bình continues to be involved with Quán Sứ Pagoda and she is still the leader of a group of the pagoda association there, so sometimes she can arrange for them to go and meet a big group of monks. And if they didn't have a relationship with her then they wouldn't be able to go. They wouldn't get the information." Others, however, are not always so successful. Such was the case in this story that was related to me of a pagoda outside of Hanoi where I knew the monk and some people that are close to him:

In the past there was a woman named Mrs. Yến. She was the group leader of the pagoda association there before the monk, Thầy Trí, took over the pagoda. With the previous monk she was the group leader. She was in charge of a lot of things at the pagoda, and conducted some particular rituals. For other rituals, she formed the group and directed people. The previous monk let her do these things and make the decisions. When Thầy Trí took over that pagoda, he made the decisions and chose a few other women to take care of various tasks with her, and so he divided up the responsibilities. For example, this person go to the market, that person buy the ritual items, that person buy the food for the feast, this one prepare money for the ritual, that person call people for meetings. Thầy Trí divided up the responsibilities to make sure no one woman had all of the power. And Mrs. Yến was very angry and didn't like Thầy Trí any more. She hated the women who Thầy Trí gave responsibilities to, and she started to spread rumors. She said, "That monk is not good at all. He likes to drink alcohol a lot and speaks nonsense. He isn't a good monk at all." And she went to all of the neighbors to tell them all about how bad he is. And in the end Thầy Trí didn't let her be the leader anymore, but he didn't do it overtly: he told the other women, "Now you should have a meeting and vote for another leader, but vote for the other woman, don't vote for Mrs. Yến." And all of the women had a meeting and said that they needed to vote for a new leader. So Mrs. Yến was not elected and this made her even angrier. She spoke badly to everyone in the community. Now she says, "I am not going to that pagoda anymore! On the ritual days I won't go anymore. I don't need Thầy Trí to do the rituals, I can do them myself." And she does the spirit possession rituals by herself. The rest of the women who you met were the ones that Thầy Trí suggested take over. The women there say that Mrs. Yến is not good because she spreads rumors, all kinds of stories. Old women often say bad things about each other. It is very funny!

In another example that Mrs. Tu related to me, the power of Mrs. Bình was challenged and defended:

Mrs. Bình speaks badly, but in general she isn't a bad person. But there is something about her that doesn't sit well with everyone, which can lead to problems. For example, when Mrs. Trang was required to contribute money she said, "It's a lot!" By this she was referring to how the expected contribution had increased. Mrs. Bình explained that it was the same for everyone. Mrs. Trang replied, "So if we have to give more, does it mean Buddha's price has gone up?" It's true, that is what she said! Then Mrs. Bình said to me, "Mrs. Trang is saying bad things. Who dares to speak like that?!" And Mrs. Bình then went around telling other people how bad Mrs. Trang is. She told a lot of people. With a lot of things if you don't make Mrs. Bình happy she will do that kind of thing to you.

CONCLUSION

The nonhierarchical aspect of Buddhism in Vietnam that has been stressed by authors such as Hickey and Jamieson, especially when juxtaposed with the male structure of the communal house, does not provide an adequate understanding of the dynamics at work within the field. The communal house is regarded as the seat of village hierarchy par excellence, and by comparison the pagoda is egalitarian and relatively undifferentiated; nevertheless, status competition still exists in a more subtle form. That is, competition in the pagoda has a different logic, but nonetheless there are struggles over the capital that will command access to the profits of the field. The most obvious asymmetry of power and status in the pagoda is between men and women and is manifested most tangibly through seating arrangements, with men inevitably sitting in front of women. As I have shown, there is a more subtle form of competition that transpires through the conspicuous performances of devotion. These performances ultimately seek status through recognition in the pagoda community.

The presence of uniforms, symbols on the walls of houses, and other markers of conspicuous devotion are not only markers of inclusion, but also markers of distinction. There was a performative aspect to people's practice that indicated that their individual identity was embroiled in public recognition of their Buddhist piety. While it would be incorrect to view conspicuous devotion as a conscious attempt to gain capital in the Buddhist field, this aspect is frequently present.

The impulse to identify Buddhist activity with overall views of the self causes women to be increasingly engaged, as it does for a few men, as will be discussed in the next two chapters. It also leads to increased efforts by those women to be seen as Buddhist. However, the measure of worth is not personal satisfaction as much as it is public recognition. Thus, in a sense the anticipation of profit for performances of conspicuous devotion have as much to do with public affirmation for the sake of giving meaning to lives than it does for the acquisition of naked power.

8   Interpretive Distinctions

Mr. Trung was born in the late 1920s, and describes his life as having been difficult. He never really knew his father, who died when Mr. Trung was four years old. He was the youngest of six children, and was moved around quite a bit, living for periods with various members of his mother's family. At a young age he joined the revolution to fight against the French and spent some time in a notorious prison, the "Maison Centrale," which is called Hỏa Lò by the Vietnamese and "Hanoi Hilton" by American POWs who were later imprisoned there. He proudly told me that his name and picture remain on exhibit today in the museum that replaced the prison, along with those of others who had been imprisoned there. He says that he was an undercover agent, receiving orders from a handler for a variety of covert tasks, but he was unable to discuss the exact details of what he did because it remained secret. After liberation, he continued to work for the government, still doing undercover work that, again, he was unable to describe. By his account, he had been very successful with the tasks that his handlers gave to him and he received recognition, a monthly pension, and other benefits from the government for his effort. Every year the government pays for a vacation for him and other former undercover agents (which I understood is a reunion of sorts), though he told me that in recent years it has been reduced from ten days to five.

He started to become more interested in Buddhism as he grew older, though at first he only went to the pagoda on occasions when he returned to his home village, and he kept it secret from the people in Hanoi where he lived (presumably to avoid being labelled as "superstitious" by his peers—a descriptor that would have impeded his career). When he retired at the age of fifty-five, the age established by state policy at that time, he believed that he wanted to contribute something to society, so he focused his efforts on learning more about Buddhism. He lived close to Phúc Lộc Pagoda, and he used to stop by occasionally, especially on the death anniversary of the nun who had resided there. On one occasion he saw that there was a neglected palanquin, used for carrying the spirit of the pagoda during festivals, sitting on the ground. He went to the current nun to ask why such a precious object was not being better treated. He then volunteered to clean it up and put it on a proper stand for storage. Later the nun asked him to help with the organization of some feasts and he gradually became more involved. Then he started to study more about how to do rituals (*cúng*). After the Renovation, when the pagoda was being restored, he was part of a Buddhist study group and the people in the neighborhood elected him and one other (Mr. Lê, described in Chapter 9) to lead the reorganization of the pagoda. They believed that it was important that the proper rituals be performed at a pagoda, so he invited an old ritual master to teach him and Mr. Lê how to conduct the rituals. He studied several years with the old ritual master before the master became too old and had to return to his home village. When I first met Mr. Trung in 1997 he was the head of the ritual group (*ban cúng*) and was busily teaching other older men how to perform the rituals. When I last met him in 2010, he had moved some distance from the pagoda, but still returned (one hour by bicycle) to perform rituals on the first and fifteenth of every lunar month and on other important ritual days.

As described in Chapter 3, young men often deride religion. In doing so, they tend not to differentiate between various aspects and activities, labelling all religious practice as superstition. One young man who had come from a village close to Hanoi in order to get a job in construction summed it up when he told me, "It's all a bunch of superstition." Devotional practices that involve making offerings and praying for material benefits are seen by many men as signifying weakness and dependency, and are antithetical to the hegemonic masculine ideal. Thus, young men, who are most actively engaged in the reproduction of this kind of masculinity, avoid religious practice altogether, taking a stance of skepticism instead. They joke about women being superstitious, but regard superstition as an inevitable aspect of women's nature. The practices that are most targeted by these masculine performances of skepticism, are especially practices that supplicate the supernatural for material benefit, and those that are particularly associated with women.

Men, therefore, avoid such religious activities and are instead more actively engaged in ancestor worship. Older men, in particular, are the main actors in communal house rituals. However, aside from these two sanctioned religious activities, which have always been closely connected to male power, the formulation of masculinity in relation to religiosity makes participation for most men problematic. The presence of those who choose to engage in Buddhism is particularly anomalous because of the feminine characterization of the Buddhist pagoda. Nonetheless, and despite their incongruence, some old men are still present in Buddhist spaces and even take on central roles. Buddhist monks dominate the formal institution and are most prominent at major public rituals and male practitioners are usually found in the front of the altar, leading rituals. The male authority of the monastic institution, in particular, was clearly visible at the funeral of a prominent monk that I attended in 2004. The most notable monks in the region sat stoically drinking tea directly in front of the pagoda's monastic "ancestor" altar (the position of honor where special guests are usually received), whereas the throngs of lay Buddhists (mostly women) stood cheek by jowl in the courtyard.[1] There were also some nuns present, but even the most senior nuns were seated in an inferior position, off to the side of the ancestor altar and the monks.

The presence of men in the feminine pagoda space brings into question how older men engage with Buddhism as lay Buddhists without compromising their sense of self as masculine beings. It is clear that most men who identify themselves as Buddhist do not see themselves as engaging in feminine behavior. Instead, they rephrase their practice so that it adds to, rather than detracts from, their sense of selves as masculine. Masculinity is also redefined in ways that no longer stress strength and self-reliance as in the masculinity of young skeptics. Instead, the masculinity of older men stresses self-cultivation (*tu thân*), casting Buddhism in a way that is much more amenable with their gender projects.

RETIREMENT AND THE REPHRASING OF MASCULINITY

Old men sometimes denigrate certain practices considered superstitious, but the discrimination between religious and superstitious practices becomes more nuanced as they age. Age permits them to express interest or even sympathy with religious practice, though it may not prompt them to actively participate. Some will become actively involved with Buddhist practice but, generally speaking, men continue to look down on beliefs and practices in which women are typically engaged.

There is also some official sanction for religious participation today that opens an opportunity for older men to become more involved. Religious practice is now often linked to nationalist concerns to preserve an "authentic" Vietnamese culture that many fear is being overwhelmed by western-inspired materialism. Old people told me of their concern that Vietnamese tradition and culture were in danger of being lost. The youth are perceived as the weak link in the defense of Vietnamese tradition against Western cultural encroachment, purportedly because they are losing values such as filial piety and public responsibility, and these values are being replaced by crass materialism. Most old men, even those who have never been religious and who continue to maintain a lifestyle removed from religious spaces, speak favorably of the connection between religion and Vietnamese tradition in certain contexts.

Despite the problems that Buddhist practice poses to masculine identities, there clearly remain compelling motivations for becoming involved in Buddhist life. Religion addresses many of the same kinds of concerns for aging men that were mentioned for aging women in Chapter 6. Death is no less a frightening prospect for men than it is for women, and becoming more engaged in Buddhism may be one way to address this anxiety by more actively influencing what happens after death. Although never directly expressed to me, the way that reincarnation is formulated necessarily implicates questions of morality, and morality was frequently expressed by men as a motivation for starting to take part in Buddhism.

Comparable to the way that many women become more active when family duties are reduced, retirement provides the opportunity and time for men with the inclination to become more involved in religious activities. From a social perspective, Thanh Tùng points out that with retirement comes a deprivation of many markers central to masculine identities, such as salary, honors, privileges, access to informal sources of income (e.g., bribes), and the feelings of power that these markers accord (Thanh Tùng 1998, 41). With retirement, especially in urban areas, men's usefulness tends to diminish. A few of the men I knew at Phúc Lộc Pagoda had previously held positions that had some prestige, but retirement essentially stripped them of that crucial component in their self-identity. Public life was also drastically curtailed, and if they stayed at home, many were recruited to take care of grandchildren.

Boredom is also an important impetus for finding avenues in a new public life. One of the attractions of Buddhism for retired men stems from the fact that there are few activities available in urban Hanoi once the demands of a career cease. Old men can be seen stretching, running, playing badminton, and doing Tai Chi under the trees. The music and the slow-count that drives the Tai Chi groups can be heard remotely throughout Hanoi. The elderly's participation in early-morning exercises is so common that it has been called a "mass movement among the old," which "not only allows a good intellectual, physical and social activity [sic], but also remedies or relieves many infections: asthma, high blood pressure, nervous breakdown, chronic colitis, rheumatism, etc." (Nguyễn Khắc Viện 1998, 94).

With a few exceptions, such as the state-controlled Elderly Association (Hội Cao Tuổi, which organizes events for retired citizens) and morning exercise groups, however, there are few opportunities to meet the needs of old men. Religious practice of one kind or another is one of the few options. It can start to be an appealing alternative to isolation at home, and is consequently no longer avoided as it is by young men, as in the case of Mr. Trung. Men who go to pagodas are drawn by the sense of community that can be gained through friendship with the other men there and they consequently group together to form internal subgroups within the pagodas. The pagoda becomes a viable option for some as a way to reconnect socially and provide these men with an activity that, for many, is completely new and has some challenges. For some, the prestige of the workplace can even be recreated within the pagoda by setting themselves up as experts and taking on leadership roles. Thus, involvement can bring some limited benefit and prestige of a different kind. Mr. Trung, for example, felt proud about the recognition that his knowledge brought within the pagoda:

> So, since I started following Buddhism, everywhere I go people are very nice to me. For example, when I visit my home village people call out to me, people know me, and that makes me very happy. When I go there the monk and the people at the pagoda really value me, welcome me, and ask about my family, and I can sit and talk to them right away about Buddhism. When I go back to the village and talk about Buddhism a lot of people listen to me, even though I am not really very special and don't really know that much … though I do know some things: I know about real life and I know how Buddhism relates to actual experience, so people really enjoy listening to me.

However, in order to make Buddhist practice acceptable, the feminine associations first need to be neutralized. This is done by making distinctions with women's practices by avoiding some practices and rephrasing others, so as to avoid the connotations of dependency and superstition. Instead of accentuating the benefit that Buddhist practice brings to the family, men tend to stress self-cultivation as being central to their practice.

Whereas women's Buddhist practices are emphasized as being devotional and emotional, men's practices are described as being intellectual, philosophical, moralistic, and emotionally detached. Whereas women see their practice as being an extension of their role as family caregiver and the goal as usually bringing materialistic and immediate benefit to their lives, men never drew any relationship between their Buddhist practice and the welfare of their family in conversations with me. Men instead viewed their practice as involving self-cultivation without the help of the buddhas. The life of quiet retreat is an ideal commonly associated with old age for men who find the image of a contemplative life dedicated to self-cultivation compelling.

I knew a man in 1997 who was about to retire, who expressed sympathetic views towards Buddhism to me. He was thoughtful and soft-spoken. He had never been religious, although his wife was very active in Buddhism, and one of his daughters regularly went to pagodas, especially to wish for success in exams. He was not entirely pleased with this, particularly if it replaced study as a means for her to succeed. He once defined superstition as being different from religion because the latter contained a moral element, indicating a view that was more measured and thoughtful than most antireligious rhetoric. He told me that he would not mind living in a monastery when he grew older because it would be a peaceful life. His interest in living in a pagoda was not due to feelings of devotion to the buddhas and bodhisattvas. Rather, he was attracted to the quiet of a contemplative life associated with Buddhist monasticism. When he said this, he contrasted the monastic life with his active life in the world, where he was plagued by worries about his family and finances. This ideal of self-cultivation has connotations that reach across the different aspects of religion in Vietnam.[2] In many ways, this ideal of masculinity replaces the masculinity of youth that focuses on strength and self-confidence.

The individualistic practice of Buddhism that is valued by men is perhaps one of the reasons that Zen is valued as the main tradition of Vietnam.[3] While Zen receives prominence, however, and is claimed as the central tradition to Vietnamese Buddhism by internationally recognized monastic figures such as Thích Thiên Ân, Thích Nhất Hạnh, and Thích Thanh Từ, the reality is that few Vietnamese Buddhists practice meditation. Nonetheless, the Zen archetype, whose practices accentuate personal experience, self-reliance, and cultivation, resonates with notions of masculinity that avoid devotional reliance on the supernatural. It, therefore, is perpetuated at a rhetorical level by the masculine academy and institutional Buddhist organization, and by associated figures with both of these who write about the Buddhist tradition in Vietnam. In Thích Thanh Từ's (1992) book *Zen Masters of Vietnam* (*Thiền Sư Việt Nam*), four of the one-hundred and forty-one entries describe female monastics.[4] Thích Đồng Bổn (1995) has edited a work entitled *Biography of Vietnamese Monks of the 20th Century*, Volume I (*Tiểu Sử Danh Tăng Việt Nam Thế Kỷ XX, Tập 1*) that excludes nuns completely. I do not know of any books devoted solely to the biographies of nuns. Virtually all notable Buddhist figures in Vietnam are male, and are described as Zen masters. The written record stresses elite, male, orthodox practice, while ignoring that the vast majority of regular devotees who sustain the monastic institution are, and appear always to have been, women. In fact, it would be fair to say that women are entirely responsible for Buddhism's continued existence in Vietnam, as the main participants and donors. Nor is this only a twentieth century trend: during the

Nguyễn dynasty, it was often queens who sponsored the constructions of pagodas in the Huế area.[5]

This attempt by men to distinguish their Buddhist practice from women's is part of a general discourse of masculine practice by which men, as a group, gain ascendancy over women. This is not to say that the pagoda is a primary site for the reproduction of a particular vision of masculinity, or that the pagoda is a critical site for the subordination of women. Rather, the pagoda is one space in which we can see the processes and reproduction of gender-based power relations, both mirroring broader patterns and contributing to male hegemony in Vietnamese society. Within this field, men attain cultural capital through particular performances of male-based knowledge. At the same time, this cultural capital is in some ways convertible across different fields. Men, as a whole, benefit from being regarded as more intellectual, rational, and in control of their emotions than women. Although Buddhist practice may contribute to the production and naturalization of this belief (at both an individual and a general level), the symbolic capital gained in the pagoda has the most value within the boundaries of the religious field. These dynamics will be made clearer below.

MALE REPHRASING OF PRACTICE: THE PENITENCE RITUAL

I have heard many descriptions of men as having a more rational and intelligent nature than women, though exceptions were recognized. It was, for example, stated in this way in explaining to me why higher positions in government, the academy, and business are usually held by men. Men's ascendency was further described by some as being derived from the karmic results of past lives. Men are understood as being higher in the hierarchy of possible reincarnations and are consequently seen by many as having greater intellectual capacity. The product and evidence of this intelligence is manifest in knowledge, particularly of abstract philosophical ideas, such as those found in Buddhism. The following statement by Mr. Trung underscores the belief that women are not equal to men when it comes to higher religious and philosophical ability: "Today there are more nuns than monks [in Vietnamese Buddhism]. Now this might be a little bit sexist, but by my understanding if there are a lot of monks Buddhism then develops, but if there are too many nuns then Buddhism declines." The association of intellectual capacity with being a man is a critical determinant of the way that men engage in Buddhism. This expected higher capacity for knowledge is performed as part of the masculine *habitus*, both demonstrating maleness and providing de facto justification of gendered assumptions. Women's lack of performative capacity, on the other hand, is taken as evidence of their lower karmic status. Assumptions of gendered capacity have a formative effect that simultaneously encourages (and creates expectations of) male performances of knowledge, and discourages the same in women. This, then, has a strong effect on the way that women and men practice and interpret their practices, and can be clearly seen in the very different ways that they approach the act of chanting sutras.

There are a variety of interpretations as to the effect and goal of chanting sutras. Whereas some chant sutras purely as a devotional act with the aim of enlisting the help of the Buddhist pantheon, others believe that there is a philosophical and moral value, and that reciting is, therefore, not an end unto itself. After you leave the pagoda you must actively try to be a better person. There is a notable division in the benefit that is perceived to come from participation in this activity. There are some (mostly women) who are quick to mention that their participation will ensure a better future for their families, and especially their children, but most men would also mention that chanting is primarily done for moral and spiritual betterment of the individual practitioner. Men believe that chanting will not bring more immediate, material, benefit and should be done for self-cultivation in a purely individual way. An example of this belief is the way that men interpret the penitence ritual called the Sám Nguyện.

At most pagodas in Hanoi, the group of lay Buddhists gathers four times every lunar month in the sutra hall to perform the penitence ritual. It is always performed and led by the laity, with resident monastics of the pagoda playing a limited role. The group that takes part in sutra recitals is cohesive and has a sense of shared purpose. It is a group of devoted Buddhists, made up mostly of older women. The time and day of the penitence ritual remains constant, and most people who participate do so regularly. Though there is someone who leads the recital, there is no official rank given to distinguish people who have achieved "levels." During the year and a half when I regularly attended the event at Phúc Lộc Pagoda it was led by laymen who formed "the ritual group" (*ban cúng*). Men always sat in front of the altar and women sat behind them, with the oldest women usually sitting closer to the front. The men who led the ritual at Phúc Lộc Pagoda generally waited in the reception area sipping tea and talking until it was time to start, whereas the women sat in the main shrine room, perhaps to ensure a good seat. When the time arrived, the men got up, put on their brown robes, and entered the shrine room.

Though the Sám Nguyện is a ritual of penitence, there is no opportunity provided for people to think specifically about their past actions (for example, in the form of a reflective silence). Nor is there an opportunity for people to pray individually or to speak about their moral infractions. It is formally structured and emphasizes the group rather than the individual. Although there are other rituals performed throughout the year, and the monastics of a pagoda are supposed to chant sutras in the main shrine room several times every day, the penitence ritual is one of the principal rituals performed regularly by the laity. At Phúc Lộc Pagoda, the men also get together on the first and fifteenth of the lunar month to perform a specialized ritual called *cúng*, and then chant sutras—the Medicine Buddha Sutra (Kinh Dược Sư, dedicated to Bhaiṣajyaguru) on the first and the Universal Door Sutra (Kinh Phổ Môn, dedicated to Quan Âm Bodhisattva) on the fifteenth. However, these male-led rituals are done separately, mostly without women attending, and before the penitence ritual in which the lay women participate.

Opportunity is created for reinterpreting the significance of the penitence ritual because of the lack of systematic explanation as to its meaning and purpose. The stress is instead on the performance itself, resulting in a wide variety of understandings regarding what it will achieve. These range from a doctrinal understanding of karma as being purely causal and salvation coming through personal effort, to a totally devotional stance of reliance on the buddhas or bodhisattvas for any spiritual gain. Closely related to these two interpretative stances is the issue of what the practitioner is actually supposed to be doing.

At one end of the spectrum of interpretative possibilities is the notion that the performance of the penitence ritual is sufficient to absolve the performer of their transgressions. An example of this interpretation was given to me by a sixty-seven-year-old woman: "In our life everyone is put in the position where they transgress [*tội lỗi*], so you have to repent [*sám hối*] in order to get the pardon [*xá*] of the Buddha."[6] Thầy Tâm, the nun at Phúc Lộc Pagoda, agrees that the Buddha has the capacity to give atonement: "Everyday you are in a bad environment, and it makes you say bad things. When you go to the pagoda, you have to talk to the Buddha [Thích Ca Mâu Ni Phật] because the other buddhas are just the followers of the Buddha. Therefore, you need to ask his pardon." Others expressed a more mixed view, saying that participation in the penitence ritual needed to be accompanied by efforts to curtail future immoral behavior. One woman who was around fifty years old expressed it in this way: "Penitence is, for example, if today you did something wrong, not right with someone, and you feel uncomfortable, and you repent to the Buddha to get release for your heart, and next time you will do better."

In all of these opinions there is a sense that individual action is not sufficient for correcting bad karma and that the Buddha needs to intervene on behalf of the supplicant. This view differs dramatically from the interpretation that men gave me, stating that the penitence ritual is merely a tool to focus one's mind on one's behavior. For men, therefore, the penitence ritual must be accompanied by moral action, and it is this nonritual action that has sole significance. Penitence alone would have no effect on one's life and future rebirths. The men who held this conceptualization condemned the view that the performance of the penitence ritual is an end unto itself, or that the Buddha could have any effect on a person's life, as superstitious. This is seen, for example, in Mr. Trung's explanation of how taking part in the penitence ritual affects his life: "When I go to repent I think of what I did wrong and thereby build trust with my family. Then I go home and feel very peaceful, relaxed and happy—when I see my children and grandchildren I don't feel guilty or uncomfortable at all. I can see that my repentance is very useful. So if I don't repent, when I come home I feel very troubled and uncomfortable and easy to get upset with other people in the family and involve the whole family in my bad feelings." In the explanation from one monk about the purpose of chanting sutras there is also a denial of the Buddha intervening in one's karmic path:

> During the recitation, your mouth may chant but you must also focus your mind. Why do we have sutras? Because the Buddha taught us, and when he attained nirvana, his follower—Ananda, also called Đức Thánh Hiền—collected all of the utterances of the Buddha and it became the sutras. When we chant we should think about the meaning. For example, the Buddha said if you do meritorious actions you will get good things, and if you do wicked things, you will get the consequence. This is to make us scared to no longer do those bad things. That is why we chant.

INTERPRETATIONS OF CAUSALITY

The interpretive spectrum of the penitence ritual points to very different views of the nature of karma and whether the Buddha is able to assist in changing one's present and one's future. The views of the women who believe that participating in the penitence ritual will result in the Buddha absolving the participant's transgressions moves away from the doctrinal Buddhist formulations of karma that is reflected in men's interpretations of the penitence ritual. In the doctrinal view of karma, an individual remains culpable for his or her actions because of the inevitable consequences of cause and effect. Emotional attachment to actions produces karma, which in turn influences future rebirths. All karma, by this definition, is bad in the sense that it propels someone from one rebirth to the next, while the formal goal of Buddhism is to escape the cycle of rebirth entirely.[7] Enlightenment is recognized as a process that may take many lifetimes, so, through moral cultivation, the hope is that in the next life one will be born in a better position to achieve this goal.

It should not be presumed that this doctrinal position is held by everyone. As mentioned, while some participants believe that the Buddha can absolve the devotee from bad karma, others think of it more as an opportunity to reflect on past actions and as a launching pad for future self-improvement. However, it must be noted that in neither case is there an idea of sin in the Christian sense. Especially by those who hold the latter interpretation, karma is thought of as being produced through one's actions in a causal manner. According to my informants, immoral actions are not "against" the Buddha, but instead produce bad results.[8]

In the interpretation of the effect of the penitence ritual that holds that the Buddha has the power to absolve someone of his or her sins and improve his or her fortune, karma is not held to be eradicated so much as turned to one's favor. Spiro proposed in the context of Theravada Buddhist practice in Burma that there are in fact different kinds of Buddhism that had divergent goals, rather than presuming that Buddhism was monolithic. In the Buddhism most popularly practiced by lay Buddhists, which he called Kammatic Buddhism, the goal of people was to work towards a better life by improving their karma through good acts, rather than striving for enlightenment (called Nibbānic Buddhism) (Spiro 1982, 114–139).[9] In Vietnam, most Buddhists are also striving for a goal similar to the goal of Kammatic Buddhists in that they are ultimately concerned with karma. Where it differs is that it is more common for women to speak about the merit accrued from chanting sutras as having the immediate effect of causing good luck, rather than concentrating on future rebirths. For these people, the motivation for participating in the penitence ritual was not significantly different from making offerings and distributing *lộc*. Women believed that their participation would have the effect of aiding their own and their families' lives in an immediate and material way.

When interlifetime understandings of karma were brought up (by both men and women), it was usually as a passing explanation for the sufferings of life or in reference to women's lower karmic birth. This suggestion came mostly from women as an explanation for why women went to pagodas more often than did men, saying it was out of necessity because they have a heavier karmic burden. At Quán Sứ Pagoda, one informant, a woman in her late forties, explained, "The Buddha taught people how to behave morally, to have manners. In short, women have a heavier karmic burden than men [*nặng nghiệp hơn*], therefore they have to go to the pagoda to repent [*sám hối*].... This karma is from the former life, from very long ago; many lives. Now they have a very heavy fate [*số nặng*].[10] Now they have to pay."

This construction of gender places women on a lower position in cosmological conceptions, but is also a justification for women having fewer privileges in this world. This same point—of women being karmically disadvantaged, or owing a moral debt as evidenced by their birth—crept into discussions with others as well. A woman at Phúc Lộc Pagoda in her sixties told me, "Women usually go to pagodas to get rid of bad karma, and men don't." When I asked another, older, woman why there were more women than men at the pagoda, she replied, "Because women are the ones in the family who have a heavy fate."[11]

Another divergence in the way that causality is understood is regarding whether merit accrued from good actions can be transferred between people. Some informants have explained to me that participation in the penitence ritual not only affects the individual participant by lightening their karmic burden, but will also bring luck to the participants and their families. This represents another important distinction between men's and women's perceptions of the objectives of performing the penitence ritual. Whereas men stress self-cultivation, women often stress that performing the penitence ritual enlists the assistance of the Buddha on behalf of the entire family in order to bring them all good luck. This notion was expressed by Mrs. Phương, a woman in her early fifties:

Me: After you have confessed you don't have to worry about going to hell any longer, is that right?

Mrs. Phương: Of course your fault or mistake is only partly released, and you will still go to hell, but the punishment will be less. If people do good things they will feel very happy and good. And those good things will bring luck and virtue to the mother's children.

Thus, in this case the performance of the penitence ritual is understood much in the same terms as is the distribution of *lộc*. Here too, the generation of sentiment and the creation of *ơn* (moral debt) in the family remains an important impetus to religious practice. This requires a fairly radical divergence from the Buddhist doctrine of causality, which is usually adhered to more closely by men than by women. In making these different claims regarding the actual effect of the penitence ritual, men are conforming and women diverging from doctrinal Buddhist ideology, but both are closely following the gendered expectations in Vietnamese society.

THE IMPORTANCE OF COMPREHENSION

Closely related to the discussion of whether or not the buddhas and bodhisattvas could intervene in the karmic process is a disagreement on whether or not comprehension was a necessary correlate to practice in the recitation of sutras. This is an especially important issue in Vietnam, because sutras are usually written in very formal and archaic Sino-Vietnamese, though they are then transcribed in the modern Romanized script. This allows practitioners to make the correct sounds regardless of whether they understand the meaning. The archaic Sino-Vietnamese is almost entirely incomprehensible for the average Vietnamese today, and so comprehension requires purposeful action independent from recitation. Either a practitioner has to seek out and read the sutra in translation (available for only some sutras), or to make the effort to study Sino-Vietnamese.

When I asked participating women whether meaning was important, the answers generally stressed the physical performance, and placed little value on comprehension. One forty-four-year-old female accountant summed up the opinion of most women when she told me, "If you can understand [the sutras], then it is good, but if you can't then never mind." Thảo, the young professional, stressed the performative aspect above all:

Me: When you chant sutras, is it important if you understand?
Thảo: Not very. If you don't, you just follow exactly, but you have to read very carefully, and if you say something wrong—make a mistake—you will be punished.
Me: So you have to be very careful when you read it?
Thảo: But not for people who don't know that. [For them] it is no problem, but for people like me, I know that if I read something wrong I will be punished, so I have to be careful. But for other people who don't know [they will be punished], no problem. They will not be punished in the afterlife because they don't know that, but for people who know [they will be punished], they have to take care.

A woman in her late sixties expressed a similar lack of interest in the sutras' meanings, saying that you get benefit from its recitation, not from understanding its meaning. By contrast, men stressed comprehension as essential when chanting sutras. One fifty-year-old retired man said, "In my opinion only by understanding Buddhist sutras and philosophy can you love the Buddha and be a Buddhist according to the Buddha's teachings." An old man who is considered by all in Phúc

Lộc Pagoda to be an expert in ritual, Mr. Lê, holds a similar opinion: "The most important thing is to understand the sutras, which is even more important than reciting them. Chanting sutras without understanding is like the sutras steering you. If you understand them then you are in control. Chanting sutras like a parrot doesn't do anything at all. Understanding, however, is essential." On another occasion Mr. Lê, Thầy Tâm, and I had the following conversation:

> Thầy Tâm: [Speaking to Mr. Lê] Alec asks why you often come to the pagoda and talk about the Buddha's sutras but never recite them yourself. Is that right? You say you don't chant sutras but you study them and understand them, and that is better than the people who recite them but don't understand anything.
>
> Mr. Lê: First, I follow the teachings of Buddhism. It isn't only when I became old that I started to pay attention to the Buddha's teachings. All of my life I haven't done anything wicked, I haven't done anything ugly, double-faced or dishonest. *That* is following the Buddha. I have always followed the Buddha in this way. So then, chanting sutras is in a way the repetition for the sake of respectfulness. And what is a sutra but the summary of [the Buddha's] speeches.... It is done this way to enable people to understand and remember.

Thus, despite the fact that Mr. Lê was considered to be the expert (something to which I will return in Chapter 9), he himself did not chant sutras.

Similarly, Mr. Toàn was seventy-two-years old when I met him in 2010. He came to Phúc Lộc Pagoda only on important days, but did not involve himself in chanting sutras or in rituals. He told me that he did not have a "fated attraction" (*duyên*) for such things.[12] He considered himself Buddhist, and as his main practice read books about Buddhism. He told me that it was more important to understand sutras than to recite them. Another old man at Phúc Lộc Pagoda recognized that most people would not be able to understand the sutras, and that, for them, reciting was sufficient: "For monastics, it is essential to recite and understand the sutras, but for ordinary people it isn't important. If they can [recite them], it is good enough." Nonetheless, when asked specifically about his practice, he emphasized that he believed that comprehension was very important.

While almost every man would give explanations of the penitence ritual that were intended to sound erudite, and men tended to conform more closely than women with doctrinal Buddhist conceptions, the stress on understanding was not exclusively found with the men. A few women also voiced it in similar ways. Thầy Tâm, for example, told me, "It is important that if you chant sutras you understand them. If you recite like a parrot, then you return to doing bad things."

There are some notable points that arise out of this range of opinions. The first is that men generally believe that comprehension is important, while women are mixed in their opinions. For men, the intellectual component is particularly prominent in reference to their own practices, though they typically concede that different people are at different levels and so recitation without comprehension is better than nothing. The implication is that chanting sutras is particularly appropriate as a practice for women in their view, whether or not it is accompanied by efforts to understand the content. Thus, there seems to be a double standard expressed by men that emphasizes the importance of understanding for men only, while saying that recitation alone is a lower practice that is suitable for women. The outcome of this is that the image of women as intellectually inferior is subtly perpetuated. Most women, for their part, did not challenge this interpretation and would instead either totally accept the view that recitation is sufficient, or concede that comprehension is desirable but not essential. Only a very few would join Thầy Tâm in saying that comprehension was crucial.

ABSOLUTION OR SELF-IMPROVEMENT

In examining these wide interpretive variations there are a number of points that must be taken into account. The perceived motivations and processes are divided between the desire for absolution and transcendental grace, most commonly by women, and self-cultivation and inner strength, most commonly by men. These two views align with the performative expectations of femininity and masculinity. As with the practices associated with *lộc*, it is considered to be unmanly to ask for help or to rely on others, in either this world or the supernatural realm.

Women are, as we have seen, both expected and taught to be weak. This emphasized femininity not only is manifested in images and expectations of feminine behavior at large in Vietnamese society, but also affects women's approach to the supernatural, as seen in interpretations of the goals of the penitence ritual that stress the Buddha's absolution. For men who are practicing Buddhists, the dependence expressed in this view of the penitence ritual directly conflicts with constructions of masculinity. Therefore, men choose a language of individualism, inner strength, and self-reliance to phrase their practice (Soucy 1999, 2000).

The different interpretations stem from distinct social positions. Men's social relations are based on prestige as measured by individual achievement.

Thus, men are judged by their position in society, which depends on such things as education and occupation. They are measured against yardsticks of knowledge and virtue (often expressed as generosity); their position in society largely relies on these yardsticks, and on social recognition gained through their performance. This leads to a *habitus* of individual striving that resonates well with the view of religious practice being closely related to an individualistic self-cultivation. The male interpretation of the penitence ritual as being primarily an exercise in self-reflection that must be followed by moral action, reinforces a view of masculinity that stresses individual effort and steers well clear of interpretations of religious practice as reliance on the Buddhist supernatural.

Women, on the hand, are judged, and judge themselves, according to entirely different criteria, often not on their own merit but on their family's: if they come from a good family, what their husbands are like, if their children are successful, if they have sons to continue the patrilineage, if they have been successful in creating "happy families" (Gammeltoft 1999, 217). In the Taiwanese rural family described by Margery Wolf, women are largely outside of the patriarchal structure and therefore build a "uterine family" based on the family that they have borne rather than the one to which they only ever marginally belong through marriage (M. Wolf, 1968, 1972). Wolf attributes many tensions within the family, including household schisms and difficulties between mothers and daughters-in-law, to the structural dynamics created by the uterine family. In Hanoi, women's lives are directed more towards families and less towards careers because of the same inducements to form a uterine family. Although severance with the natal family is nowhere near as complete as described by Wolf of Taiwan at the time of her research, nonetheless, wives often still take up residence with the husband's family in Hanoi, and have essentially the same difficulties with mothers-in-law. This has the effect of women resting more of their identity and energy with their children than with their husbands.

The social position of women is at the root of women's particular understandings of the gains achieved by performing the penitence ritual. Women's stress on the benefits that their performances of the penitence ritual would have on their whole families reflects a view of women's identity as being tightly tied to the family. Karma is no longer the consequence of individual action, but has become both collective and transferable. For example, people spoke to me about being affected by the karma of their ancestors. One woman told me, "Having a heavy karmic burden is the reason behind misfortune. This burden is from a previous life, or often from the bad actions of your ancestors." Another young married woman spoke of bad karma as being transferable:

If a married woman doesn't get pregnant after around a year, the neighbors from around her husband's home will start to say that she or her family must have done something bad in a previous life. They will start to say really mean things about her and her family. My friend has been married for a long time already. She is very nice, but she has no children. So her mother-in-law and the neighbors of her husband's family say that there must be a problem with her or her parents for her to have this trouble. Her family must be a bad, immoral family. You know, there is an expression: "A poison tree has no fruit, an evil woman has no child" [*cây độc không trái, gái độc không con*].

This interpretation reflects the realities of women's social worlds much more closely than does the authoritative, orthodox individualism that constitutes the social realities of men. Women did not usually speak to me of apprehensions about retribution in hell, which I had expected to be an important motivation for increased religiosity in older women when I started research on the topic. Instead, they tied their fate to their families. Their expressed motivations for participation were focused on concern for their children and on the hope for family prosperity. Older women are freed from many of the burdens of housework, but their care and aspirations to create the "happy family" lead to an increased focus on enlisting the help of the supernatural.

As we have seen in Chapter 6, one of the concerns of old women is that their children care for them properly after their deaths. This arises from their structural insecurity in the patrilineage that makes the uterine family—children and grandchildren—of particular concern. Thus, the emphasis on the mother as the creator of the happy family continues to be reiterated until the very end of women's lives, and often is intensified as death approaches and concerns regarding the treatment they will receive from their children become paramount.

Men, on the other hand, approach Buddhism in a way that strongly resonates with Confucian ideals of self-cultivation, which in turn underlie the masculine ethos of individual effort and achievement. Thus, the penitence ritual for men does not involve atonement from the Buddha, but instead stresses that it is part of a process for correcting one's own behavior. Views of karma emphasize the necessity of this process. By stressing this interpretation they are in conformity with both doctrinal Buddhism and the state discourse on superstition. We thus see a convergence between masculine ways of being and these dominant discourses, which creates a distinctly separate mode of practicing and of understanding practice. The notable divergence between interpretations should not be seen as women's misapprehension of Buddhism and men's superior understanding, but rather as reflecting very different concerns and needs. It should not be surprising that Buddhist and state institutions, and the language and symbols they control (i.e., orthodoxy), reflect a masculine view of religious practice. Nor should it be surprising that the male view is placed in a preeminent position, given the overall hegemonic structure of gender in Vietnam.

However, this does not mean that there is any need for men to force women to adopt their religious views. In fact, the gender structure is actually strengthened by maintaining these distinctions between practices and interpretations to a much greater degree than if women were compelled to adopt a male, orthodox, understanding through more rigorous indoctrination. By women continuing to stress dependence on the Buddha's grace, and by both men and women describing women as holding these "inferior" views, the expectations perpetuated by the gender structure are met and reinforced.

CONCLUSION

Chanting sutras is a core activity at the pagoda. Although the vast majority of Buddhists in Vietnam do not chant sutras, all, even those who do not chant, regard chanting as essential. In fact, for the most part chanting sutras is considered the definitive activity of the Buddhist pagoda. Nonetheless, there is wide variance in participation. It is only those who are considered most devout that take part in this activity. These devotees are mostly old women, though there are a few old men who also take part in the rituals. However, they do so with a very different understanding of what their practice represents and what it achieves.

Men tend to hold a more authoritative, doctrinal stance about the reasons for chanting sutras that places an emphasis on individualism. Men's interpretation of the penitence ritual is aligned with a more doctrinal understanding of karma when they claim that participation in the ritual is significant only in that it provides the opportunity for change through self-cultivation. Women, on the other hand, see their religious practice as reverberating throughout their social relationships. They stress the assistance and blessings that the Buddha gives, and say that penitence can get rid of their sins through his grace and that their participation brings benefit to their whole family.

Thus, there is a significant difference that cleaves along gender lines. Other sociological variables, such as wealth or education level, do not appear to be as important a determinant on these views. Men who participated in Buddhist activities—whether their background was as a laborer, a spy, or a company director—expressed similar opinions, though they may not have articulated them in the same way. The overall education of women that I encountered at pagodas tended to be lower (though not universally so), but, regardless of education level, women nonetheless tended to assert that the welfare of their families was a prime motivation for their religious activities.

By ignoring the understanding that women have of their practice, the significance of participation cannot be fully understood. On the other hand, we ignore motivations for men's orthodoxy at our peril, for they cannot be taken as any less grounded in social realities then women's, though they are, on the surface, in greater conformity with authoritative understandings of Buddhist doctrines on karma. Religious practice can hold very different meanings for different people, and the explanations given fit into larger discourses that arise from the position of the speaker as embroiled in the struggles of life. Thus, while no Vietnamese Buddhist I know would dispute the orthodox stance, many women place greater emphasis on concerns that are more immediate to them: their position as women in Vietnam and their roles as caretakers of their families.

The labels of orthodoxy and heterodoxy reflect a hegemonic discourse that fuels the reluctance of individuals to express the ways that they conceptualize the symbolic meanings of their practice. By claiming authority, men achieve status vis-à-vis women within the field, which both draws on and extends into a wider societal power imbalance. However, although there is a differentiation and hierarchization between men's and women's practice as subgroups within the field, there is also competition within these subgroups. For women, this competition often takes the form of conspicuous devotion. For men, it is often involved with performing knowledge and self-cultivation—a subject to which we now turn.

9 Language, Orthodoxy, and Performances of Authority

In the bright summer morning, a group of old Vietnamese men and women chatted quietly in the courtyard of Phúc Lộc Pagoda. The air hung with moisture as usual, but the oppressive sun had not yet stolen away the cooler morning air. Outside the pagoda gates the fury of market activity and the signature bustle of Hanoi's pedestrian traffic and honking motorcycles had been under way for hours. Inside the courtyard, however, was an oasis where birds sang in bamboo cages that hung from the branches of a starfruit tree. The group of elders formed into loose ranks for their morning Tai Chi exercise. The leader, Mr. Lê, turned on the tape recorder and a male voice started calling out the positions while tranquil music played in the background, signalling the start of their morning ritual and of a new day.

I first met Mr. Lê while doing research in 1997–1998. At that time, he was seventy-nine years old and a long-retired former director of a state-owned construction company. His leisurely days started every morning by leading the Tai Chi group in the front courtyard of the pagoda. Most participants in the group described their activity as a form of exercise and were not inclined to ruminate on any deeper significance. Mr. Lê, however, would point out the metaphysical meanings behind the practice as trying to balance the *yin* and *yang* within his body, and would describe the significance of each of the postures.

He enjoyed speaking, and rarely did I need to ask more than one question before he would go into a monologue that could last as long as an hour. He was often so engaged in his discourse that his cigarette would burn itself out from neglect, virtually untouched. Many times he needed no prompting in order to commence orating about aspects of Vietnamese tradition, history, philosophy, or religion.

He had earned high status among not only the Tai Chi group, but also the whole community centered on the pagoda because of his phenomenal memory and ability to speak authoritatively on a variety of topics, but especially about Buddhism. He spoke French quite well and when explaining something, would often pepper his speech with French words or sentences in a display of his erudition. He would do this especially with me, but would sometimes use French words even if the person he was addressing spoke only Vietnamese. When speaking to me about Buddhism he often used Sanskrit Buddhist terms in addition to his French vocabulary. Even more important for his prestige was his knowledge of Chinese characters. The first time we met, someone sitting near him pointed out his virtuosity to me by making specific reference to his ability to explain the Chinese inscriptions in the pagoda. Responding to this cue, he started to explain the meaning of the inscription on the pillar behind me using the Sino-Vietnamese pronunciation.[1] This first speech was to be our introduction and henceforth I often would wander by the pagoda in the early morning so that I could sit and listen to him as the group sat on the floor of the great hall and drank tea while taking a break between their sessions of Tai Chi.

The people in the group would stop and listen intently to what he was saying. He was not interrupted, and allowed to speak at length on whatever subject he thought would benefit me. He responded to this attention by directing his lectures not only to me, but also to everyone in the group. He was not only an informer feeding information to the anthropologist, but also a performer, lecturing the whole group about the glories of Vietnamese tradition and Buddhist philosophy. So, when he used French, Sanskrit, or Sino-Vietnamese he would immediately provide a vernacular Vietnamese translation and an explanation for my sake as well as for the others who spoke only Vietnamese.

He also wrote booklets and distributed them to members of the pagoda community. At the feast for the saint at Phúc Lộc Pagoda in 2010, after the ritual was concluded, one of the women who was part of the community (but who never chanted sutras) sang to the saint (*chầu văn*: a kind of ritual music extolling the virtues of the god and usually used in spirit possession rituals). The history that her singing recanted came from a booklet that had been written by Mr. Lê in 1992. A few weeks later, when I went to meet Mr. Trung to interview him about his practice as a member of the ritual group, he brought me another booklet that he and Mr. Lê had written. It was a photocopied booklet that had been written by hand and titled, *Tam Giáo Đồng Nguyên: Phật—Lão—Khổng* (Three religions from the same source: Buddhism, Daoism, and Confucianism).

Mr. Lê was a key informant in the classic anthropological sense, as the person in the community who thought and studied about Buddhism and Vietnamese traditions, could speak eloquently about these subjects, and to whom people would turn as an authority. He had answers to my questions (though often formulaic as if they had been taken straight from a book) when most people struggled to articulate assumptions that were usually unspoken and unquestioned. His knowledge and proclivity to explicate would have been a boon if my interests lay in uncovering symbolic systems according to orthodox Vietnamese Buddhist discourses. Instead, it was sometimes an impediment to my desire to obtain a range of opinions, though it was nonetheless illustrative of the power and authority that his knowledge accorded him in the community. One old woman insisted virtually every time I met her that I should go to his house and speak with him. People would even provide me with questions to ask him. On one occasion another old woman helpfully took my notebook and wrote down a question that she believed I should ask Mr. Lê next time we met, telling me that it was something important that I should know. Apparently, she believed herself unqualified to tell me about it herself.

Phúc Lộc Pagoda's one nun stood in sharp contrast to Mr. Lê. Thầy Tâm was not, by self-admission, a very authoritative nor particularly knowledgeable woman, although she was charming, got on well with everyone, and competently managed the affairs of the pagoda. She studied Chinese characters in order to be able to chant sutras as a requirement of office, but she was more intent on learning the pronunciations for practical purposes than for reasons of translation or comprehension of the sutras. She confided to me in 2005 that she doubted she would ever be able to learn to read the Chinese characters beyond the level of liturgical functionality, or to understand their meaning, and by 2010 she no longer studied at all. Even she, the resident monastic of the pagoda, would send me to Mr. Lê to find out the meaning of specific rituals and symbols. On one occasion when I asked the meaning of a ritual dedicated to Bhaiṣajyaguru Buddha that she had performed the day before, she told me that I should go to ask Mr. Lê.

On another occasion I asked her the significance of some aspects of the ritual sequence of funerals. She started off by explaining to me the schedule of the different rituals that were performed in the days, months, and years following a death. However, for a deeper explanation, she suggested that I speak with Mr. Lê. At this point he happened to walk by and she persuaded him to sit and explain funerals to me, insisting that he was far more knowledgeable about the subject, despite the fact that it was she who actually performed the rituals.

Mr. Lê was very engaged in thinking, reading, and speaking about Buddhism, but his engagement did not mean that he was interested in participating in rituals. In fact, he resolutely avoided taking part in rituals and did not chant sutras either at home or at the pagoda. Despite his lack of participation, he described himself as a Buddhist, stating that his studies, lectures, and moral practices constituted his own form of religious practice. It was a practice that, far from leading to criticism for his lack of ritual participation, accorded him authority and status within the pagoda community.

The performative nature of Mr. Lê's religious practice is grounded in the constitution and marking of social identities. It is part of an ongoing identity project, the production of social capital, and assertions of legitimacy and authority. For the men like Mr. Lê, who undertake performances of knowledge, what is at stake is status recognition within the pagoda community and, correspondingly, a sense of self-worth and power within the field, which can become more significant with retirement and its attendant diminishment of access to power and prestige in the public realm. Religion can be described as a form of theatre—a theatre of constructing and displaying social identities (youth, old age, masculinity, femininity, authority, and so on).

The male performances of expertise are sometimes transparently inauthentic, but also can be powerfully persuasive. As a whole, they succeed in achieving their intended goal of creating authority, prestige, and status within the pagoda field vis-à-vis essentially all women, as well as other men whose performances are less convincing. These performances have an advantage in that they are already backed up by a gender structure that asserts that men are more intelligent and can achieve a deeper understanding than can women. They are successful in the sense that women accept the normative Buddhist understanding that these "experts" put forward as holding authority. Nonetheless, if the intention is to convert women to men's understanding, they should be seen as a near total failure: women continue engaging in the religious practices that resonate with their particular concerns and ascribe meanings that contribute to their own identity projects. The result is that the performances of authority are ambivalently recognized; authority is acknowledged but the message is almost entirely ignored as meaningless relative to the practices of women. For this reason, male performances of authority should not be understood as primarily aimed at winning over female listeners or readers to their understanding of Buddhism. Instead, it is the performance rather than the actual content of the discourse that is important.

MASCULINITY AND KNOWLEDGE AS PERFORMANCE

At Quán Sứ Pagoda, I was struck by the spatial division that seemed to coincide with modes of practice: the main sanctuary, the Research Institute, the lecture hall, and the library. I found that, as I made my way around the premises, there were certain people I met only in specific places. Many that I knew only by sight appeared exclusively in the main sanctuary during the penitence ritual. Others spent all their time in the Research Institute.

On occasion I made my way up to the office in Quán Sứ Pagoda that was in charge of publications. Out of this office emerged the quarterly magazine on Buddhism, *The Research Journal of Buddhist Studies*. Inside the office was a long meeting table that ran the length of the room. Against the far wall were three desks, for the man in charge of publications and for the two women who worked as his part-time assistants.

There were often men who would visit the journal's office, many of whom submitted articles regularly to the magazine. One man that I occasionally saw there was a former army colonel. When we first met, he presented me with a name card printed in English on one side and Vietnamese on the other. The English side read:

Tâm Tịch
COLONEL (RETIRED)
Senior Editor
Editorial Board of
VN ENCYCLOPEDIA
Journalist (since 1945)
Researcher on Buddhism

Colonel Tịch always made his way straight from the gate to the Research Institute, where he would have a cup of tea and talk with the people there. I never met him in any other location or saw him engaged in any other activity; he did not chant sutras, he did not go to the Sunday lectures, and he did not make offerings. He was a proud man with a friendly disposition and a good sense of humor. He would speak to me in French and English as well as Mandarin, and he made a point of showing me that he had written articles in the Buddhist magazine. The conversations we had were usually related to Vietnamese and Buddhist history.

His religious practice was focused on researching and writing about Buddhism, and was spatially situated in the Research Institute rather than the main sanctuary. Although he agreed that rituals need to be held in the pagoda, he made vague excuses for why he did not take part in them. Once he said that, on a personal level, it was more important to study and behave morally than it was to perform rituals or chant sutras. Not only was his practice scholarly rather than devotional, but also the space for that practice was entirely separate from the women who were chanting sutras in the main sanctuary.

In order to transform the feminizing Buddhist space into something that does not threaten their masculinity, older men such as Colonel Tịch draw on traditions rooted in the image of the Confucian literati that esteem scholarship as a supremely masculine activity. This scholarly gentleman ideal is the dominant form of masculinity guiding the behavior of old men. Hồ Chí Minh, for example, was given a Confucian image tempered with revolutionary zeal in the process of his mythologization. His hagiographies accentuate his Confucian background as the son of a principled scholar: "He was born in 1890 into a poor peasant scholar's family of Kimlien hamlet, Namlien village, Namdan district, Nghean province, a place with long-standing revolutionary traditions. His father was a Pho Bang [doctor of classical humanities], who out of patriotism had refused to collaborate with the French colonialists and Nguyen feudalists and lived in poverty" (Trường-Chinh 1966, 9).

Accounts of him point to a man who was simple in taste, kind (especially to children), and selflessly devoted to service of the nation. In fact, his image is reminiscent of the ideal Buddhist monastic life: he is pictured as frugal, chaste, peripatetic, virtually homeless, and eschewing luxuries. Even his eating was mindful of those who had worked to grow and prepare the food (Pham Van Dong 1990, 64).[2] However, while his lifestyle had a definite monastic character, it is the image of the Confucian scholar that is stressed; Nguyễn Khắc Viện wrote of him, "The most vivid example of a Confucian scholar who changed from one philosophy to the other is surely President Ho Chi Minh" (1974, 51); Pham Van Dong wrote, "Ho Chi Minh was a man who lived a life which consistently aimed for lofty ideals set from the start and was a man of ideals and these ideals materialised in him" (1990, 64); and Trường-Chinh wrote, "He has developed the traditional virtues of the East: intelligence, humanity and courage on a completely new basis" (1966, 60). In short, in order to create an image of Hồ Chí Minh that resonates with the highest ideal for older men, he is pictured as being rigorous in his efforts at personal self-cultivation in order to transform the nation. This behavior is the very essence of the Confucian scholar.

Education, and the idea that men (in relation to women) have superior intellectual ability, is one important means through which women as a group are subjugated to men. In conversations I had with a number of people, I asked whether they thought that men were more rational and therefore ought to make the most important decisions in the family. All men agreed that this was the case, and the majority of women agreed or were not sure. When I asked one young woman why so many women chose to get degrees in accounting instead of sciences, she explained, "Women are naturally good with money, but they aren't as intelligent as men when it comes to abstract thinking. That is why most men are scientists. It is the same for subjects like history or philosophy. Women are just better at practical things."

A higher education for women also affects their eligibility for marriage. One man told me that he did not want his wife to have a higher education, because it would only cause problems within the family. It is commonly believed in Hanoi that women with higher education will be at a disadvantage when it comes to finding a suitable marriage partner. One young woman who held a job in a joint venture company said to me, "If I have a daughter, I don't think I would want her to get a higher education. She should get a practical degree, but after she graduates she should find a job. If she studies to a higher level, she would have trouble finding a husband and it will be harder for their relationship to succeed. If a woman has education to the same level they won't be able to follow their husband because they will feel too equal. Women with high education are more stubborn, and that will cause trouble in their families."

Through constructions that make education more easily obtainable for men, as well as through performances of knowledge, an aura is created that men are wiser, more knowledgeable, and more intellectual. This, of course is not necessarily the case at all, but it is a fiction that is reified through male performances of knowledge and thereby made "real" in the sense that it is universally accepted. The performances of knowledge as a form of Buddhist practice draws on the image of men as being more knowledgeable and studious than women. For old men, this expectation takes the form of the Confucian ideal of self-cultivation as a prominent trope. The performances make the act of study and the possession of knowledge, indicated through speech acts and displays of ritual mastery that are designed to establish symbolic capital in the Buddhist field, a central focus of Buddhist engagement for these men.

LANGUAGE AND AUTHORITY

Language is used in a performative way to build symbolic capital in the Buddhist field and to transform it from a feminizing space. Actors, largely unconsciously, seek to maximize symbolic profits by anticipating acceptability, which determines the type of linguistic production by fixing "price" or "value" of the product, and leads people to be selective in their choices of language. With the appropriate cultural capital, they can choose to employ varying levels of language, add words or phrases from other languages (code switching), and make other choices that will maximize symbolic profit (Bourdieu 1991, 177). This could be seen, for example in a discussion I had with the caretaker at Quán Sứ Pagoda who found out I was from Canada and immediately exclaimed, "Are you from Canada!" (as a statement), in order to demonstrate that he knew English, though in fact he could say little else. Linguistic performances by men in pagodas include strategies similar to the caretaker's, the most prominent being utterances of foreign language as well as the employment of a specialized Buddhist vocabulary. In some cases, these utterances represent a true understanding of these languages and terms, as with Mr. Lê, but in most cases, their value is symbolic and the men who use them have no more than a superficial vocabulary that is employed in linguistic performances.

Using French, which has had special significance in Vietnam, is a common strategy. During the colonial period starting in 1859 and running to 1954, French supplanted Chinese as the language of power and became a new avenue for social mobility. At the end of the last century, "most educated Vietnamese assumed that Chinese or French, or both, were essential modes of 'higher' communication" (Marr 1981, 137). At the village level, French became an alternative avenue to local power. Luong describes how in Son Duong, northern Vietnam, this replacement was reflected in the ritualized seating at communal house feasts, with the highest level of seating being given both to Confucian scholars and to men who had attained the Franco-Vietnamese *certificat d'études élémentaires* (Luong 1992, 71).

French colonialism is a distant memory to most, and English now dominates as the foreign language of advancement, but French is still regarded as a more cultured language than English. Even young people I knew in Hanoi spoke of French as a more beautiful language, though its practical value had distinctly diminished relative to English. Older men recall their early education in French and would often try out a few words or phrases on me, usually in attempts to be recognized as knowledgeable.

The continued power of French in performances of authority was displayed at a small festival that I attended at Đình Thổ Khối just outside Hanoi in 1998. Two German friends, who were doing research on communal houses, had been invited to attend, and my wife and I tagged along. We arrived just as things were getting under way. When we walked through the gates, we (as foreign guests) were led over to a gentleman in his sixties or seventies. After ushering us to seats, he stood up in front of the four of us, surrounded by a crowd of locals, and pulled a neatly folded piece of paper out of his jacket pocket. He unfolded it, cleared his throat, and proceeded to read a very formal welcome speech to us in French. Afterwards, there were a number of other old men who approached us with pride, offering a smattering of half-remembered French greetings. These men clearly were leaders in the community that centered on the communal house, and these performances were not so much done for us as they were for their fellow villagers.

The use of French was part of a production of symbolic capital that, particularly because of the public nature of these utterances, built and reinforced status within their community.

Mr. Lê used French, Sino-Vietnamese, and a Sanskrit vocabulary when speaking, occasionally throwing in an English word as well. A typical discourse, given in Vietnamese with French interjections, went like this: "This 'virtue' can be understood as *âm* [*yin*]...So then *âm* is *tout ce qui est passive, froid, obscure, lunaire. Dương* [*yang*] is *tout ce qui est active, chaud, clair, solaire, masculine.* That is, *âm* is symbolic for things that are dark, cold, passive, and whatever pertains to the moon. *Dương* represents things that are positive, luminous, warm, and towards the sun and pertaining to things masculine. These two things the French translate as *les deux éléments,* but this is not correct. They should be called *les deux modalités cosmiques.*"[3]

It meant little whether these foreign words were understood by the people with whom Mr. Lê was speaking, because they were usually explained in Vietnamese, as in the passage above. Although I gave an example of French here, he would also use Sanskrit terms in his discussions, again providing translation and explanation for them to me and others who were listening. The use of foreign words in Vietnamese was an effective way to build symbolic capital, as seen in a comment once made about him by Thầy Tâm: "When you have the time you should come here or go to Mr. Lê's house. He also does research about the same thing as you and he is really excellent. He has a lot of very interesting books which he reads and remembers very well. He remembers everything that the books say from any passage. He is really clever—he even speaks French!"

French is often used by old men to display education more generally, but Chinese (written in Chinese characters, but spoken with the Vietnamese pronunciation [Sino-Vietnamese]) is ritually the most important language in Vietnam. The symbolic value of the Chinese written language cannot be understood separate from the ambivalent relationship between Vietnam and China. Although on the one hand China is feared and hated as the invading foreigner par excellence, Chinese culture has for millennia represented the pinnacle of human cultural achievement, and Vietnam has politically benefited in the region by borrowing important Chinese innovations, from currency and printing to centralized government. Classical Chinese was the dominant written language of court right up to the end of the Nguyễn Dynasty. It was regarded as the language of the learned, and it was only through knowledge of written Chinese that one was able to participate in the imperial examinations that were the only real avenues to power (Luong 1992, 228; Woodside 1971, 1988; see also Luong 1990, 92–93).

The importance of Chinese diminished considerably in importance since its replacement by French as the language of power during the colonial period, and then by the language policies of the twentieth century that used Vietnamese Romanized script for the assertion of a national identity (Marr 1981, chap. 4). Written Chinese has nonetheless continued to have symbolic importance in Vietnam as a language intimately connected to Vietnamese culture through art and architecture. Couplets and other inscriptions written in Chinese characters are prominent features of religious architecture of Vietnam. Even when inscriptions are in the modern Romanized letters, they are sometimes written in a calligraphy that intentionally mimics Chinese characters.

The continued symbolic importance of written Chinese is particularly evident in its ritual usage. All of the Vietnamese religious expressions (Buddhism, spirit cults, communal house rituals, and so on) make use of Chinese at some level. For example, at every sutra recital and ritual performance, there is a petition to the buddhas, called a *sớ*, that is read out loud with the Sino-Vietnamese pronunciation and then burned. Included on the petition are the names of the individuals in the group that performed the ritual, and the location of its performance. Although this petition can be written in regular Vietnamese, it is believed to be more efficacious when written in Chinese characters, as are charms that are written for such things as bringing good luck when writing examinations, to ward off bad luck, or to smooth out domestic problems that have supernatural causes. At important religious sites there are usually old men who can be paid to write both petitions as well as charms in Chinese. All ritual masters are able to write Chinese characters, and Buddhist monastics (especially monks) are also expected to be able to know Chinese characters. Spirit mediums in possession rituals will often parody the action of writing Chinese when possessed by the highest level (male) mandarin spirits.[4] The sutras commonly recited are also mostly in Sino-Vietnamese, but are written in the Romanized Vietnamese script. Thus, even when they can be read, the meanings of the sutras are not comprehensible to most people. The ritual use of Chinese characters takes on a value that transcends its communicative use, and becomes fetishized in such a way so as to be thought of as having superior efficacy.[5]

The complexity of learning to write Chinese characters, to recognize and understand them, and to pronounce them in Sino-Vietnamese means that these skills give anyone who has mastered this ritual language de facto authority and respect in the same way that mastery of written Chinese gave the literati status prior to French colonization times. Consequently, there is an opportunity for some to gain considerable capital by the study of Chinese. Because study such

Spirit medium possessed by a mandarin, feigning to write Chinese calligraphy

as this is generally thought to be better suited to men, these avenues of status become, in practice, shut to women. Old men frequently offered me explanations of pagoda and temple inscriptions as overt performances of their knowledge. By contrast, women never offered me an explanation of meaning for temple inscriptions. At Phúc Lộc Pagoda, the nun Thầy Tâm would perform the daily rituals. However, when important rituals required someone to read out the Chinese characters, a lay ritual specialist would be hired because of his specialized knowledge. So, because of the value of Chinese language for ritual, a layman would take precedence at the pagoda over the resident female monastic.

It was the ability to read Chinese and speak authoritatively about Buddhism that gave Mr. Lê status at Phúc Lộc Pagoda, rather than any ability to perform rituals, for he never took part in any rituals. He placed central importance on understanding the sutras, denying entirely the importance of recitation:

> Mr. Lê: Chanting sutras is good, but not important. Like myself chanting sutras, I understand them quite well but I never recite them.
>
> Me: If a person chants sutras but doesn't understand any of it, does it have any purpose or meaning?

Mr. Lê: The activity of chanting sutras and understanding them is the most important, but reciting without understanding also has small advantages.

Thầy Tâm: That's right There is still an advantage.

Mr. Lê: The meaning is like this: when I chant sutras my mind doesn't think of wicked things, my hands don't do wicked things and my mouth doesn't say wicked things any more. The idea is that the heart, speech, thought—all of them are virtuous. This is okay, but understanding the sutras is still better.

Thus, there is a denial of the most commonly held view of women, that chanting sutras will bring supernatural benefit. Mr. Lê openly admitted that he never recited sutras. However, he made a point of displaying his knowledge of their contents, and his ability to do so gave him status in the pagoda. His authority rested not only on the content of his pronouncements, but also on the form that they took, with formal language and the use of non-Vietnamese vocabulary.

The librarian at Quán Sứ Pagoda, Mr. Đức, similar to Mr. Lê, concentrated on studying and professing Buddhist orthodoxy, while neglecting the ritual aspects of Buddhism. Also similar to Mr. Lê, he would frequently use French, English, and Sanskrit words when describing Buddhist philosophy. He was passionate when he spoke to me about how to live a Buddhist life. He was orthodox in his understanding of Buddhism—perhaps more than any other person that I met in Hanoi. He was also very firm in his criticism of superstition and what one ought to do in order to be a Buddhist.

Mr. Đức never attended sutra-recital rituals. He preferred to stay with his books. For him, understanding the teachings of the Buddha was central to his Buddhist practice. He tended to look down on many who went to sutra recitals:

Mr. Đức: After you chant sutras you will feel joyful, you will promise to follow the Buddha forever. But there are some people who do it wrong. They hope that when they chant sutras they can wish for things like health, wealth, or success in business from the Buddha. This way of thinking is wrong.

Me: Do you think that most people do it correctly or not?

Mr. Đức: That depends on the level of enlightenment of each person. If their level of instruction is enough, then they are "cultured" (*có văn hóa*) and will be able to understand that you have to rely on yourself to gain enlightenment. Those who have only studied a little in the village think that reciting the sutras alone is enough to bring happiness.

Similar to Mr. Lê and Colonel Tịch, Mr. Đức described himself as Buddhist, but steadfastly declined to take part in the rituals. Instead, his practice focused on study and his authority rested on his performance of knowledge.

These performances of knowledge are grounded in the linguistic and behavioral *habitus* of Vietnamese men, and reproduce the appearance of men being more intellectual than women. It is useful to think of the male performance of knowledge in terms of what Erving Goffman (1959) has described as a "working consensus," which involves "not so much a real agreement as to what exists but rather a real agreement as to whose claims concerning what issues will be temporarily honored" (pp. 9–10).

The performance of knowledge by men needs to be understood as simultaneously resting on and reinforcing hegemonic gender structures. Nonetheless, these performances cannot be seen as always effective. Performances are evaluated, so that those with a greater competence may come to be recognized as authoritative (such as Mr. Lê's), but others are less convincing. I witnessed an example of a failed performance after a group of men had just performed a ritual for the main (non-Buddhist) spirit of the pagoda. The men were sitting in a circle, eating and drinking the leftover offerings that had been made to the spirit. At one point an old man asked me to pass him a plate and gave me a warm, "Merci, thank you" when I did so. In response, someone at the other side of the circle bluntly said, "You don't understand Western languages," and the first man fell silent. Countless times when sitting with Mr. Lê other men would try to offer up a piece of information, only to be dismissed as being incorrect or drowned out by Mr. Lê. These performances lacked persuasion and, therefore, were rejected outright. Less-persuasive performances nonetheless draw on the same views of gender and are propped up by those performances that are more successful. Although they may not result in authoritativeness, they nonetheless serve to achieve a higher position relative to women.

The success of Mr. Lê's performance relative to other men (and women) was clearly demonstrated at an annual feast at Phúc Lộc Pagoda in honor of the pagoda's monastic ancestors called Lễ Giỗ Tổ. Local Communist Party officials were given the first servings at the best table. They were joined by Mr. Lê as representative for the pagoda (rather than Thầy Tâm) and myself as a "foreign expert." All other men who had roles in pagoda rituals were served later at a separate table, followed by the crowds of women who ate together at tables that were placed on the ground rather than a raised platform, as were the men's tables.

In this context, knowledge is not as important as the performance of it. These performances are accepted as "natural" because they rest on established gender structures. Language becomes a crucial aspect for these performances and the consequent generation of symbolic capital that creates authority and hierarchy within the Buddhist space.

RITUAL SPECIALISTS

As we saw in the last chapter, although Mr. Lê, Colonel Tịch, and Mr. Đức avoid rituals entirely, not all men do. However, men and women tend to engage in the practice of chanting sutras in very different manners. As we saw in the last chapter, men describe chanting sutras in ways that distance themselves from the religious aspirations of women. Mr. Lê's emphasis on understanding rather than practice is also upheld by men who actually engage in chanting. These men insisted that chanting sutras is intended to be for self-development and to assist in learning Buddhist teachings through repetition, thereby nullifying feminine associations. At the same time, however, men do not simply follow along, but try to assume leadership roles in rituals in order to distance themselves from women's practice in a more demonstrative way.

In 1997–1998 at Phúc Lộc Pagoda, sutra recitals were held four times every month and were always led by men in conjunction with Thầy Tâm. The ritual group that led the weekly rituals with Thầy Tâm was made up entirely of male laity. In 2010, sutras were chanted only once or twice a lunar month, but the ritual group still met on the first and fifteenth to conduct their rituals before the performance of the penitence ritual. Every man who takes part in sutra recitals at the pagoda becomes a member of this group. Their role is to perform what they termed a "ritual" (cúng lễ) before the sutra-recital sessions and sometimes to lead the much larger group of women in the sutra recital. The cúng is a specific type of ritual that, as explained to me by a number of sources, is intended to invite the gods and buddhas to come and partake of the offerings that are made for them and to witness the sutra recital. In form, the ritual did not differ substantially from other sutra recitals other than that they were accompanied by percussion instruments and they were more intricate: the chanting alternates between different individuals and sections of the group and involves more complicated tonal shifts.[6] Certain sections are chanted by one of three leaders. The leader in the middle strikes the bowl-gong to indicate sections and transitions in the ritual and strikes the wooden fish (a hollowed-out wooden block) to keep time while chanting sutras. The leader on the left plays the large drum, and the leader on the right plays the small drum. Behind them are men who play other percussive instruments such as the cymbals and a brass plate that is hit with a stick. Some sections are chanted by one of two parts of the group, and sometimes by the entire group. The phrases of the sutra are timed in relation to the percussion accompaniment, involving concentration and counting out the beat in order to phrase correctly. Each section has a leader, who alternately performs on his own or with the group, making the recital even more complex. Thầy Tâm usually led the entire ritual, sitting front and center, counting the beat with the wooden fish and signaling transitions with the bowl-gong in 1997–1998, but by 2010 she was no longer participating in the *cúng*. Due to the complexity, the men who do it (all old, retired men) practiced two days every week, with the more knowledgeable teaching those who had more recently joined. The sutras from which they read are, notably, written in Chinese characters (though the Sino-Vietnamese is hand-written in the Romanized alphabet beside the characters by some in the group), unlike the regular liturgy used by women, which only has the Romanized writing.[7]

On certain occasions in 1997–1998 Thầy Tâm was not always able to lead the ritual—for example, if she was not present on that day for a special reason, such as if she was menstruating and therefore forbidden to enter the main sanctuary of the pagoda. In those cases, one of the leaders of the ritual group would take her place. The men who sat in the front and played the big and small drums had the highest status in the group by virtue of their superior knowledge and mastery of the liturgy and their virtuosity in performing the percussion accompaniment, one of whom was Mr. Trung. It is these leaders that acted as instructors for the whole group at the twice-weekly rehearsals.

The two rehearsals that took place every week to train for the ritual performance started at 8:00 in the morning and continued until 10:30.[8] They then resumed in the afternoon at 2:00 and continued until around 4:00. This time was spent partly on rehearsing the rhythms with the percussion instruments, partly on rehearsing the timing and pronunciation of the sutra, and partly on drinking tea and chatting.

The positions of leadership in this group are achieved by virtue of the individual's superior ability and knowledge. The hierarchy is not rigid, but is a recognition of authority and virtuosity. There are no formal ranks or insignia. The leaders are simply recognized as being more knowledgeable than the others and therefore assumed leadership.[9] Not surprisingly, they had participated longer than most others, but there were some men in the group who had virtually no sense of rhythm, and would never be able to achieve a high status in the group because of their lack of ability. These people, too, were tolerated and accepted in the group.

Only men may participate in the ritual group, for though Thầy Tâm would sometimes lead the ritual, she was not part of the ritual group. Exclusion of women is not so much prescribed as it is tacitly understood. No woman ever complained to me about the fact that only men are in the group. Nor were there any opportunities for men to feel obliged to refuse women's participation. When I asked about this, people responded that women were not excluded, but that it was not really their place to participate. One man said that it was because women are too busy taking care of their houses, which was more an expression of stereotype than a statement about this specific practice. Others stated that it was simply something that only men did. Part of the reason for the exclusion of women was the notion that women were not fit or somehow unable to study the required procedures. It is not for reasons of pollution, but simply an attributed "naturalness" to the way that things are.

By joining this group, the old men are transformed into ritual specialists. Regardless of the level of competence, all men who take part in sutra recitals also take part in rituals and are members of the ritual group. They sit at the front and most are given instruments to play. If there are not enough instruments to go around, the men take part in reciting without an instrument.

Not all of these participants are viewed equally, however. An important marker of performative competence is the ability to read Chinese characters without the use of Romanized prompts (though the Sino-Vietnamese passages could just as easily have been rendered fully in Romanized script). The ones who are able also play the most important instruments (the wooden fish and bell, and the drums) and sit at the front. Those who rely on Romanized script are always followers rather than leaders, sit at the back, and play the less-prestigious instruments (cymbals or the brass plate), or are not given any at all.

Nonetheless, relative to women, they all gain status by inclusion in this group. The ritual has higher standing because it is seen as being essential to the ritual life of the pagoda rather than for the benefit of the individual, as the penitence ritual is believed to be. Thus, members of the group become essential for the pagoda, whereas women are never seen as essential to the ritual life of the pagoda in the way that the men of the ritual group are. Furthermore, they are participating in study, through which they produce cultural capital that gives them authority within the pagoda. When they take part in regular sutra recitals (e.g., penitence ritual), they are the ones who sit closest to the front and lead the service.

When there are special rituals, men also play a prominent role beside the monastic. For example, I went to the Ritual for the Opening of Summer in 1998, which was sponsored on this occasion by a woman for her family. It is a seasonal ritual that is performed to ensure, on a general level, that the weather is good, crops are abundant and there are no epidemics. For the woman who sponsored the ritual, it was also meant to ensure a successful financial summer for her family's business. The greater part of the ritual was done by a male ritual master. When Thầy Tâm was required to recite a particular portion, the ritual master sat beside her and cued her when she stumbled over the pronunciations of certain Chinese characters in the sutra.

Both the example of the ritual master and that of the ritual groups have in common that they require study or rehearsal, and therefore again draw on stereotypical views of men's capacity to study. The reason why men are seen as having the ability to perform ritual largely ties in with attitudes towards study. Consider the conversation I had with Thầy Tâm:

> Me: Thầy, how come yesterday there were only men practicing the drums, not women?
> Thầy Tâm: They are called the "ritual group." Of course, it is mainly men who do rituals. Seldom do women do them.
> Me: Why don't women also perform ritual?
> Thầy Tâm: Women usually don't study about ritual.
> Me: Women don't study about ritual? But if they study, can they do it?
> Thầy Tâm: If they studied they could also do it, but they don't study.
> Me: Why don't they study?
> Thầy Tâm: It's not our way.
> Me: What do you mean?
> Thầy Tâm: It isn't an activity for women.
> Me: Then why do you still study, and you are a woman?
> Thầy Tâm: Because monastics have to study. For example, at the many rituals, if there isn't anyone else, I have to perform the ritual, but if there are monks present, then we (nuns) don't have to do it.
> Me: What activities are for women, then?
> Thầy Tâm: Nuns only prepare offerings for feasts, and chant sutras, that's all. Rituals are for the monks. Nuns don't perform rituals.
> Me: But chanting sutras is also for men, right?
> Thầy Tâm: Chanting sutras is for everyone, performing rituals is something separate.

In a more abstract way, another monk also described women's exclusion as being a result of inherent qualities of women, though he also insisted that it was not because of intelligence:

Rarely do women do rituals because according to the laws of nature women have a heavy karmic burden [*nặng nghiệp*]. I don't know if overseas you have this custom or not, but in Vietnam it is thought that men have seven life forces [*vía*] women have nine. When they die women have only seven life forces. Because of this, rarely do women do rituals. You can say it is because of life forces or you can say it is because of their karmic burden. But it is not because women are less intelligent. Women have been queens—just think of the Two Trưng Sisters!

Thus, Thầy Tâm fulfilled her liturgical role, and saw her participation as necessary, but not ideal. She viewed her gender as a liability because, as she explained on another occasion, she believed that the fact that she was a woman stood in her way to properly understanding Chinese characters and being able to remember their pronunciations.

The idea that women are not intelligent enough to grasp the linguistic requirements for taking part in Buddhist rituals is undermined in practice by the fact that young women, more than young men, are gaining proficiency in modern foreign languages and are more commonly employed as interpreters and translators. Nonetheless, most older women who frequent pagodas have received a much lower level of education than men of the same age, making assumptions of male superiority in the field pass as realistic. These views are not directly challenged by women insisting on joining the ritual group. In fact, women do not feel the need to take part in the performance of rituals, as the underlying motivations for practice are very different from those of men who are actively Buddhist. The performances of women are based to a greater extent on a desire to show piety and concern for the family, whereas the performances of men are based on presenting sagacity and learning in a manner that reflects the valued image of a scholar and defeminizes the pagoda as a locus for male practice. Whereas all of the men at the pagoda (sitting front and center before the women during sutra recitals) try to give the appearance of knowledge of ritual language, the fact is that many can do no more than follow along, reading the Romanized transliterations of the characters that they handwrite next to each character, and understanding little. Nonetheless, within the Buddhist field there is an aura of difficulty around ritual language that lends the appearance of it being the domain of learned men, and in turn lends authority to the men who take part in the ritual group.

The linguistic and ritual presentations of older men allow for a reframing of masculinity in a way that moves away from the younger male image of self-reliance, strength, and material success, and towards an equally acceptable, and equally masculine, view of a retired gentleman-scholar. This is done not only through linguistic and ritual performances, but also by denying the validity of women's interpretations of their practices and replacing them with their own explanations that stress self-cultivation rather than devotion. Rather than being authoritative in their own right, scholarly activities and ritual mastery can be seen primarily as performances of authority that serve the particular goals of the men who are active in the pagoda.

CONCLUSION

The male religious practice of study is intimately connected with the building of symbolic capital through performances of knowledge. These performances are made valid through the use of language, ritual expertise, and overall manner. There is a tendency to deny female understandings of practice and to sublimate devotion in favor of a normative Buddhist stress on morality and philosophy. This interpretation resonates with contemporary internationalized forms of Buddhism that increasingly gained currency through the twentieth century. These performances of knowledge also include the production of religious texts and oratory about religious and cultural subjects.

This chapter has tried to bring to light some of the ways that authority is built up, especially by men, in Buddhist pagodas of northern Vietnam. The need for male lay Buddhist practitioners in northern Vietnam to be authoritative is grounded in their experience of masculinity, and in turn is a component in the overall production of gender hegemony. Men's performances of knowledge and authority in the pagodas of northern Vietnam are not only a product of the male *habitus*, but also are attempts at reconstruction of identity and an important precursor for men's participation in the Buddhist field.

There are many men who call themselves Buddhist, read books about Buddhism, but never attend sutra-recital rituals. It must be recognized that their study is not an abstract activity, unrelated to cultural production, especially in relation to gender and power. Study brings knowledge, and knowledge (or the appearance of knowledge) gives status to men in the pagoda community. The practices that are regarded as superstitious are those that do not conform to the orthodox views held by those who hold the greatest amount of symbolic capital. It is not surprising that this opinion often focuses on women and their motivations for Buddhist involvement as well as non-Buddhist religious practice in which women are primarily involved. One can say that men's practice is understood as being precisely not women's practice. At the core of the discourse on religion and superstition is an attempt by certain individuals to raise their status by showing that they possess superior (i.e., male) knowledge.

The few men who engage in Buddhist practice do so as men, with the orientation towards status seeking that masculinity entails. Status and hierarchy are not definitively part of pagoda practice, but are created through the *habitus* of those who practice. Thus, men join ritual groups to become specialists or they study to the exclusion of Buddhist ritual, not necessarily condemning it, but maintaining an unwillingness to engage in it. Through all of these practices, the way that language is used plays a key role in raising asymmetrical status out of what is arguably an essentially egalitarian religion.

Conclusion

The people introduced in these chapters expressed a range of possibilities for what it means to be Buddhist in Hanoi. Thảo, the young woman who considers herself to be a fervent Buddhist, neither meditates, recites sutras at the pagoda, nor reads extensively about Buddhist philosophy. Her primary religious activity is making offerings on the first and fifteenth of every lunar month, reclaiming them as *lộc,* and distributing them to her family. Mrs. Tu, also, is assiduous in making offerings on these days, but in addition she takes part in sutra recitals at her local pagoda four times every month, goes on pilgrimages at the beginning of the new year, hangs Buddhist calendars on the walls of her house, buys recordings of Buddhist sermons and magazines published at Quán Sứ Pagoda (although these are mostly left unread), and recites sutras daily in her home. The sum of these activities marks her as a lay-devotee. Mr. Lê, an elderly man, takes no part in sutra recitals and makes no offerings to the buddhas. Nonetheless, he is regarded, and thinks of himself, as an exemplary Buddhist because of his knowledge of Buddhist philosophy and his moral cultivation.

In addition to Buddhist practices, these people also involve themselves in other religious activities. Mr. Lê's religious involvement is limited to ancestor worship at home, though he has a comprehensive understanding of the religious landscape of Vietnam. Thảo and Mrs. Tu, however, often make offerings at non-Buddhist shrines and temples, and express a belief in every aspect of the Vietnamese religious landscape—from fortune-telling, to séances, to spirit possession rituals. Thảo self-consciously, but confidently, admits that she believes in all "superstitions," including omens of bad luck, charms, and ghosts.

The way that the Vietnamese involve themselves in a wide range of religious activities has led some scholars to state that people in this country are not Buddhist at all. For example, Cadière—the grandfather of the study of religion in Vietnam—claimed that the Vietnamese were animist and that very few of them practiced Buddhism, even among the monastics (1958, 5–6). More recently Đặng Nghiêm Vạn (1998) expressed an opinion that reflects the state position:

> Except for a number of monks, priests and a few of the faithful who declare that they embrace only one religion, such as Buddhism or one of the traditional religious doctrines, the majority of Hanoi believers, although setting

up Buddhist altars at home, still go to pagodas for worship, attend medium services, worship their ancestors, consult diviners, and, simply, put faith in something friendly whispered in their ear. Since they have faith in a variety of religions, most of them keep up worship practices but few of them are fully committed. In reality, they could be seen as credulous people seeking satisfaction for a momentary spiritual need (p. 246).

However, to dismiss people's assertions of faith and identity leads to a cul-de-sac for understanding the positions from which these claims are made. Instead of contributing to an objective understanding of Buddhism, such academic summations fall prey to constructions of legitimacy and end by contributing to structures of power in the Buddhist field. In other words, by creating categories that parse "true Buddhists" from practitioners of folk religion (or some other label), the academic discipline strays into the discourses and structures that should be the object of our study. True objectivity is an impossibility, of course, but there is nonetheless merit in aiming as close as possible to this goal.

As a start, we need to acknowledge the ways that people define and describe themselves in relation to their worldview. I have found it advantageous to begin studies of Buddhists in Hanoi from an acceptance that whoever self-identifies as Buddhist and takes part in activities that are commonly understood to be Buddhist, is indeed Buddhist.

The common phrasing of the landscape as Buddha side / spirit side given by many of my informants offers a holistic understanding of the Vietnamese religious landscape from which to start an exploration of Buddhist practices. The distinctions made between buddhas and spirits are not mutually exclusive, but instead can be viewed as being engaged in a complementary relationship. In this scheme, the Buddhist pantheon represents a group within an array of beings who all have certain characteristics. The Buddha did not deny the existence of other powerful spirits, but denied that they were the highest truth. This suits my informants just fine, as they do not address the spirits for matters regarding salvation, but instead approach them for matters of this world. For them, it would be foolish and dangerous to not acknowledge, respect, and hopefully benefit from the supernatural potency that permeates the landscape of Vietnam. This does not make them less Buddhist, even when they tend to approach the Buddhist pantheon in much the same way as the spirits—by entering into mutually beneficial relationships that exhibit many of the rules of reciprocity that characterize relationships between humans. However, whereas the majority of religiously active people hold these views, they are also subject to criticism as part of a total discourse on religion in Vietnam.

Taking claims to be Buddhist at face value as my starting point, I have tried to show that Buddhism in Vietnam cannot be understood without looking at how practice links to the overall construction of masculinity and femininity in Vietnamese society. Privileging the authoritative view of Buddhism, while ignoring alternative views and practices, in effect disassociates religion from society, resulting in an incomplete understanding of Buddhism that leaves out the lived realities of most practitioners. The interpretations of religious specialists and key informants are inevitably those that are given primacy because of the coherence of their explanations. There is no doubt that such explanations are valid, but they represent a viewpoint and a form of religious practice that is grounded in constructions of masculinity and do not possess an essential truth. Specialists are usually men, and the practice of offering coherent explanations is part of a male disposition. To regard them as more than one among many ways of being Buddhist disallows the possibility for exploration of how religious practice draws on gender discourses. Understanding explanations of specialists as discourses rather than as statements of fact is crucial to understanding the differences between men's and women's religious engagements.

Nor does women's inarticulateness mean that they do not understand what they are doing. Rather, the inability to articulate is a result of society not generally expecting or valuing intelligence in women, leading to a feminine *habitus* of avoiding displays of knowledge. Expectations of women's low intellectual capacity, and the way that structures of gender make particular forms of behavior more sexually desirable, condition women to be unable or unwilling to articulate their cosmological understandings (Gal 1991, 176). Despite an often-met unwillingness among women to articulate their broader cosmological understandings, they nonetheless have understandings of their practices that they relate back to their daily lives. Their explanations were no less meaningful than Mr. Lê's or Mr. Đức's doctrinally based interpretations of Buddhism. To accept the explanations of ritual specialists to the exclusion of other possible interpretations is to ignore the fact that the very explanation given to the anthropologist (or religionist or Buddhologist) is part of the production of symbolic capital by which (usually male) ritual specialists maintain their positions of authority.

The relation between gender and dispositions towards religion is seen most clearly by looking not at those who are religiously active, but at those who are most skeptical towards religion. Many young men entirely avoid participation in religious activities and often criticize all religious practice as superstitious, irrational, and wasteful. Their view, which has as its basis the idea that men are strong and independent, stems largely from the perception that to rely on the supernatural (much less to believe in it) is an admission of personal weakness antithetical to the construction of masculinity. Young women, on the other hand, are more ambiguous in their views of religion. Some of them express a fervent belief in the efficacy of making offerings and wishes to the spirits or the buddhas, whereas others make offerings only half-believing that doing so will have any effect whatsoever. They make the offerings "just in case." Few young women, however, dismiss these practices entirely. For them, religious practice is tied to the construction of emphasized femininity that is, as with young men, partly driven by expectations of sexual desirability. Many women become increasingly devout as they age, especially after the age of forty, and participate in Buddhist practice to a much greater extent than do young women. They often explain their practice as being concerned with the welfare of their family, tying it to social expectations of women's concern and self-sacrifice for the sake of their children. Old men seldom dismiss religion out of hand, as do young men. Rather than being concerned with reproducing an image of outer strength that women will find desirable, they are more often concerned with demonstrating inner strength through ascetic forms of self-cultivation.

I have looked at three specific forms of Buddhist practice: making offerings, chanting sutras, and studying. These are not exclusive categories of Buddhist practice, but represent major ways that people practice Buddhism in Hanoi. At the same time, these forms of practice clearly demonstrate the way in which gender and age differentiates practitioners, and the manner in which religious practice expresses gender differences.

The first practice that I discussed involved making offerings and wishes at the altars of the buddhas or spirits, or both, and then reclaiming these offerings, called *lộc*. Creating and distributing *lộc* is a practice that is done almost exclusively by women, both young and old. Although some men (primarily businessmen) will offer incense and make wishes to the supernatural, they do not usually offer items that can be reclaimed as *lộc*. *Lộc,* being a gift from the spirits or buddhas, or a talisman, is seen as spiritually charged by the supernatural and so able to bring good luck to the bearer. Its subsequent distribution, usually to family members, can therefore be seen as part of the fulfillment of expectations for women to be primarily concerned with the family. For younger women, making offerings and wishes contributes to the construction of a femininity that focuses on receptivity and dependence, while at the same time indicating future orientations towards the creation and care of a happy family.

The group that recites sutras is mixed in terms of gender, but more exclusive in terms of age, with the majority of members being elderly women. The penitence ritual provides an opportunity to see the different approaches and understandings of men and women to common activities. Many women express the same motivation for taking part as younger women do for making offerings. They stress the benefits their fervent Buddhist practice would have for their families. At a personal level, they describe the ritual as seeking absolution from the Buddha. Men usually deny that taking part in the recital has any direct effect on their karma—an interpretation that is doctrinally sanctioned. Men also say that participation is intended to draw one's attention to past errors in conduct, with the aim of self-correction in the future. Furthermore, men generally augment this practice by studies of specialized rituals or the study of Buddhist Philosophy and Chinese characters. At Phúc Lộc Pagoda especially, all of the men who attend the penitence ritual also take part in the ritual group, effectively transforming all men into ritual specialists of varying degrees, and thereby raising their practice above the level of women's practice.

The sutra recitals are performed by a cohesive group. For the men and women who take part, sutra recital offers the possibility of inclusion and a shared sense of purpose that transforms their lives. Usually, participation in these rituals starts in later age, after retirement, when children have grown up. Thus, an intensification in pagoda ritual activity comes at a time when masculinity and femininity have to be personally redefined. For women, direct care of their children is no longer as time-consuming, and while many old women spend a great deal of time taking care of grandchildren, their responsibilities are lessened. An intensification of pagoda activity as a way to enlist the help of the supernatural can be seen as a transference of this caring role to a different level. For older men, participation in pagoda life takes place after retirement. Because the masculinity of youth draws heavily on the centrality of the career, retirement can be an emasculating experience. This is especially the case for men who held good positions with some status. By becoming ritual specialists, men reestablish their sense of status, although within a different field.

Inclusion is an important dynamic that draws people to become part of a pagoda community, but within the pagoda there is often competition. I have used the term "conspicuous devotion" to describe how women, especially, try to display the fervency of their belief. Their level of devotion is often ostentatiously performed by adopting a specific style of clothing, donations, or overt forms of devotional behavior. Within the Buddhist field, such displays serve to create a hierarchy of belief and dominance. Men, by virtue of the capital they already hold by being male in Vietnam, are in a position of dominance over women. However, there is further differentiation and assertions of authority made by performances of linguistic and ritual competence, or of philosophical knowledge. Such observations of the way that status is established within the pagoda serve to counter the claims of some scholars that the pagoda is essentially a feminine, egalitarian space.

Study is an important aspect for most of the men who become engaged with pagoda life. For many, the performance of knowledge is more important than ritual participation. Mr. Lê has a dominant position at Phúc Lộc Pagoda because he displays a high level of competence in Buddhist philosophy and an understanding of the meaning of ritual, rather than actual participation in the ritual itself. Although such performances of knowledge establish dominance within the Buddhist field, study and knowledge are also central to the construction of masculinity. This construction in many ways draws on Confucian images of the literati as an ideal for older men. Today the hegemonic masculine ideal is urban and stresses success in business or politics, but for older men the ideal of self-cultivation and wisdom maintains currency and is a valid alternative to the younger hegemonic masculinity. Performances of knowledge help maintain an overall dominance of men over women, because they normalize the perception that women are intellectually inferior to men, emotional rather than rational, and generally unfit for high-level positions.

There are multiple forms of engagement with Buddhism in Hanoi, all of them inextricably entangled in social life. As such, Buddhist practice participates in the overall construction of gender in Vietnamese society, both being affected by gendered expectations, and reifying gender structures. By linking gender and Buddhist practice in this way, we can see the importance of taking seriously individual experiences of what it means to be Buddhist.

Notes

Introduction

1.   Following standard practice in essays dealing with Vietnamese Buddhism, I call Buddhist temples "pagodas," not to be confused with the architecture type consisting of a multistoried, tiered tower. The usage likely comes from French scholarship, but has been perpetuated by Vietnamese scholars, and is useful in providing an easily recognized distinction between Buddhist and non-Buddhist sacred sites (which are usually called temples).

2.   This is the common chant used when counting prayer beads. The meaning is something like, "Hail to Amitābha Buddha," and comes from the Pure Land Buddhist belief that by reciting the name of this Buddha in faith one can be reborn in the Pure Land.

3.   *Sám Nguyện* is the name of the ritual, *sám hối* is the verb, meaning "repent (of), be remorseful (of)" according to Bùi Phụng (1993, 1174). This definition reflects the way that my informants referred to it.

4.   Although *vàng* refers specifically to gold, my informants used the term *vàng mã* to refer specifically to spirit money, including symbolic gold bars and paper currency of various kinds, usually printed to look like old Chinese currency or American bills, and including the words "Bank of Hell." The term "*hàng mã*" was used more generally to refer to all objects that are ritually burned for spirits, including money as well as objects like houses, clothing, cell phones, and motorbikes made of colored paper.

5.   This percentage has roughly held true from what I have seen in southern Vietnam as well as among the overseas Vietnamese in Canada (see Soucy 1993, 1994, 1996).

6.   I do, however, refer to an "elite," "orthodox," or "doctrinal" view. It can be seen as shorthand for elite, hegemonic cultural pronunciations on "popular" practice, and should not be seen as having implications of what is "correct" or "true."

7.   I am drawing on Erving Goffman's use of "performance," which resonates with Bourdieu's notion of *habitus* in that it emerges from embodied dispositions that are not necessarily recognized by the performer. Performance is also understood as a total act that includes not just speech, but setting, appearance, and manner, together called a "front" by Goffman (1959, 17–30). I am intentionally avoiding Butler's understanding of performance because, although her critique of Bourdieu's *habitus* as not sufficiently accounting for the creative role of transgressive language in counterhegemonic actions (Butler 1997, 142–145) may be true to a point, Butler accords too much agency in linguistic innovation and fails to account for a whole set of social shifts that must occur as a precondition for the linguistic innovations that she uses to critique Bourdieu. In the context of Hanoi (and especially within the particularities of the religious field), these shifts were not taking place, and consequently instances of

resignified speech as a form of resistance (where an offensive term is "taken back" by the group at which the derogatory word was aimed) were absent, making Butler's notions of performance irrelevant.

8. I am borrowing Bourdieu's term "field" as shorthand for a structured space in which positions are determined and negotiated through the production of social capital. In the way that I view this production of social capital within the Buddhist "field," the transferability of capital outside the field is variable, but usually is fairly limited for all but the most serious and nationally prominent monks.

9. The connection between increased religiosity and the drastic changes that have taken place in southern Vietnam since the late 1980s has been well documented by Philip Taylor (2004) and in northern Vietnam by Endres (1998), Malarney (2002), Marr (1994, 15), Pham Van Bich (1999, 95), and Hy Van Luong (Luong 1993).

10. See Kleinen (1999, 171), Malarney (2002), and P. Taylor (2004, 37–39).

11. Although religious belief (*tín ngưỡng*) is mentioned in the constitution, words such as "religion" (*tôn giáo*), "religious dogma" (*giáo chỉ*) and "religious path" (*đạo*) are absent.

12. See Soucy (1993, 1994, 1996).

13. According to the 2007 census, the population was 3,398,889 (VN Express 2007), although this number has increased drastically since the city incorporated outlying districts in 2008.

14. These migrant workers are largely temporary, and still call their village "home." Li Tana (1996) and Nguyen Van Chinh (1997) both have written studies on migrant labor in Hanoi.

15. Robert Connell calls this sexual aspect "cathexis," referring to the attachment of emotion to particular objects. By recognizing the idea of cathexis as part of a component in the reproduction of gender structures, Connell acknowledges that culture shapes desire and that these desires are very much a part of the processes that uphold the hegemonic play of power and gender (Connell 1995, 74–75).

1: Views of the Religious Landscape

1. The center is organizationally under the leadership of Thích Thanh Từ, who is headquartered in Đà Lạt in the south, and the abbot (from Huế) is one of his close monastic disciples. See Soucy (2007).

2. Theravada is the tradition mostly practiced in South and Southeast Asia, whereas Mahayana is practiced in China, Japan, Korea, and Vietnam. Most Theravadins in Vietnam are ethnic Khmer. The two traditions hold in common the central teachings of the Buddha, but their view of the historical Buddha is radically different. Theravada Buddhism regards the Buddha as a man who discovered the truth of existence and leads us to our own eventual discoveries solely through example. Mahayana Buddhism, by contrast, sees the Buddha as both a historical figure and a cosmic emanation. In the Mahayana tradition, the

historical Buddha is only one of many buddhas and bodhisattvas who have the capacity to assist people in their spiritual quests and with other difficulties experienced on Earth and in other realms. It is unusual for people to follow both, though adherents to either would offer respect to monks of the other.

3.   I have rendered *hội phật tử* as "pagoda association," rather than as the more literal "Buddhist association" because of the association's unofficial status and relationship to a particular pagoda. In the literature, it also seems to be commonly called the Elderly Women's Buddhist Association (*hội chư bà*), reflecting the character of most of the participants (Lê Thi 1998, 82; Luong 1992, 58, 1993, 271; Malarney 1999, 196). I have never heard the groups referred to by this term in Hanoi, however, and informants I spoke with were puzzled when I asked about it.

4.   The belief in ghosts in Vietnam has recently been the topic of two books: *Ghosts of War in Vietnam* (Heonik Kwon [2008]) and *War and Shadows: The Haunting of Vietnam* (Mai Lan Gustafsson [2009]), and two documentary films: *Psychic Vietnam* (Phua 2006) and *Wandering Ghosts* (Lojkine 2005). All of these works deal especially with the concern for ghosts that resulted from lost remains because of the war. In addition, Nash and Nguyen have written about the belief in ghosts by Catholic overseas Vietnamese in New Orleans (1995, Ch. 7).

5.   Hungry ghosts (*ma đói*) are spirits that were potentially someone's ancestors, but for one reason or another have been neglected, and have literally become hungry, marauding beings. They are sentenced to roam the Earth in a near-permanent state of starvation. Before most important rites, whether Buddhist or otherwise, an offering is made to hungry ghosts so that they will not interfere with the proceedings.

6.   To the best of my knowledge there is no specific term for a spirit caller. People speak about attending a séance or "spirit calling," and address the spirit caller as "teacher."

7.   The literal meaning of "*bà*" and "*ông*" are "grandmother" and "grandfather," respectively, but they are also used as respectful pronouns. In the case of Thầy Linh, who was in his early thirties, the pronoun "*ông*" was used out of respect for him as a monk rather than because of age when he was not in the context of spirit mediumship, but his followers addressed him as *bà* (grandmother) when in his role as a medium, indicating his ambivalent gender identity, especially when engaged in mediumship. Barley Norton (2006, 55–75) deals with sexuality and mediumship.

8.   Her full name in Vietnamese is Quan Thế Âm Bồ Tát, but she is often referred to as Lady Buddha (Phật Bà).

9.   Sangren (1983) suggests that Guanyin's power arises from the fact that she is not associated with aspects of women that are threatening to Taiwanese traditional kinship structure (e.g., wives and daughters-in-law who might try to split brothers in order to increase their share of property). Sangren's argument is also compelling in the Vietnamese context with Quan Âm.

10.   The process by which mediums are called to service by experiencing illness or insanity

is also described by Endres (2006, 80, 83); Fjelstad (2006, 97–99); and Fjelstad and Maiffret (2006, 112–116).

11.   Arthur Wolf has written a substantial essay on the close connections between ghosts and ancestors in the context of Taiwan. His overall observations regarding the ambivalent and contextual nature in which spirits of the dead are regarded largely hold true for Vietnam as well (A. Wolf 1978, 146).

12.   The masculine nature of the state, the academy, and the Buddhist institution are so overwhelming that they need not be elaborated at length here. However, it can be substantiated by a few facts: (1) Only 10 percent of people in Communist Party Committees are women, and women have never held the top government positions of either prime minister or president (Vuong Thi Hanh and Doan Thuy Dung 2007, 3). At the provincial, district, and city levels the number of women representatives rarely exceeded 20 percent during the period 1985 to 1999 (Lê Thị Nhâm Tuyết 2002, 205; United Nations Economic and Social Commission for Asia and the Pacific [UNESCAP] n.d., 9). (2) Women hold only 37.6 percent of university-level teaching positions (National Committee for the Advancement of Women in Viet Nam [NCFAW] 2006, 56). (3) Although there are no statistics on women in Buddhism, all notable figures reported in Buddhist magazines are men, as are all leaders in the Vietnamese Buddhist Association.

13.   My translation, from TV broadcast.

14.   Among the more significant borrowings that gave Vietnam a relative advantage were the adoption of paper money and wood-block printing techniques in the fourteenth century that "gave Vietnamese a lead of about four centuries over their Southeast Asian neighbors in such matters as the organization and storage of political and scientific information" (Woodside 1988, 25).

15.   There are several terms for Confucianism. I think that the traditional term is Nho Giao and the others might be relatively recent inventions that have emerged with the Western notion of "religion" and "world religions."

16.   Hue-Tam Ho Tai points out that the state or Confucian concern with orthodoxy is partly due to the idiom of rebellion taking a religious form (Ho Tai 1987, 134). Li Tana shows that a hybrid official religion was integral to the Nguyễn establishment of authority in southern Vietnam, though it could hardly be called Confucian. Instead, and as opposed to the more Confucian north, the religious ideology of the south relied much more on Mahayana Buddhism (Li Tana 1998, 102–103) than it did in the north. Woodside also points out that tensions existed between state orthodoxy and local beliefs to a greater extent in Vietnam than they did in China (1971, 228).

17.   See also Fjelstad and Nguyen (2006a) for a number of accounts of spirit possession rituals being practiced during the pre-Renovation period. Phạm Quỳnh Phương (2006, 49), in particular, describes how one male medium of Saint Trần kept his shrine and continued to perform possession rituals privately after the land reforms of the 1950s, despite his brother being arrested and having to undergo reeducation for owning a shrine.

18.   Trần Ngọc Thêm's (1997) overview of Vietnamese culture, for example, implicitly follows the scheme by devoting a chapter each to Buddhism, Confucianism, and Taoism, while all other aspects of Vietnamese religion are covered in a chapter entitled "beliefs." Thanh Huyên writes in "An Overview of Beliefs and Religions in Vietnam," "Probably only Buddhism, Taoism and Catholicism can be counted among organized religions" (1996, 12). He dismisses Confucianism from being included because he insists it is more of an ethic than a religion.

19.   Fjelstad and Nguyen (2006b) note, "Practice of the [spirit medium] ritual is still not officially allowed. State instructions on cultural and religious activities consider *len dong* spirit possession as a 'social evil,' and a list of condemned superstitious practices released by the Ministry of Culture and Information in 1998 states that astrology, horoscopy, ghost calling, spirit petitioning, making amulets, performing exorcism, and magical healing are superstitious practices. This ban was supported by a 2003 resolution that 'strictly forbids using religion and belief to carry out superstition'" (p. 15). The "Ordinance of the Standing Committee of the National Assembly NO. 21/2004/PL-UBTVQH11 OF 18 JUNE 2004 Regarding Religious Belief and Religious Organizations" continues to state that it is illegal to "spread superstitious practices" (Standing Committee of the National Assembly [SCNAC] 2004, Chapter 1, Article 8, Clause 2). However, it is not made clear what activities are considered superstitious, other than the following found in Chapter 1, Article 3, Clause 1: "Activities which arise from religious beliefs [*hoạt động tín ngưỡng*] manifest themselves as ancestor worship [*tôn thờ tổ tiên*]; memorializing and honoring those who have rendered great services to the country and the collective; the worship of saints and deities [*thần, thánh*], traditional symbols and other folk beliefs and activities [*hoạt động tín ngưỡng dân gian*] that inspire responsibility towards valuable historical, cultural, moral and social values" (SCNAC 2004). The 2006 *Law on Information Technology,* under Article 12, "Prohibited Acts," includes, "Exciting [*sic*] violence, propagating wars of aggression; sowing hatred among nations and peoples, exciting obscene, depravation [*sic*], crime, social evils or *superstition;* undermining the nation's fine traditions and customs" [my emphasis] (National Assembly, Socialist Republic of Vietnam 2006).

20.   As the essays in *The Country of Memory: Remaking the Past in Late Socialist Vietnam* illustrate, the manipulation of symbols has been broad-ranging, and is not just limited to religion (Ho Tai 2001). For example, art (N. Taylor 2001), cinema (Bradley 2001) and tourism (Kennedy and Williams 2001) have also been subject to this process, as has traditional culture and religion.

21.   By institutionalized violence, I am referring to the threat of arrest and punishment that was most manifest during the pre-Renovation period. Nonetheless, while the threat of state violence and its institutions of enforcement (i.e., the police and army) are often hidden, the possibility of their employment is always present. This is true not just of Vietnam, but of all states. While in Vietnam there has been increasing lenience towards religious practice since the Renovation, in recent years, there is still some trepidation that control can be reinstated at the whim of forces well beyond the control of those engage in marginalized practices, such as spirit mediumship. These concerns are perhaps intentionally perpetuated by continuing the lack of legal clarity and unevenness in the way that the law is prosecuted.

2: Space and the Ranking of Buddhisms

1.   Ullambana (Vu Lan), is sometimes translated as Mother's Day by my Vietnamese informants. It is a festival particularly associated with relieving the suffering of relatives (especially mothers) who may be in hell (which is temporary in Buddhist and East Asian traditions). It involves activities that build merit to transfer to those souls in order to gain their early release.

2.   Trần Văn Giáp's uncritical reading has mostly been repeated by subsequent writers, including Bechert and Vu (1976), Durand (1959), Mai Thọ Truyền (1959), Minh Chi, Ha Van Tan, and Nguyen Tai Thu (1993), Nguyễn Tài Thư (1992), Thich Nhat Hanh (1967), and Thich Thien-An (1975). C. T. Nguyen (1995, 82–83, n. 5) gives a concise appraisal of all available works dealing with Vietnamese Buddhist history. Since the time that Nguyen completed his important work, descriptions by Western academics have adopted his assessment (e.g., McHale 2004).

3.   These books include Hà Văn Tấn, Nguyễn Văn Kự, and Phạm Ngọc Long (1993); Phan Cẩm Thượng (1996); Trần Đại Vinh, Nguyễn Hữu Thông, and Lê Văn Sách 1993; Võ Văn Tường (1993, 1994); and Võ Văn Tường and Huỳnh Như Phương (1995). There is a similar coffee-table book about communal houses (*đình*) in Vietnam (Hà Văn Tấn and Nguyễn Văn Kự 1998), and another about Christian churches (Nguyễn Hồng Dương 2003). Around 1998, a CD ROM on pagodas was released, but no longer seemed to be available by 2005.

4.   Tourism, which is increasingly important for the economy, is also an important factor in the production of these books.

5.   The organization he joined was the Hưng Yên Province Buddhist Society to Save the Country (Hội Phật Giáo Cứu Quốc Tỉnh Hưng Yên).

6.   I am not certain when the portico was built, but the use of the Romanized writing system played a prominent role in the struggle to modernize Vietnam and establish independence from French colonial rule in the first half of the twentieth century (Marr 1971, 183, 214–215; Marr 1981, 33, 137, 150).

7.   In the north, there has been little in the way of resistance to this control. This is probably because there was no organization that successfully unified the disparate Buddhist pagodas in the north prior to independence, despite reformers' attempts. In the south, however, there were movements towards organization, prompted by repression of the Catholic President Ngô Đình Diệm. The Unified Buddhist Church was formed in 1964; although the organization was fractured by leadership struggles and never represented all Buddhists, it was nonetheless an important force. After Reunification, the organization moved to resistance of Communist control over Buddhism. Backed by the large diasporic community, the Unified Buddhist Church of Vietnam today continues to resist the government, and its leaders, consequently, are often jailed or put under house arrest.

8.   A new complex has been built in Sóc Sơn on the outskirts of Hanoi, with the groundbreaking ceremony for construction held in February 2005. There are similar institutes in Huế and in Ho Chi Minh City.

9. Only two other pagoda bore such a plaque in 1998: the One Pillar Pagoda and Trấn Quốc Pagoda.

10. This is especially true since the late 1950s, when much of their lands were confiscated and buildings were erected around them.

11. It was not clear how they would be replaced after they were no longer able to perform this task, because no new people were being trained.

12. To preserve anonymity, I have not provided the spirit's name, which is here represented by "X."

13. Văn Thù Sư Lợi and Phổ Hiền Bồ Tát are generally paired. They are both celestial bodhisattvas that appear in the *Lotus Sutra*.

14. I have never encountered such a structure in Buddhist pagodas of the south, though Ngọc Hoàng Pagoda in Saigon, which is a converted Daoist temple built by the Chinese community at the beginning of the century, has a room dedicated to mother goddesses of a different cult.

15. What is distinctive about these representations of the supernatural is not the cosmological view, but the ritual by which that view is addressed: the spirit possession ritual. This fact has allowed for the main figures to be interchangeable in various parts of Vietnam. For example, in Huế the goddess of heaven, Thiên Y A Na, who is of Cham origin, stands at the centre, whereas in the north another goddess, Liễu Hạnh, is much more prominent (Bertrand 1996, 272).

16. Here I am following Charles Taylor's notion that modernity has brought about a disembedding of the individual, whereby religion no longer expresses the individual as part of a social nexus, but instead is replaced by "a new self-understanding of our social existence, one that gave an unprecedented primacy to the individual" (C. Taylor 2007, 50). There is a disenchantment that dispels the world of spirits and places us unequivocally in a secular time (Taylor, 186).

3: Masculinities and Performances of Skepticism

1. Cigarettes are often offered to ancestors and other spirits (particularly to the Earth God, Ông Địa). It is usually done by pushing the stick left after burning a regular incense stick into the cigarette butt and then burning it upright as if it were incense.

2. I call it a "pseudopilgrimage" because the intent for most of the group was entirely pleasure, and even the more devout saw the trip as having a dual purpose of entertainment and supplication.

3. I received questionnaires back from 114 men and women, randomly sampled: eleven men younger than twenty, twenty-two men from twenty to forty, five men from forty to sixty, two men over age sixty, thirteen women under twenty, forty-six women from twenty

to forty, eleven women from forty to sixty, and four women over age sixty. The questionnaire was not intended as quantitative data and cannot be considered statistically valid.

4.   "Structure," as I use it, recognizes that there are broad patterns that shape practice. Practice is not always completely circumscribed by structure, forcing actors to mindlessly reproduce and conform to structure unreflexively. Nonetheless, practice must reckon with the constraints imposed by structure, whether through conformity or through resistance. Thus, practice does not float freely, but is grounded in a broad pattern or context. Furthermore, structure is not fixed and rigid. Instead, it is culturally and historically constituted and changes with time, though it is remarkably durable. Part of the durability of the gender structure lies in the fact that it is not monolithic, but contains "internal differentiation, historical unevenness and internal contradiction" (Connell 1987, 96).

5.   For a discussion of how hegemonic masculinity and emphasized femininity are constructed in the Western context, see Connell (1987).

6.   Barley Norton describes how *đồng cô* refers to effeminate gender identity when applied to male mediums, and not to their sexuality. Many were also homosexual, though they did not see their sexuality as being in any way related (2006, 71–72).

4: Offerings and Blessings

1.   *Oản* is made from sweet bean powder that is pressed into truncated cone shapes and then wrapped in colored cellophane.

2.   Although *đức* is translated as "merit," I am not convinced that it is used in the same sense as it is in Theravada Buddhism. However, in common speech it was more often used in a Buddhist context. While no one was able to explain concisely, the general idea was that it coincided with the idea of improving moral virtue, mixed with the idea that the fruits of these actions would be realized both in the next life as well as immediately through good luck and fortune, and would benefit not only the individual, but also the whole family.

3.   *Mừng tuổi* (i.e., the money given at Tết) is called "*lì xì*" in southern Vietnam (Toan Ánh 1996, vol. 2, 333), and is related to the Cantonese term, "*lai see.*"

4.   A similar process takes place at communal house and pagoda festivals or death day anniversaries for ancestors, where the offerings form a main part of the feast that follows the ritual.

5.   *Có thờ, có thiêng, có kiêng, có lành.* "The dangerous things" refer to practices of avoidance, like staying out of the wind to prevent sickness, or avoiding water after childbirth.

6.   Donations to the *sangha* (or to pagodas) are made in Vietnam, and there is the belief that these acts of generosity will have an impact on one's karma. In Hanoi, however, these donations are not stressed as being centrally important. Furthermore, the connection between individual monastics and devotees is potentially distanced because there are donation boxes in which people make contributions, rather than giving directly to a monk. (Vietnamese Mahayana Buddhist monks do not beg for food.) There seemed to be little perception that

the merit accrued is relative to the status of the person to whom the offering is made. Thus, it is not felt that giving money at a pagoda of nuns is substantially different from giving to a monk's pagoda, though most people tend to put cash directly on altars or to hand money directly to monastics rather than putting the money in the box.

7.   The main explanations people give me for misfortunes are leading an evil life, failing to take care of one's ancestors properly, or random acts of ghosts and malevolent spirits. However, there is also a belief that moral actions of the family, as a collective (including ancestors), influence the fate of individuals.

8.   While this downward flow of *lộc* is true in a broader sense, it is not exclusive. *Lộc* is distributed to everyone in the family, so that wives (supposedly lower status) also give *lộc* to husbands (who are presumed to be socially higher). Likewise, people can, and do, give *lộc* to elders.

5: Women, Offerings, and Symbolic Capital

1.   Within the family there continue to be substantial inequalities in the division of labor. Most wives are expected to cook and care for the family, even if they have a full-time job outside the home. Women's labor, both inside and outside the home, tends to be devalued. Childcare is still mostly the responsibility of women and men generally help very little (Pham Van Bich 1999, 67). One study from 1997 reported that whereas women do 68.1 percent of the sweeping and cleaning, men do 6.8 percent; whereas women wash clothes 83.7 percent of the time, men do it 3.6 percent of the time; and whereas women do 75.4 percent of the cooking, men do only 4.9 percent of it (with the remainders presumably being done by children) (Hoàng Bá Thịnh 2002a, 153).

2.   In the Western context, Connell describes the phrasing of emphasized feminity as "the display of sociability rather than technical competence, fragility in mating scenes, compliance with men's desire for titillation and ego-stroking in office relationships, acceptance of marriage and childcare as a response to labor-market discrimination against women" (Connell 1991, 187). The way that emphasized feminity is played out is somewhat different in Vietnam, but the overall themes do not vary greatly.

3.   Hà Đông is a town south-west of Hanoi.

4.   Men can marry at any age, with remarriage for men being considerably easier than for women, and has no social stigma attached to it.

5.   Spirits of unmarried women, with no children, are among the spirits considered "deserted and forsaken," destined to roam around homeless, desperate and hungry, and are among those spirits considered dangerous to the living (Đỗ Thiện 2007, 162).

6.   If a woman does have an outside job that is more prestigious or that pays more than her husband's job, she must be careful to diminish the fact as much as possible so as not to bruise her husband's ego (Pham Van Bich 1999, 66).

7.   For more on the role of *ơn* in gender negotiations, see Gammeltoft 1999, 122; Jamieson 1993, 16–17; Marr 1997, 296; O'Harrow 1995, 173; and Soucy 2000, 192–194.

8.   Margery Wolf has similarly argued in the context of rural Taiwan that because women's positions in their husband's families are tenuous and peripheral, they expend much effort to construct a "uterine family" by instilling, and guarding, feeling of emotional obligation in their children (M. Wolf 1968, 1972).

9.   "*Hiếu: Đi khắp thế gian; Không ai tốt bằng mẹ; Gánh nặng cuộc đời; Không ai khổ bằng cha; Nước biển mênh mông; Không đong đầy tình mẹ; Mây trời lồng lộng; Không phủ kín công cha; Tần tảo sớm hôm; Mẹ nuôi con khôn lớn; Mang cả tấm thân gầy; Cha che chở đời con; Ai còn mẹ; Xin đừng làm mẹ khóc; Đừng để buồn; Lên mắt mẹ nghe con.*"

6: Sutra Recital and Buddhist Identities

1.   Sutra recitals are held four times a month, following the lunar calendar. Special rituals, such as the Ritual for the Opening of Summer, also follow the lunar calendar, while other occasions are timed at the whim of the fortune-teller who determines auspicious dates and times for certain rituals.

2.   Rogers describes four purposes that religion serves for aging people: (1) dealing with the approach of death by providing an explanation of what happens after death, (2) giving meaning to lives that are put into question by the approach of death, (3) compensating for diminished roles and significance in society, and (4) meeting secular needs by providing inclusion in a community (Rogers 1976, 406–411).

3.   In every pagoda there are other sutras that are chanted daily by the monastics, but I am not concerned with these here. For an explanation of the schedule of Buddhist liturgy, see Nguyễn Thuyết Phong (1983) and Revertegat (1974, 24–33).

4.   The distinction is entirely instrumental for the purposes of my description, for chanting sutras is itself a ritual. The difference I draw for the purpose of this discussion is based on Vietnamese terminology, which describes the two activities differently.

5.   The all-male ritual group consists of old men who practice and perform rituals at the pagoda. This group will be discussed at greater length in Chapter 9. The name *Thỉnh Phật Khoa* is not translatable.

6.   In 1997–1998 these occasionally also took place at Bà Đá Pagoda (headquarters of the Hanoi Buddhist Association [Nguyễn Thế Long and Phạm Mai Hùng 2003, 17–18]), but the event at Quán Sứ Pagoda was the largest. Sùng Phúc Thiền Tự in Gia Lâm, which has been set up as a Zen meditation center, also holds regular Dharma talks.

7.   Their presence during funerals is not absolutely essential, and only tends to be done at the request of family members who are devout Buddhists. This stands in juxtaposition to funeral musicians, who are always seen as essential to keeping the soul from wandering, and can be heard playing more or less continuously during the period when the body is being displayed and, even more importantly, during the procession. This usage of funeral musicians

is much the same as has been described by James Watson in the Cantonese context (1991 [1988], 122–124).

8. King Lý Thánh Tông (1023–1072) was the third son of Lý Thái Tông. During his reign he strongly supported Buddhism, had many temples and stupas built, and was even said to have been a patriarch in the Thảo Đường Zen School. At the same time, he promoted Confucian studies, had the Temple of Literature built, installed statues of Confucian sages to be worshipped, and institutionalized Confucian court etiquette (Nguyen, C. T. 1997, 440–441, n. 644; Nguyễn Khắc Viện 1993, 52–53).

9. Côn Sơn Pagoda is also known as Chùa Tư Phúc. It was built during the Lý dynasty. It is famous as the pagoda where the fourteenth-century Zen master Huyền Quang lived and died. He was the third patriarch of the Trúc Lâm Thiền sect (Võ Văn Tường 1994, 202). Đền Kiếp Bạc is dedicated to the thirteenth-century deified hero Trần Hưng Đạo. See Pham Quynh Phuong (2009) for a discussion on Trần Hưng Đạo's cult.

10. When it is undertaken twice a month it is on the first and fifteenth. Other days on which Buddhists eat vegetarian are on the eighth, fourteenth, twenty-third, twenty-fourth, twenty-seventh, twenty-eighth, twenty-ninth, and thirtieth. Monthly abstinences are done on the first or seventh lunar month.

11. Hy Van Luong describes the Elderly Women's Buddhist Association as fairly hierarchical, with requirements for entry into the group and strict seating order based on seniority and age. He notes, however, that a male Party member of Son Duong village is impressed that there is little dispute over where people should sit (Luong 1993, 271–272). My experience in Hanoi was that there was no strict hierarchy, nor was there any regulation of entry into the group. However, there was a tendency for older women to sit closer to the altar and for younger women to voluntarily relinquish their seats for them, which was more a part of the general disposition of respect towards elders than it was an indication of hierarchy in the pagoda association.

12. The original Vietnamese written on the bags was "Tổ Kinh Tinh Tiến; Phật Tử Chùa Nôi Đồng; Tây Thiên Tự—PL2553."

13. Whereas sexuality is a key focus of young women's gender projects, seen through the concern with fashion, after childbirth and with middle age women's sexuality is virtually nullified, so that it becomes almost incomprehensible that a woman of fifty or older could be sexually attractive, and those who try to continue are ridiculed. For men, sexuality is never as central when young (there is no prominent stress on virility in the Vietnamese structures of hegemonic masculinity) and their sexual potential never fully extinguished (old men may still marry young women, though the opposite never happens). Thus, for women, old age becomes particularly problematic.

7: Conspicuous Devotion and Devotional Distinctions

1. For descriptions of the way that the communal house hierarchy was achieved and marked, see Gourou (1975, 73–74); Hickey (1987, 5–7); Jamieson (1986, 99–100; 1993,

31, 36); Kleinen (1999, 164); Lê Văn Hảo (1998 [1962], 203); Luong (1992, 70–71); Nguyễn Khắc Viện (1974, 167); P. Taylor (2007, 21); Thanh Tùng (1998, 41); and Toan Ánh (1996, 275–279). Horim Choi describes that local officials also take part in communal house rituals, in the Hanoi district where he did his fieldwork, as a way to "augment their authority" (Choi 2007, 111). Women's exclusion from the communal house meant that they played no part in official community decision making and were barred from this avenue of formal village power (Lê Văn Hảo 1998 [1962], 201), though they almost certainly played a large role in informal ways through pressure exerted on husbands and through networks of women. Malarney has described women as being a driving force behind the reconstruction of communal house ritual life in northern Vietnam (2002, 193–195). However, the main rituals are still performed by old men.

2.   In another essay I describe how imperatives that emerged from immigration to Canada affected this division in a Vietnamese Buddhist pagoda (Soucy 1996).

3.   For a discussion of this, see Rey (2007, 66–68).

4.   The disjuncture between the ways that outside and inside audiences perceive these performances can be explained by the fact that fields have internal logics that do not necessarily transpose very well outside the boundaries of that particular field. The pagoda can be seen as a particular field, which, though intersecting with other fields (e.g., the family) has its own specific rules.

5.   In April 2010, when this conversation took place, one million *đồng* equalled a little over US$50.

6.   While these critical comments are commonplace, and are engaged in by everyone to one degree or another, some (usually, but not always, women) gain a negative reputation for being too critical and quick to gossip.

8: Interpretive Distinctions

1.   The pagoda's monastic ancestors, comprising deceased monks or nuns who once resided at the pagoda, are structurally parallel to the family's ancestor altar, and the table and benches for meeting guests are placed in a manner similar to the arrangement most commonly seen in village houses. It is frequently situated directly in front of the altar or off to one side.

2.   Đỗ Thiện (2003) writes, "The meaning of the word *tu* (Chinese *hsiu*—to correct, repair, reform, improve) has long entwined the Confucian trajectory of *tu thân* (self-correction, perfectibility), or *tu tâm* (cultivate the heart/mind), with Daoist *tu luyện* (training—as in various meditative arts including alchemy and magic) and with the Buddhist *tu niệm* (perfecting thought and imagination)" (p. 133). The men who become active in the pagoda focus on cultivation, particularly in a way that distinguishes their morality and knowledge-based forms of practice from more devotional exercises, aimed at receiving the Buddha's blessing. This accent on self-cultivation, as I saw it, put a strong accent on moral and mental perfection. Unlike the practices of women, which stressed the family, the practices of men

were starkly individualistic. Furthermore, interpretations of their practices usually stressed self-reliance and denied the possibility for intervention by buddhas.

3. See C. T. Nguyen (1995, 1997) and Soucy (2007) for a discussion of the construction of Zen as the definitive form of Buddhism in Vietnam. Miriam Levering (1992) convincingly argues that in the rhetoric of Ch'an (Zen) Buddhism there is an inherent androcentricism that excluded the possibility of women's experience and language having an influence.

4. Interestingly, all of the four nuns (Ni Sư Diệu Nhân, Ni Sư Tuệ Thông, Ni Cô Họ Lê, and Ni Cô Họ Tống) came from rich or noble families. They are described as being virtuous, pious, filial, and beautiful, and two had been widowed before they became nuns.

5. For example, Báo Quốc Pagoda was restored in 1808 by Emperor Gia Long's mother and Quốc Ân Pagoda in 1805 by Gia Long's sister (Trần Đại Vinh et al. 1993, 154, 164).

6. The words that I have translated as "transgress" (tội lỗi) and "pardon" (xá) are judicial metaphors. They can mean sin, trespass, crime, offence, fault (Bùi Phụng 1993, 1477), and forgive, amnesty, exempt, free (from obligation) (Bùi Phụng, 1666), respectively.

7. In fact, it is karma rather than the individual that carries over into the next life. Buddhism holds that there is no "self" to be reborn, only the energy that is created through one's actions, or more precisely, through one's attachment to those actions. Escaping rebirth remains the goal in Theravada Buddhism, though in Mahayana Buddhism the goal of individual escape is replaced by the goal of compassionately remaining behind to help all other sentient beings until such a time that we can all get out of the cycle of rebirth. This goal is regarded as potentially unattainable, which makes the self-sacrifice involved even more significant in terms of the ideal of compassion.

8. However, David Marr claims that he has known believers who felt guilty at missing a vegetarian day, and often felt that the Buddha was watching (personal communication).

9. "Kamma" is Pali for karma, and "nibbāna" is the Pali word for nirvāṇa.

10. I did not hear people refer to having a heavy fate in this way very often, though one woman had heard the phrase "căn cao số nặng" (high spirit root, heavy fate) to describe someone who needed to perform a ritual to improve his or her fate. In the Buddhist context, people more often refer to this as nghiệp (karma) rather than fate. In the context of spirit possession rituals, people speak of having nặng căn, or heavy spirit root, because of events that took place in a past life as a way to explain how they were called to serve the spirits. All of these terms seemed to be used to indicate the same thing.

11. In a Vietnamese pagoda in Montreal, this opinion was most often given to me in the context of a discourse against traditional values, which was used as an explanation of men's absence: men believed that because they were karmically superior, they need not worry about producing good merit, whereas women do worry. I was assured by the head nun (a dedicated feminist) that this was an erroneous belief, and that men were arrogant fools for thinking this (Soucy 1994, 75). I never came across this formulation in Hanoi. Where women's lower status was stressed, it was to show the inferiority of women rather than the superiority of men.

12.   The word "*duyên*" is used to denote why some people, objects, or activities are attractive to someone. It implies that there is a connection that is related to attachments formed in past lives and one's fate. The term is often used, but the meaning is not easily articulated. I seldom received a satisfactory explanation when I asked about its meaning.

9: Language, Orthodoxy, and Performances of Authority

1.   No Vietnamese person ever reads characters with a classical Chinese pronunciation. Instead, they are always read with the Sino-Vietnamese pronunciation, and, unless specifically stated, it can be presumed throughout this chapter that I am referring to this pronunciation when I indicate that characters are read.

2.   Such an image of masculinity has some striking resemblances with the way that men in Java are described as gaining access to power through ascetic practice and the control of their passions (Anderson 1972, 1990, 23–26; Brenner 1995, 28–31). The main difference between masculinity in Java and Vietnam is that self-cultivation and the control of passions is more directly associated with social power and prestige without intermediation of spiritual power. Đỗ Thiện (2003), however, convincingly argues that self-cultivation in the popular sense in southern Vietnam is implicated to a much greater extent with obtaining spiritual power.

3.   In the translation of this discussion with Mr. Lê I have translated all the Vietnamese to English, with the exception of *âm* and *dương*, which are the Vietnamese terms for yin and yang. All of the French is written out as he said it.

4.   The usage of writing as a symbolic act that evokes images of masculine power is particularly telling of the close association between literacy and the construction of male gender in Vietnam.

5.   In a similar argument, Emily Martin Ahern has pointed out that in China the petitions that were written to gods were structurally similar to the kinds of petitions that would be made to the incumbents of bureaucratic office (1981, 16). Thus, we could say that, just as Chinese was the language of court and power on Earth in imperial Vietnam, Chinese continues to be the presumed language of the supernatural world.

6.   The percussion instruments included a large drum and a small drum, and two sets of cymbals. There was a wooden fish and a bowl-bell, and a number of small plates made of brass that would make a clanging sound when hit with the drumstick. For more information on the instruments used in Buddhist liturgy, see Nguyễn Thuyết Phong (1985, 1986).

7.   The liturgy is a compilation of the following texts: Thỉnh Phật Khoa (請佛科), Nhiếp Phật Khoa (攝靈科), Triệu Linh Khoa (召靈科), and Chúc Thực Khoa (呪食科).

8.   They no longer practiced in 2010 and the number of members had diminished to half due to deaths.

9.   I never saw a power struggle take place, but presumably it could happen (and perhaps has happened).

Bibliography

Ahern, Emily Martin. 1981. *Chinese Ritual and Politics*. Cambridge: Cambridge University Press.

Anderson, Benedict. 1972. "The Idea of Power in Javanese Culture." In *Culture and Politics in Indonesia*, ed. Claire Holt, 1–69. Ithaca, NY: Cornell University Press.

———. 1990. *Language and Power: Exploring Political Cultures in Indonesia*. Ithaca, NY: Cornell University Press.

Arthur, Linda B. 1999. "Introduction: Dress and the Social Control of the Body." In *Religion, Dress and the Body*, ed. Linda B. Arthur, 1–7. Oxford: Berg Publishers.

Barry, Kathleen. 1996. "Introduction." In *Vietnam's Women in Transition*, ed. Kathleen Barry, 1–20. New York: St. Martin's Press.

Bechert, Heinz, and Vu Duy-Tu. 1976. "Buddhism in Vietnam." In *Buddhism in the Modern World*, ed. John C. Maraldo, 186–193. New York: Collier Books.

Bertrand, Didier. 1996. "Renaissance du *Lên Đồng* à Huế (Việt Nam): Premiers Éléments d'une Recherche." *Bulletin de l'École Française d'Extrême-Orient* 83:271–285.

Bourdieu, Pierre. 1990. *The Logic of Practice*. Stanford, CA: Stanford University Press.

———. 1991. *Language and Symbolic Power*, ed. John B. Thompson. Cambridge, UK: Polity Press.

———. 1998. The Laughter of Bishops. In *Practical Reason: On the Theory of Action*. Stanford, CA: Stanford University Press.

Bradley, Mark Philip. 2001. "Contests of Memory: Remembering and Forgetting War in the Contemporary Vietnamese Cinema." In *The Country of Memory: Remaking the Past in Late Socialist Vietnam*, ed. Hue-Tam Ho Tai, 196–226. Berkeley: University of California Press.

Brenner, Suzanne A. 1995. "Why Women Rule the Roost: Rethinking Javanese Ideologies of Gender and Self-Control." In *Bewitching Women, Pious Men: Gender and the Body in Southeast Asia*, ed. Aihwa Ong and Michael G. Peletz, 19–50. Berkeley: University of California Press.

Bùi Đình Thảo, and Nguyễn Quang Hải. 1996. *Hát Châu Văn* [Singing *châu văn*]. Hanoi: Nhà Xuất Bản Âm Nhạc.

Bùi Phụng. 1993. *Từ Điển Việt-Anh* [Vietnamese–English dictionary]. Hanoi: Nhà Xuất Bản Giáo Dục; Công Ty Phát Hành Sách Hà Nội.

Butler, Judith. 1997. *Excitable Speech: A Politics of the Performative*. New York: Routledge.

Cadière, Leopold. 1958. *Croyances et Pratiques Religieuses des Vietnamiens*, Vol. 1. Saigon: Nouvelle Imprimerie d'Extrême Orient.

Chau, Adam Yuet. 2006. *Miraculous Response: Doing Popular Religion in Contemporary China*. Stanford, CA: Stanford University Press.

Choi, Horim. 2007. "Ritual Revitalization and Nativist Ideology in Hanoi." In *Modernity and Re-Enchantment: Religion in Post-Revolutionary Vietnam*, ed. Philip Taylor, 1–56. Singapore: Institute of Southeast Asian Studies.

Chú-Kinh Nhật-Tụng [Sutras for daily use]. 1964. Saigon: Chùa Dức Hòa.

Connell, Robert. 1987. *Gender and Power: Society, the Person and Sexual Politics*. Stanford, CA: Stanford University Press.

———. 1995. *Masculinities: Knowledge, Power and Social Change*. Berkeley: University of California Press.

Đặng Nghiêm Vạn. 1998. *Ethnological and Religious Problems in Vietnam*. Hanoi: Social Sciences Publishing House.

DeVido, Elise Anne. 2007. "'Buddhism for This World': The Buddhist Revival in Vietnam 1920 to 1951, and Its Legacy." In *Modernity and Re-Enchantment: Religion in Post-Revolutionary Vietnam*, ed. Philip Taylor, 250–297. Singapore: Institute of Southeast Asian Studies.

Diệu. 2010. *"Mê Tín Và Lãng Phí Trong Mùa Vu Lan"* [Superstition and waste in the Vu Lan season]. *Tuần Báo Giác Ngộ* 502:28–29.

Đỗ Thiện (or Do, Thien). 1998. "Enlightenment and Cultural Identity: Buddhism in Contemporary Vietnam." Unpublished paper. Near Brisbane, Australia.

———. 2003. *Vietnamese Supernaturalism: Views from the Southern Area*. London: Routledge Curzon.

———. 2007. "Unjust-Death Deification and Burnt Offering: Towards an Integrative View of Popular Religion in Contemporary Southern Vietnam." In *Modernity and Re-Enchantment: Religion in Post-Revolutionary Vietnam*, ed. Philip Taylor, 161–193. Singapore: Institute of Southeast Asian Studies.

Đoàn Lâm. 1999. "A Brief Account of the Cult of the Female Deities in Vietnam." *Vietnamese Studies* 131(1):5–19.

Drummond, Lisa B. W. 1999. "Mapping Modernity: Perspectives on Everyday Life in Vietnam's Urbanizing Society." PhD diss., Australian National University, Canberra.

Durand, Maurice. 1959. *Technique et Panthéon des Mediums Vietnamiens (Dong)*. Paris: École Française d'Extrême-Orient.

Endres, Kirsten. 1998. "Culturalizing Politics: Doi Moi and the Restructuring of Ritual in Contemporary Rural Vietnam." Unpublished paper. Ludwig-Maximilians-University, Munich.

———. 2001. "Local Dynamics of Renegotiating Ritual Space in Northern Vietnam: The Case of the *Dinh*." *Sojourn* 16(1):10–101.

———. 2006. "Spirit Performance and the Ritual Construction of Personal Identity in Modern Vietnam." In *Possessed by the Spirits: Mediumship in Contemporary Vietnamese Communities*, ed. Karen Fjelstad and Nguyen Thi Hien, 77–93. Ithaca, NY: Cornell Southeast Asia Program.

———. 2007. "Spirited Modernities: Mediumship and Ritual Performativity." In *Modernity and Re-Enchantment: Religion in Post-Revolutionary Vietnam*, ed. Philip Taylor, 194–220. Singapore: Institute of Southeast Asian Studies.

———. 2008. "Fate, Memory, and the Postcolonial Construction of the Self: The Life-Narrative of a Vietnamese Spirit Medium." *Journal of Vietnamese Studies* 3(2):34–65.

Fahey, Stephanie. 1998. "Vietnam's Women in the Renovation Era." In *Gender and Power in Affluent Asia*, ed. Krishna Sen and Maila Stivens, 222–249. London: Routledge.

Fjelstad, Karen. 2006. "'We Have *Len Dong* Too': Transnational Aspects of Spirit Possession." In *Possessed by the Spirits: Mediumship in Contemporary Vietnamese Communities,* ed. Karen Fjelstad and Nguyen Thi Hien, 95–110. Ithaca, NY: Cornell Southeast Asia Program.

Fjelstad, Karen, and Lisa Maiffret. 2006. "Gifts from the Spirits: Spirit Possession and Personal Transformation Among Silicon Valley Spirit Mediums." In *Possessed by the Spirits: Mediumship in Contemporary Vietnamese Communities,* ed. Karen Fjelstad and Nguyen Thi Hien, 111–126. Ithaca, NY: Cornell Southeast Asia Program.

Fjelstad, Karen, and Nguyen Thi Hien, ed. 2006a. *Possessed by the Spirits: Mediumship in Contemporary Vietnamese Communities.* Ithaca, NY: Cornell Southeast Asia Program.

———. 2006b. "Introduction." In *Possessed by the Spirits: Mediumship in Contemporary Vietnamese Communities,* ed. Karen Fjelstad and Nguyen Thi Hien, 7–17. Ithaca, NY: Cornell Southeast Asia Program.

Gal, Susan. 1991. "Between Speech and Silence: The Problematics of Research on Language and Gender." In *Gender at the Crossroads of Knowledge: Feminist Anthropology in the Postmodern Era,* ed. Micaela di Leonardo, 175–203. Berkeley, Los Angeles, and Oxford: University of California Press.

Gammeltoft, Tine. 1999. *Women's Bodies, Women's Worries: Health and Family Planning in a Vietnamese Rural Community.* Surrey, UK: Curzon.

Gimello, Robert M. 2004. "Icon and Incantation: The Goddess Zhunti and the Role of Images in the Occult Buddhism of China." In *Images in Asian Religions: Texts and Contexts,* ed. Phyllis Granoff and Koichi Shinohara, 225–255. Vancouver: UBC Press.

Giran, Paul. 1912. *Magie et Religion Annamites: Introduction à une Philosophie de la Civilisation du Peuple d'Annam.* Paris: Librairie Maritime et Coloniale.

Goffman, Erving. 1959. *The Presentation of Self in Everyday Life.* Edinburgh: University of Edinburgh, Social Sciences Research Centre.

Gourou, Pierre. 1975. *Man and Land in the Far East.* New York: Longman.

Gustafsson, Mai Lan. 2009. *War and Shadows: The Haunting of Vietnam.* Ithaca, NY: Cornell University Press.

Hà Văn Tấn, and Nguyễn Văn Kự. 1998. *Đình Việt Nam—Community Halls in Vietnam.* Ho Chi Minh City: Hồ Chí Minh City Publishing House.

Hà Văn Tấn, Nguyễn Văn Kự, and Phạm Ngọc Long. 1993. *Chùa Việt Nam—Buddhist Temples in Vietnam.* Hanoi: Nhà Xuất Bản Khoa Học Xã Hội.

Hickey, Gerald Cannon. 1987. "The Vietnamese Village Through Time and War." *The Vietnam Forum* 10:1–25.

Ho Tai, Hue-Tam. 1987. "Religion in Vietnam: A World of Gods and Spirits." *The Vietnam Forum* 10:113–145.

———, ed. 2001. *The Country of Memory: Remaking the Past in Late Socialist Vietnam.* Berkeley: University of California Press.

Hoàng Bá Thịnh. 2002a. "Relationship Between Family Members." In *Images of Vietnamese Woman in the New Millenium,* ed. Lê Thị Nhâm Tuyết, 139–156. Hanoi: Thế Giới Publishers.

———. 2002b. "Lonely Elderly Women." In *Images of Vietnamese Woman in the New Millenium,* ed. Lê Thị Nhâm Tuyết, 192–202. Hanoi: Thế Giới Publishers.

Hữu Ngọc. 1997. "Buddhist Vegetarian Meals." *Vietnamese Studies* 55(3):89–106.

Jamieson, Neil L. 1986. "The Traditional Village of Vietnam." *The Vietnam Forum* 7:88–126.

———. 1993. *Understanding Vietnam.* Berkeley and Los Angeles: University of California Press.

Jayawardena, Kumari. 1986. *Feminism and Nationalism in the Third World.* London: Zed Books.

Jellema, Kate. 2007. "Returning Home: Ancestor Veneration and the Nationalism of *Đổi Mới* Vietnam." In *Modernity and Re-Enchantment: Religion in Post-Revolutionary Vietnam,* ed. Philip Taylor, 1–56. Singapore: Institute of Southeast Asian Studies.

Kapferer, Bruce. 1997. *The Feast of the Sorcerer: Practices of Consciousness and Power.* Chicago and London: The University of Chicago Press.

Kendall, Laurel. 1985. *Shamans, Housewives, and Other Restless Spirits: Women in Korean Ritual Life.* Honolulu: University of Hawai'i Press.

———. 1996. "Korean Shamanism and the Spirits of Capitalism." *American Anthropologist* 98(3):512–527.

Kendall, Laurel, and Diana Lee (producer/director). 1992. *An Initiation Kut for a Korean Shaman* (film). Distributed by University of Hawai'i Press, Honolulu.

Kennedy, Laurel B., and Mary Rose Williams. 2001. "The Past Without Pain: The Manufacture of Nostalgia in Vietnam's Tourist Industry." In *The Country of Memory: Remaking the Past in Late Socialist Vietnam,* ed. Hue-Tam Ho Tai, 135–163. Berkeley: University of California Press.

Khánh Duyên. 1994. *Tín Ngưỡng Bà Chúa Kho* [Religious beliefs regarding the Lady of the Storehouse]. Hà Bắc: Cục Văn Hóa Thông Tin Và Thể Thao Hà Bắc.

Kipnis, Andrew. 1997. *Producing Guanxi: Sentiment, Self, and Subculture in a North China Village.* Durham, NC: Duke University Press.

Kleinen, John. 1999. *Facing the Future, Reviving the Past: A Study of Social Change in a Northern Vietnamese Village.* Singapore: Institute of Southeast Asian Studies.

Kwon, Heonik. 2008. *Ghosts of War in Vietnam.* Cambridge: Cambridge University Press.

Larsson, Viveca, and Kirsten W. Endres. 2006. " 'Children of the Spirits, Followers of a Master': Spirit Mediums in Post-Renovation Vietnam." In *Possessed by the Spirits: Mediumship in Contemporary Vietnamese Communities,* ed. Karen Fjelstad and Nguyen Thi Hien, 143–160. Ithaca, NY: Cornell Southeast Asia Program.

Lê Thị Nhâm Tuyết. 2002. "Women and Politics." In *Images of Vietnamese Woman in the New Millennium,* ed. Lê Thị Nhâm Tuyết, 203–215. Hanoi: Thế Giới Publishers.

Lê Văn Hảo. 1998 [1962]. "Introduction à l'Ethnologie du Đình" [Introduction to the ethnology of the communal house]. *The Vietnam Review* 4:185–217. Originally published in *Bulletin de la Société des Études Indochinoises, Nouvelle Série* 36(1).

Leshkowich, Ann Marie. 2003. "The *Ao Dai* Goes Global: How International Influences and Female Entrepreneurs Have Shaped Vietnam's National Costume." In *Re-Orienting Fashion: The Globalization of Asian Dress,* ed. S. Niessen, A. M. Leshkowich, and C. Jones, 79–116. Oxford: Berg Publishers .

Levering, Miriam L. 1992 [1985]. "Lin-chi (Rinzai) Ch'an and Gender: The Rhetoric of Equality and the Rhetoric of Heroism." In *Buddhism, Sexuality, and Gender,* ed. J. Cabezón, 137–156. Albany: State University of New York Press.

Li Tana. 1996. *Peasants on the Move: Rural–Urban Migration in the Hanoi Religion.* Singapore: Institute of Southeast Asian Studies.
———. 1998. *Nguyễn Cochinchina: Southern Vietnam in the Seventeenth and Eighteenth Centuries.* Ithaca, NY: Cornell Southeast Asia Program.
Lojkine, Boris (producer/director). 2005. *Wandering Ghosts* (film). 4A4 Productions.
Luong, Hy Van. 1990. *Discursive Practices and Linguistic Meanings: The Vietnamese System of Personal Reference.* Philadelphia: John Benjamins.
———. 1992. *Revolution in the Village: Tradition and Transformation in Northern Vietnam, 1925–1988.* Honolulu: University of Hawai'i Press.
———. 1993. "Economic Reform and the Intensification of Rituals in Two Northern Vietnamese Villages, 1980–90." In *The Challenge of Reform in Indochina,* ed. Borje Ljunggren, 259–292. Cambridge: Harvard Institute for International Development.
Mai Thọ Truyền. 1959. *Le Bouddhisme au Việt-Nam.* Saigon: France-Asie.
Malarney, Shaun Kingsley. 1993. *Ritual and Revolution in Vietnam.* PhD diss., University of Michigan, Ann Arbor.
———. 1999. "Buddhist Practices in Rural Northern Việt Nam." In *Liber Amicorum: Mélanges Offerts au Professeur Phan Huy Lê,* ed. Phillippe Papin and John Kleinen, 183–200. Hanoi: Nhà Xuất Bản Thanh Niên.
———. 2001. "'The Fatherland Remembers Your Sacrifice': Commemorating War Dead in North Vietnam." In *The Country of Memory: Remaking the Past in Late Socialist Vietnam,* ed. Hue-Tam Ho Tai, 46–76. Berkeley: University of California Press.
———. 2002. *Culture, Ritual and Revolution in Vietnam.* Honolulu: University of Hawai'i Press.
Marr, David G. 1971. *Vietnamese Anticolonialism: 1885–1925.* Berkeley: University of California Press.
———. 1981. *Vietnamese Tradition on Trial, 1920–1945.* Berkeley: University of California Press.
———. 1987. "Vietnamese Attitudes Regarding Illness and Healing." *The Vietnam Forum* 10:26–50.
———. 1994. "Religion and Money." *Vietnam Today* 67:14–15.
———. 1997. "Vietnamese Youth in the 1990s." *The Vietnam Review* 2:288–354.
Mauss, Marcel. 1969 [1950]. *The Gift: Forms and Functions of Exchange in Archaic Societies.* London: Cohen and West.
McHale, Shawn Frederick. 2004. *Print and Power: Confucianism, Communism, and Buddhism in the Making of Modern Vietnam.* Honolulu: University of Hawai'i Press.
Minh Chi, Ha Van Tan, and Nguyen Tai Thu. 1993. *Buddhism in Vietnam—From Its Origins to the 19th Century.* Hanoi: Thế Giới Publishers.
Nash, Jesse W., and Elizabeth Trinh Nguyen. 1995. *Romance, Gender and Religion in a Vietnamese-American Community: Tales of Beautiful Women.* Lewiston, NY: Edwin Mellen Press.
National Assembly, Socialist Republic of Vietnam. 2006. *Law on Information Technology.* No. 67/2006/QH11. Accessed July 2011 at http://www.investip.vn/uploads/vanbanphapluat/Tu%20van%20dau%20tu/Luat/en/Law%20on%20Information%20Technology.pdf.

National Committee for the Advancement of Women in Viet Nam (NCFAW). 2006. *The Gender Statistics Book*. National Committee for the Advancement of Women in Vietnam (NCFAW) and General Statistical Office (GSO).

Needham, Rodney. 1972. *Belief, Language and Experience*. Chicago: University of Chicago Press.

Ngô Đức Thịnh, ed. 1992. *Hát Văn* [Singing literature]. Hanoi: Nhà Xuất Bản Văn Học Dân Tộc.

———. 1996a. "The Cult of the Female Spirits and the Mother Goddesses 'Mẫu.'" *Vietnamese Studies* 121(3):83–96.

———. 1996b. *Đạo Mẫu ở Việt Nam, Tập I—Khảo Cứu, Tập II—Các Bản Văn* [The mother goddess religion in Vietnam, part I—investigation, part II—texts]. Hanoi: Nhà Xuất Bản Văn Hóa Thông Tin.

———. 1999. "The Pantheon for the Cult of Holy Mothers." *Vietnamese Studies* 131(1):20–35.

———. 2006. "The Mother Goddess Religion: Its History, Pantheon, and Practices." In *Possessed by the Spirits: Mediumship in Contemporary Vietnamese Communities,* ed. Karen Fjelstad and Nguyen Thi Hien, 19–30. Ithaca, NY: Cornell Southeast Asia Program.

Nguyen, Cuong Tu. 1995. "Rethinking Vietnamese Buddhist History: Is the *Thiền Uyển Tập Anh* a 'Transmission of the Lamp' Text?" In *Essays into Vietnamese Pasts,* ed. K. W. Taylor and John K. Whitmore, 81–115. Ithaca, NY: Cornell Southeast Asia Program.

———. 1997. *Zen in Medieval Vietnam: A Study and Translation of the Thiền Uyển Tập Anh*. Honolulu: University of Hawai'i Press, The Kuroda Institute for the Study of Buddhism and Human Values.

Nguyễn Đình Cẩn. 2010. "Người Tu Hành Luon Hướng Về Những Điều Tốt Đẹp Nhấy Cho Dân, Cho Nước…" ["The monastics wish all the best for the people, the country…"]. *Tạp Chí Nghiên Cứu Phật Học* 1:5–7.

Nguyễn Hồng Dương. 2003. *Nhà Thờ Công Giáo Việt Nam* [Catholic churches of Vietnam]. Hanoi: Nhà Xuất Bản Khoa Học Xã Hội.

Nguyễn Khắc Viện. 1974. *Tradition and Revolution in Vietnam*. Berkeley: Indochina Resource Center.

———. 1993. *Vietnam: A Long History*. Hanoi: Thế Giới Publishers.

———. 1998. "Gymnastics for the Years of Retirement." *Vietnam Studies* 128(2):92–95.

Nguyễn Minh San, Ngô Đức Thịnh, and Đoàn Lâm. 1999. "Typical Rites of the Cult of Holy Mothers." *Vietnamese Studies* 131(1):36–55.

Nguyễn Tài Thư. 1992. *History of Buddhism in Vietnam*. Hanoi: Social Sciences Publishing House.

Nguyễn Thế Long, and Phạm Mai Hùng. 1997. *Chùa Hà Nội* [Pagodas of Hanoi]. Hanoi: Nhà Xuất Bản Văn Hóa Thông Tin.

———. 2003. *130 Pagodas in Hà Nội*. Hanoi: Thế Giới Publishers.

Nguyen Thi Hien. 2002. "The Religion of the Four Palaces: Mediumship and Therapy in Viet Culture." PhD diss., Indiana University, Bloomington.

———. 2006. "'A Bit of a Spirit Favor Is Equal to a Load of Mundane Gifts': Votive Paper

Offerings of *Len Dong* Rituals in Post-Renovation Vietnam." In *Possessed by the Spirits: Mediumship in Contemporary Vietnamese Communities,* ed. Karen Fjelstad and Nguyen Thi Hien, 127–143. Ithaca, NY: Cornell Southeast Asia Program.

Nguyễn Thuyết Phong. 1983. "La Liturgie Bouddhique du Việt-Nam et Son Répertoire." *The Vietnam Forum* 2:44–55.

———. 1985. "Les Instruments Rituels de la Musique Bouddhique au Viêtnam." *The Vietnam Forum* 5:174–213.

———. 1986. "Les Instruments Profanes dans la Musique Bouddhique du Viêtnam." *The Vietnam Forum* 7:72–86.

Nguyen Van Chinh. 1997. *Social Change in Rural Vietnam: Children's Work and Seasonal Migration.* Canberra: Department of Political and Social Change, Research School of Pacific and Asian Studies, Australian National University.

Norton, Barley. 2000a. "Music and Possession in Vietnam." PhD diss., School of Oriental and African Studies, University of London.

———. 2000b. "Vietnamese Mediumship Rituals: The Musical Construction of the Spirits." *The World of Music* 42(2):75–97.

———. 2002 "The Moon Remembers Uncle Ho: The Politics of Music and Mediumship in Northern Vietnam." *British Journal of Ethnomusicology* 11(1):71–100.

———. 2004. "Lên Đồng Việt Nam: Cấu Tạo Âm Nhạc Của Thần Thánh" [Vietnamese mediumship rituals: The musical construction of the spirits]. In *Đạo Mẫu và Các Hình Thức Shaman Trong Các Tộc Người ở Việt Nam và Châu Á* [The Mother goddess religion and forms of shamanism among ethnic groups in Vietnam and Asia], ed. Ngô Đức Thịnh, 310–341. Hanoi: Nhà Xuất Bản Khoa Học Xã Hội,

———. 2006. " 'Hot-Tempered' Women and 'Effeminate' Men: The Performance of Music and Gender in Vietnamese Mediumship." In *Possessed by the Spirits: Mediumship in Contemporary Vietnamese Communities,* ed. Karen Fjelstad and Nguyen Thi Hien, 55–75. Ithaca, NY: Cornell Southeast Asia Program.

———. 2009. *Songs for the Spirits: Music and Mediums in Modern Vietnam.* Chicago: University of Illinois Press.

O'Harrow, Stephen. 1995. "Vietnamese Women and Confucianism: Creating Spaces From Patriarchy." In *"Male" and "Female" in Developing Southeast Asia,* ed. Wazir Jahan Karim, 161–180. Oxford: Berg Publishers.

Ortner, Sherry. 1989. *High Religion: A Cultural and Political History of Sherpa Religion.* Princeton, NJ: Princeton University Press.

Peletz, Michael G. 1995. "Neither Reasonable nor Responsible: Contrasting Representations of Masculinity in a Malay Society." In *Bewitching Women, Pious Men: Gender and Body Politics in Southeast Asia,* ed. Aihwa Ong and Michael G. Peletz, 76–123. Berkeley: University of California Press.

———. 1996. *Reason and Passion: Representations of Gender in Malay Society.* Berkeley: University of California Press.

Phạm Qùynh Phương. 2006. "Tran Hung Dao and the Mother Goddess Religion." In *Possessed by the Spirits: Mediumship in Contemporary Vietnamese Communities,* ed. Karen Fjelstad and Nguyen Thi Hien, 31–54. Ithaca, NY: Cornell Southeast Asia Program.

———. 2007. "Empowerment and Innovation Among Saint Trần's Female Mediums." In

Modernity and Re-Enchantment: Religion in Post-Revolutionary Vietnam, ed. Philip Taylor, 221–249. Singapore: Institute of Southeast Asian Studies.

———. 2009. *Hero and Deity: Tran Hung Dao and the Resurgence of Popular Religion in Vietnam.* Chiang Mai, Thailand: Mekong Press.

Pham Van Bich. 1999. *The Vietnamese Family in Change: The Case of the Red River Delta.* Surrey, UK: Curzon Press and The Nordic Institute of Asian Studies.

Pham Van Dong. 1990. *Hồ Chí Minh: A Man, a Nation, an Age, a Cause.* Hanoi: Foreign Languages Publishing House.

Phan Cẩm Thượng. 1996. *Bút Tháp: Nghệ Thuật Phật Giáo—Buddhist Art.* Hanoi: Nhà Xuất Bản Mỹ Thuật.

Phan Huy Đông. 1998. *Huyền Thoại Bà Chúa Kho* [The legend of the Lady of the Storehouse]. Hanoi: Nhà Xuất Bản Văn Hóa Dân Tộc.

Phua, Joe (producer/director). 2006. *Psychic Vietnam* (film). InFocus Asia and Productions for This World.

Prebish, Charles S. 1979. *American Buddhism.* North Scituate, MA: Duxbury Press.

———. 1999. *Luminous Passage: The Practice and Study of Buddhism in America.* Berkeley: University of California Press.

Rahula, Walpola. 1974 [1959]. *What the Buddha Taught.* New York: Grove Press.

Ramsay, Jacob. 2007. "Miracles and Myths: Vietnam Seen Through its Catholic History." In *Modernity and Re-Enchantment: Religion in Post-Revolutionary Vietnam,* ed. Philip Taylor, 371–398. Singapore: Institute of Southeast Asian Studies.

Revertegat, Bruno. 1974. *Le Bouddhisme Traditionnel au Sud-Vietnam.* Vichy, France: Wallon.

Rey, Terry. 2007. *Bourdieu on Religion: Imposing Faith and Legitimacy.* London: Equinox Publishing.

Rogers, Tommy. 1976. "Manifestations of Religiosity and the Aging Process." *Religious Education* 71(4):405–415.

Sangren, P. Steven. 1983. "Female Gender in Chinese Religious Symbols: Kuan Yin, Ma Tsu, and the 'Eternal Mother.'" *Signs* 9(1):4–25.

———. 1987. "Orthodoxy, Heterodoxy, and the Structure of Value in Chinese Rituals." *Modern China* 13(1):63–89.

Simon, Pierre J., and Ida Simon-Barouh. 1973. *Hầu Bóng: Un Culte Viêtnamien de Possession Transplanté en France.* Paris: Mouton & Co.

———. 1996. "The Genii of Four Palaces: Contributions to the Study of the Vietnamese Cult of *Bà Đồng.*" *Vietnamese Studies* 121(3):109–144.

Soucy, Alexander. 1993. "The Role of Women at the Tam Bao Pagoda, Montreal." *Journal of Religion and Culture* 8:57–72.

———. 1994. "Gender and Division of Labour in a Vietnamese–Canadian Buddhist Pagoda." Master's thesis, Concordia University, Montreal, PQ.

———. 1996. "The Dynamics of Change in an Exiled Pagoda: Vietnamese Buddhism in Montreal." *Canberra Anthropology* 19(2):29–45.

———. 1999. "Masculinities and Buddhist Symbolism in Vietnam." In *Playing the Man: New Approaches to Masculinity,* ed. Katherine Biber, Tom Sear, and Dave Trudinger, 123–134. Sydney, Australia: Pluto Press.

———. 2000. "The Problem with Key Informants." *Anthropological Forum* 10(2): 179–199.

———. 2001. "Romantic Love and Gender Hegemony in Vietnam." In *Love, Sex and Power: Women in Southeast Asia,* ed. Susan Blackburn, 31–42. Clayton, Vic., Australia: Monash Asia Institute.

———. 2003. "Pilgrims and Pleasure Seekers." In *Consuming Urban Culture in Contemporary Vietnam,* ed. Mandy Thomas and Lisa Drummond, 125–137. New York: Routledge.

———. 2006. "Consuming *Lộc*—Creating *Ơn:* Women, Offerings and Symbolic Capital in Vietnam." *Studies in Religion/Sciences Religieuses* 35(1):107–131.

———. 2007. "Nationalism, Globalism and the Re-establishment of the Trúc Lâm Thiền Buddhist Sect in Northern Vietnam." In *Modernity and Re-Enchantment: Religion in Post-Revolutionary Vietnam,* ed. Philip Taylor, 342–370. Singapore: Institute of Southeast Asian Studies.

———. 2009. "Language, Orthodoxy and Performances of Authority in Vietnamese Buddhism." *Journal of the American Academy of Religion* 77(2):348–371.

Spiro, Melford E. 1982. *Buddhism and Society: A Great Tradition and its Burmese Vicissitudes.* Berkeley: University of California Press.

Standing Committee of the National Assembly (SCNAC). 2004. "Ordinance of the Standing Committee of the National Assembly No. 21/2004/PL-UBTVQH11 OF 18 JUNE 2004 Regarding Religious Belief and Religious Organizations." Translation of *Pháp Lệnh Tín Ngưỡng, Tôn Giáo.* Hanoi.

Tambiah, S. J. 1970. *Buddhism and the Spirit Cults in North-East Thailand.* Cambridge: Cambridge University Press.

Tân Việt. 1996. *100 Điều Nên Biết về Phong Tục Việt Nam* [100 things you should know about Vietnamese customs]. Hanoi: Nhà Xuất Bản Van Hoá Dân Tộc.

Tạp Chí Nghiên Cứu Phật Học [The research journal of Buddhist studies]. Hanoi: Chùa Quán Sứ, Giáo Hội Phật Giáo Việt Nam.

Taylor, Charles. 2007. *Modern Social Imaginaries,* 4th printing. Durham, NC: Duke University Press.

Taylor, Keith Weller. 1986. "Authority and Legitimation in 11th Century Vietnam." In *Southeast Asia in the 9th to 14th Centuries,* ed. David G. Marr and A. C. Milner, 139–176. Canberra: RSPAS, The Australian National University; and Singapore: Institute of Southeast Asian Studies.

Taylor, Nora. 2001. "Framing the National Spirit: Viewing and Reviewing Painting Under the Revolution." In *The Country of Memory: Remaking the Past in Late Socialist Vietnam,* ed. Hue-Tam Ho Tai, 109–134. Berkeley: University of California Press.

Taylor, Philip K. 2004. *Goddess on the Rise: Pilgrimage and Popular Religion in Vietnam.* Honolulu: University of Hawai'i Press.

———. 2007. "Modernity and Re-Enchantment in Post-Revolutionary Vietnam." In *Modernity and Re-Enchantment: Religion in Post-Revolutionary Vietnam,* ed. Philip Taylor, 1–56. Singapore: Institute of Southeast Asian Studies.

Thanh Hà. 1996. *Âm Nhạc Hát Văn* [The music of *hát văn*]. Hanoi: Nhà Xuất Bản Âm Nhạc.

Thanh Huyên. 1996. "An Overview of Beliefs and Religions in Vietnam." *Vietnamese Studies* 121(3):5–22.

Thanh Tùng. 1998. "Actual State of Aged People in Urban and Rural Areas." *Vietnamese Studies* 128(2):40–48.

Thích Đồng Bổn (Ed.) 1995. *Tiểu Sử Danh Tăng Việt Nam Thế Kỷ XX, Tập 1* [Biography of Vietnamese monks of the 20th century, Vol. 1]. Ho Chi Minh City: Thành Hội Phật Giáo T. P. Hồ Chí Minh.

Thich Nhat Hanh. 1967. *Vietnam: Lotus in a Sea of Fire*. New York: Hill and Wang.

Thích Thanh Từ. 1992. *Thiền Sư Việt Nam* [Zen masters of Vietnam]. Ho Chi Minh City: Thành Hội Phật Giáo T. P. Hồ Chí Minh

Thich Thien-An. 1975. *Buddhism and Zen in Vietnam in Relation to the Development of Buddhism in Asia*. Rutland, VT: Charles E. Tuttle Company.

Toan Ánh. 1996. *Nếp Cũ Tín Ngưỡng Việt Nam* [Traditional beliefs of Vietnam], 2 vols. Ho Chi Minh City: Nhà Xuất Bản T. P. Hồ Chí Minh.

Topmiller, Robert J. 2002. *The Lotus Unleashed: The Buddhist Peace Movement in South Vietnam, 1964–1966*. Lexington: University of Kentucky Press.

Trần Đại Vinh, Nguyễn Hữu Thông, and Lê Văn Sách. 1993. *Danh Lam Xứ Huế—The Celebrated Pagodas of Hue*. Huế: Nhà Xuất Bản Nhà Văn.

Trần Ngọc Thêm. 1997. *Cơ Sở Văn Hóa Việt Nam* [The foundation of Vietnamese culture]. Ho Chi Minh City: Nhà Xuất Bản Giáo Dục.

Trần Văn Giáp. 1932. "Le Bouddhisme en Annam des Origines au XIIIe siècle." *Bulletin de l'École Française d'Extrême-Orient* 32:191–286.

Trungpa, Chögyam. 1973. *Cutting Through Material Spiritualism*. Boston: Shambhala Publications.

Trường-Chinh. 1966. *President Hồ-Chí-Minh: Beloved Leader of the Vietnamese People*. Hanoi: Foreign Language Publishing House.

Tuần Báo Giác Ngộ [Enlightenment weekly magazine]. n.d. Ho Chi Minh City: Cơ Quan Của Thành Hội Phật Giáo T. P. Hồ Chí Minh.

Turner, Victor. 1995 [1969]. *The Ritual Process: Structure and Anti-structure*. New York: Aldine de Gruyter.

United Nations Economic and Social Commission for Asia and the Pacific (UNESCAP). n.d. "Report on the State of Women in Urban Local Government—Viet Nam." UNESCAP. Accessed at http://www.unescap.org/huset/women/reports/vietnam .pdf.

Veblen, Thorstein. 2007 [1899]. *The Theory of the Leisure Class*. New York: Oxford University Press. Accessed July 2011 at http://lib.myilibrary.com.library.smu .ca:2048?ID=114521.

Vietnam News Agency. 2005 (November 9). "Viet Nam Attends World Buddhist Summit." Ministry of Foreign Affairs, Hanoi. Accessed at http://www.mofa.gov.vn/en /nr040807104143/nr040807105001/ns051103091401/view.

VN Express. 2007 (December 16). "*Hà Nội Có 3,4 Triệu Người*" [Hanoi has 3.4 million people]. Accessed at http://vnexpress.net/Vietnam/Xa-hoi/2007/12/3B9FD60F/.

Võ Văn Tường. 1993. *Việt Nam Danh Lam Cổ Tự—Vietnam's Famous Ancient Pagodas*. Hanoi: Nhà Xuất Bản Khoa Học Xã Hội.

———. 1994. *Những Ngôi Chùa Nổi Tiếng Việt Nam—Vietnam's Famous Pagodas*. Hanoi: Nhà Xuất Bản Văn Hóa Thông Tin.

Võ Văn Tường, and Huỳnh Như Phương. 1995. *Danh Lam Nước Việt Nam—Vietnam's Famous Pagodas*. Ho Chi Minh City: Nhà Xuất Bản Mỹ Thuật.

Vuong Thi Hanh, and Doan Thuy Dung. 2007. "Women in Politics in Vietnam." GenComNet and AA Viet Nam. Accessed at www.wedo.org/wp-content/uploads /vietnam.doc.

Watson, James L. 1991 [1988]. "Funeral Specialists in Cantonese Society: Pollution, Performance, and Social Hierarch." In *Death Ritual in Late Imperial and Modern China,* ed. James L. Watson and Evelyn S. Rawski, 109–134. Taipei: SMC Publishing Inc.

Weber, Max. 1948 [1930]. *The Protestant Ethic and the Spirit of Capitalism.* London: George Allen and Unwin.

———. 1964 [1951]. *The Religion of China: Confucianism and Taoism.* New York: The Free Press.

Welch, Holmes. 1973 [1967]. *The Practice of Chinese Buddhism.* Cambridge: Harvard University Press.

Weller, Robert P. 1987. "The Politics of Ritual Disguise: Repression and Response in Taiwanese Popular Religion." *Modern China* 13(1):17–39.

———. 1994. "Capitalism, Community and the Rise of Amoral Cults in Taiwan." In *Asian Visions of Authority: Religion and the Rise of Modern States of East and Southeast Asia,* ed. Charles F. Keyes, Laurel Kendall, and Helen Hardacre, 141–164. Honolulu: University of Hawai'i Press.

———. 1996. "Matricidal Magistrates and Gambling Gods: Weak States and Strong Spirits in China." In *Unruly Gods: Divinity and Society in Chin,* ed. Meir Shahar and Robert P. Weller, 250–268. Honolulu: University of Hawai'i Press.

Wolf, Arthur P. 1978. "Gods, Ghosts and Ancestors." In *Studies in Chinese Society,* ed. Arthur P. Wolf, 131–182. Stanford, CA: Stanford University Press.

Wolf, Margery. 1968. *The House of Lim: A Study of a Chinese Farm Family.* New York: Appleton-Century-Crofts.

———. 1972. *Women and the Family in Rural Taiwan.* Stanford, CA: Stanford University Press.

Woodside, Alexander B. 1971. *Vietnam and the Chinese Model: A Comparative Study of Vietnamese and Chinese Government in the First Half of the Nineteenth Century.* Cambridge, MA: Council on East Asian Studies Harvard University; distributed by Harvard University Press.

———. 1976. *Community and Revolution in Modern Vietnam.* Boston: Houghton Mifflin Company.

———. 1988. "Vietnamese History: Confucianism, Colonialism and the Struggle for Independence." *The Vietnam Forum* 11:21–48.

Yang, Mayfair Mei-hui. 1994. *Gifts, Favors, and Banquets: The Art of Social Relationships in China.* Ithaca, NY: Cornell University Press.

Index

Page numbers in **boldface** type refer to illustrations.

A Di Đà Phật (Ch. Amituo Fo; S. Amitābha Buddha), 26, 47, 55, 56, 121, 126, 129; chanting name, 1, 126, 205n2; evoking name, 138
A Nan Đà (S. Ānanda), 47, 48, 168
absolution. *See* Buddha: pardon from
academy, 25, 31, 35; as masculine, 164, 165, 208n12
afterlife, 20, 38, 62, 75, 95, 120, 122, 137, 171
age, 67, 98, 117, 121, 136–137; appropriate activities, 125–126; and leisure time, 123; and religiosity, 118–126, 159, 161–165, 202–203. *See also* hierarchy: and age
alcohol, 74, 76, 101, 157; men drinking, 74, 76, 101, 110, 190; women drinking, 101–102
altar, 1, 140, 213n6; ancestor, 20, 34, **47**, 81, 121, 216n1; business, **73**; home, 18, 86, 97, 119, 145, 150–151, 199; mother goddess, **58**. *See also* iconography
ambivalence, 63, 74–75, 77, 91
Amitābha Buddha. *See* A Di Đà Phật
Amituo Fo. *See* A Di Đà Phật
ancestors, 25, 63, 77, 115, 208n11; as active forces, 22; affecting karma, 174; blessings, 90; commemoration of, 32, 77; cult, 10, 70, 122–123; and ghosts, 30, 207n5, 208n11; 213n7; national, 28, 32, 35; reciprocal relationships with, 22, 94–95; secularized, 59, 62; tablets, **56**; worship of (*cúng tổ tiên*), 5, 16, 17, 23, 106, 120–121, 160, 199–200, 209n19, 212n4. *See also* altar: ancestor; Lễ Giỗ Tổ; offerings: to ancestors; pagoda: ancestors; Vu Lan
áo dài, 103, 106
architecture and art: as representative of culture, 41, 59, 187. *See also* pagoda: architecture

arhats (*la hán*), 25, 27, 45, 48, 55
aspirations, 89, 99, 133, 175, 191
astrology, 52, 209n19
attachment, 90, 168, 206n15, 217n7
audiences, 143, 148, 153, 216n4. *See also* performance
authenticity, 39, 62, 161, 181
authority, 40, 59, 65, 179–181, 187–191, 193, 196; claims of, 177, 201; of experts, 75; lack of, 7; language and, 184–191, 193, 195, 203; local, 216n1; male, 6, 31, 62, 100, 103, 160–161, 177, 196; recognition and, 155; religious, 7; of the state, 51, 65; in structure of power, 99. *See also* legitimacy
Avalokiteśvara. *See* Quan Âm
avoidance: of displays of knowledge, 201; practices, 65, 91, 109, 111, 136, 180, 189, 204, 212n5; of religions, 17, 62, 64, 68, 71, 77, 78, 160, 201; of rituals, 180, 182, 189–191, 204; of spirit possession rituals, 6; of superstition, 159, 163; of women's practices, 13, 163, 164. *See also* Đức, Mr.; Lê, Mr.

Bà Chúa Kho. *See* Lady of the Storehouse
Bà Chúa Xứ. *See* Lady of the Realm
Bà Đá Pagoda, 52, 147, 214n6
ban cúng. See ritual group
barrenness, 106, 153, 175
behavior, 77, 137; affected, 139; changing, 101–102; feminine, 19, 70, 101–102, 109; submissive, 103. *See also* conspicuous devotion; faith; performance
bên phật. See Buddha side
bên thánh. See spirit side
betel nut, 22, 30, 87, 121
Bình, Mrs., 41–42, 119, 127, 133, 155, 156–158

causality, 168–170. *See also* karma

Chân Tiên Pagoda, 79

chanting, 18, 69, 75, 138, 199; correctly, 171; at funerals, 122, 128–129, 137; goal of, 166, 188; at home, 18, 144, 151; for meaning, 168, 171–173; men and, 1, 69, 119, 126, 191; no supernatural benefit, 189–190; practice of women, 118, 126, 173, 182, 189, 191; sutras (*tụng kinh*), 28, 53, 97, 119, 121, 122, 125, 166, 172, 176, 180, 188, 194, 202. *See also* sutra recitals

charms, 83, 187, 199. *See also* talismans

children, 94, 110, 123, 137; control of, 100; debt to mothers/parents, 111, 112–113, 116, 175; imperative, 123; religious practice for, 26, 94, 108–109, 123, 202; unfilial, 113. *See also* barrenness; filial piety; sons

China, 18, 64, 81, 82, 90, 112, 149, 218n5; cultural dominance, 32–33, 186; medicine, 33; relation to Vietnam, 33, 35, 39, 208n14; religions of, 33, 35, 206n2, 208n16. *See also* resistance: against China; Taiwan; three religious traditions

Chinese language, 43, 127, 179, 180, 182, 185, 186–187, 193, 194, 218n1; inscriptions, 43, 136, 179, 187, 188; of religion, 187, **188**, 192

Christian missionaries, 39

chùa. See pagoda

class, 65, 67, 68, 97, 142; middle, 17, 97, 99, 105

clothing, 87, 97, 103, 105–106, 120, 121–122, 145, 146, 149, 153; as marker, 133–135, 146, 149, 151, 203; monastic style, 119, 133, 150. *See also* fashion; robes; uniforms

Cô Bơ, 87–88

communal house (*đình*), 8, 22, 64, 83, 130, 160, 185, 187, 210n3, 212n4; destruction of, 33–34, 65; reconstruction, 65, 216n1; rituals (*tế*), 18, 77, 160, 216n1; structured, 132, 158; women's exclusion from, 216n1. *See also* hierarchy: in communal house

Communist Party, 8, 9, 39, 190, 208n12; membership in, 64

communitas, 132–133. *See also* inclusion

compassion (*có tâm*), 29, 90, 217n7

Compendium of Outstanding Figures of the Zen Garden (*Thiền Uyển Tập Anh*), 39–40

competition, 13, 55, 137, 139–142, 149, 150, 158, 177, 203

complicity, 41, 68, 103, 104

comprehension, 54, 126, 127, 171–173, 180, 187–189, 191, 195, 201, 215n13

Côn Sơn Pagoda, 131, 215n9

conformity, 5, 41, 55, 68–71, 101, 106, 170, 172, 177, 196, 212n4

Confucianism, 7, 32, 33, 35, 67, 87, 90, 99, 110, 179, 208nn15–16, 209n18, 215n8, 216n2; Hồ Chí Minh as model of, 183; and masculinity, 14, 175, 182–184, 204; scholars of, 185

conspicuous devotion, 13, 142–148, **146**, 152–158, 177, 203; praying, 138–139, 143, 151

context, 6, 17, 24, 68, 100, 121, 143, 208n11, 212n4

contradictions, 24, 36, 78, 99, 121, 212n4

Cực Lạc. See Pure Land, The

cúng. See ritual(s)

cynicism: towards religious practice, 51, 63, 155. *See also* family: disapproval

dangerous things, 91, 212n5

Daoism, 33, 35, 179, 216n2

Dâu Pagoda, 76

dead, the, 10, 49, 115, 208n11; as active forces, 20–21, 23, 30; commemoration of, 17, 23, 53, 65, 75, 120, 144, 180; communication with, 21, 61–63, 129; needs of, 70, 106, 120; war dead, 35. *See also* ancestors; ghosts; hell; séances

death, 26, 28, 61–63, 64, 93, 137; anniversary, 17, 18, 77, 121, 159, 212n4; bad, 65; good, 120, 122; preparing for, 120–122, 124, 129, 162, 175, 214n2; unnatural, 30, 65

decision making, 21, 100–101, 104, 108, 109, 140, 157, 183, 216n1. *See also* husbands

decorations, 18, 113, 133, 137, 145–146, 158, 199

Đền Bà Chúa Kho. *See* Lady of the Storehouse: Temple for

desire. *See* cathexis

destiny (*duyên*), 172, 218n12

About the Author

Alexander Soucy is associate professor of religious studies at Saint Mary's University, Halifax. He received his doctorate degree in anthropology from the Australian National University in 2000. His research has a dual focus of Vietnamese Buddhism in Vietnam and in Canada, and he has written a number of journal articles and book chapters on Buddhism and gender in the contexts of Vietnam and the Vietnamese diaspora in Canada. These include "The Dynamics of Change in an Exiled Pagoda: Vietnamese Buddhism in Montréal" in *Canberra Anthropology* (1996) based on his research in Canada; "Pilgrims and Pleasure Seekers" in *Consuming Urban Culture in Contemporary Vietnam* (Routledge 2003); "Consuming Lộc, Creating Ơn: Women, Offerings and Symbolic Capital in Vietnam" in *Studies in Religion/Sciences Religieuses* (2006); "Nationalism, Globalism and the Re-establishment of the Trúc Lâm Thiền Buddhist Sect in Northern Vietnam," in *Modernity and Re-enchantment: Religion in Post-revolutionary Vietnam* (Institute of Southeast Asian Studies, 2007); and "Language, Orthodoxy, and Performances of Authority in Vietnamese Buddhism" in *The Journal of the American Academy of Religion* (2009). He has lived in Vietnam for a total of about four years, primarily doing research in and around Hanoi. He has coedited the volume *Wild Geese: Buddhism in Canada* and is active in promoting the study of Buddhism in Canada. His current research interest focuses on Vietnamese Buddhist transnationalism and transformation.

Production Notes for Soucy / *The Buddha Side*

Series interior designed by Elsa Carl, Clarence Lee Design
with text in Garamond Premier Pro and display in Palatino
Linotype

Composition by Wanda China

Printing and binding by Sheridan Books, Inc.

Printed on 55# House White Hi-Bulk D37, 360 ppi